"Loring's diary provides a fascinating ins[ight] [into the] legislative process—in particular at the un[...] tives have had in the legislature since the s[...] [...]g in 1820. Written with remarkable candor, grace, grit, and wit, it conveys her conviction that mutual education is the only acceptable means to establishing both the common good and justice for her people."
—Bunny McBride, author of Molly Spotted Elk: A Penobscot in Paris

"When I finished this book I remembered a Rwandan woman psychologist whose speech closed a Maine conference about survivors. She introduced a Rwandan dance group of young people and the whole, very serious audience, including survivors, got up to dance, too. The speaker said at the end of this dance, 'People ask, why dance, when there is such a serious topic? I say, what better than for the people who expected to see you disappear, see you not only survive, but dance?' This book is Representative Loring dancing, in the cool light of dawn, but on fire." —Victoria Mares-Hershey, writer, playwright

"Donna Loring has committed a brave and generous act in sharing her thoughts and observations as the representative of the Penobscot Indian Nation in the Maine legislature. Written with unflinching honesty, Loring's diary not only throws light on the legislative process, but also holds up a mirror to the dominant society's entrenched thought patterns that have allowed the members of Maine tribal nations to remain 'invisible in plain sight.' Loring's belief that understanding and communication through education will foster new harmonious relationships is the hope of indigenous peoples everywhere. In the Shadow of the Eagle places Maine's Indian tribes clearly within the global struggle of all indigenous peoples for their inherent rights of sovereignty, self-determination, human rights, and human dignity. It should be required reading for all legislators and throughout the state's school system."
—Gale Courey Toensing, reporter, Indian Country Today

Photograph by Jose Leiva, Lewiston *Sun-Journal*; Penobscot cane carved by Stanley Neptune.

IN THE SHADOW OF THE EAGLE

A Tribal Representative in Maine

Donna M. Loring

Down East Books   CAMDEN, MAINE

Down East Books

An imprint of Globe Pequot

Distributed by NATIONAL BOOK NETWORK

First paperback edition: 2008
First Down East Books edition: 2023

Library of Congress Cataloging-in-Publication Data
Loring, Donna M., 1948-
  In the shadow of the eagle : a tribal representative in Maine / Donna M. Loring. - 1st pbk. ed.
    p. cm.
  Includes index.
  ISBN 978-1-68475-122-8 (pbk. : alk. paper)

  1. Penobscot Indians-Government relations. 2. Passamaquoddy Indians-Maine-Government relations. 3. Indian legislators-Maine-History. 4. Maine-Ethnic relations. 5. Loring, Donna M., 1948- I. Title.

E99.P5L67 2008
323.11970741-dc22

2007048157

Cover photograph of S. C. Francis's sculpture *Soaring Free* by Ken Woisard, East Blue Hill, Maine. Collection of the Abbe Museum, Bar Harbor, Maine
Cover photograph of the Maine Statehouse by Alan LaVallee
Design by Geraldine Millham, Westport, Massachusetts
Copyediting: Genie Dailey, Fine Points Editorial Services, Jefferson, Maine

Let understanding and communication through education be the building blocks of a new tribal-state relationship, one that recognizes and honors the struggles and contributions of Native people.

CONTENTS

FOREWORD

Neil Rolde

If you know anything at all about the history of the State of Maine, a salient fact is our existence for more than a century and a half as part of Massachusetts. Until Henry Clay's Missouri Compromise of 1820, our political center was Boston, and not as it was later to be, Augusta, Maine. It was to "old Beantown," then, that our elected representatives flocked. Also making the trip out of the District of Maine during those 168 years were delegations of the tribal governments Down East, sent to discuss aspects of White-Indian interactions with the General Court, as the Commonwealth of Massachusetts's legislature is called to this day.

Thus began a tradition that Maine took with it when it broke from the former Bay Colony. Today, tribal representation in a legislative body is practiced in the United States only in Maine. Two of the various tribes that once existed here have been allotted this right since the state's beginning—the Passamaquoddy Tribe and the Penobscot Nation. They are the two largest tribes still in Maine and, quite possibly, owe their very existence in the state today to the fact that they fought so hard and so well on the American side against the British in the American Revolution. They were instrumental in keeping eastern Maine from ending up as a piece of Canada.

Unique in America, their two representatives also occupy a unique position in Augusta. They are members of the legislature, sport special legislative plates on their vehicles, and hold seats with the other 151 elected members in the chamber of the Maine House of Representatives. Yet their powers are limited. They cannot vote on most matters and generally are allowed to speak only on issues affecting the tribes. To be sure, they are elected like the others, but solely by their tribes, not by the general public—and consequently, their inability to be full representatives is perpetuated by the U.S. Supreme Court's "one person, one vote" edict.

As a state representative myself, first elected in 1972, I, like many of my peers, was aware of but not really connected to the Indian representatives in our time. The one I initially most remember was Albert Dana, a Passamaquoddy. A shy, quiet man, he was hardly my idea—gleaned from films—of an Indian, but struck me as indistinguishable, in the way he looked, talked, and dressed, from a backcountry Maine farmer.

I should add that, in those days, the anonymity of the Indian reps was exacerbated by the denial to them of seats on the floor of the house. In the past they had been given seats but the story we heard was that forty years before, one of their number had misbehaved and they had been banished, to linger beyond our doors with even less access than most of the lobbyists we kept in the corridors.

Action to change this situation was finally taken in 1975, when I happened to be the Democratic majority leader in the house. The issue was not a partisan one, I assure you, although the sponsor of the order to seat the Indian representatives was a Democrat, Representative Judy Kany of Waterville. Let me explain that an "order" is not a "bill." It does not need the governor's signature to go into effect, nor does it even need to be countersigned by state senate approval. It is house business exclusively, deciding whom we want to seat in our body—and after a rancorous fight (the most vocal anti-Indian opponents were Democrats), our bipartisan coalition prevailed and the banishment ended.

The effects, while not immediate, were significant. Indian voices began to be heard. I remember well the first Indian woman representative I was aware of, the late Priscilla Attean, and how unbelievably effective she was for her people. And now, a fellow Penobscot, Donna Loring, has followed in her footsteps, serving her fourth term.

Donna has done a great service to the people of Maine by revealing the intimate details of what it is like to be in the anomalous position of one of only two tribal representatives in a U.S. state governing body. (There is something of a federal counterpart in the representative from American Samoa in Congress.) *In the Shadow of the Eagle* is a unique document that sees the legislative process from an inside point of view and without the distortions that are too often the essence of news reports. Donna also reveals the human side of legislating, revealing her colleagues not just as politicos but as people like you and me with all our feelings.

It is a fascinating story, still unfolding as she goes into her next session. The Indians of Maine are a tiny fragment of the state's population, yet the issues they raise as the original owners of the state's land resound in numerous ways. Whether it is their bids for gambling privileges or cleaner river environments or the removal of offensive names like "squaw" from public usage, the pot, it seems, is always boiling on behalf of approximately 13,000 of our fellow citizens who struggle to maintain, enhance, and modernize their ancient culture and thus contribute importantly to Maine culture.

In the Shadow of the Eagle is a welcome addition to the fast-growing library of books about Native American life in Maine. Donna's journal covers a period from January 2000 to May of 2002, and a session during which there were a number of complicated and contentious Maine Indian–State of Maine issues. Some could be deemed aftermaths of the momentous Maine Indian Land Claims Settlement Act that was signed in 1980. The dramas Donna describes happening twenty years later were often still on the front pages. As one particular example, tribal chiefs were threatened with imprisonment if they did not turn over tribal records in a court case, a decision they saw as a violation of the agreement they made in the land settlement. The essence of this fight was over control of pollution in the Penobscot River, but in a larger sense, it was over the question of sovereignty. Donna's narrative often includes the word *sovereignty*, which is key to the reason the tribes and the state are often at loggerheads. The Indians consider they have a government-to-government relationship with Maine but the government of the state considers these tribes no more of a legal entity than any organized town or city, and thus subservient. Donna Loring's difficult task is to navigate her way through such incompatibilities and at the same time protect and promote the interests of her constituents—the Penobscot Nation—and, in extended fashion, other Indian groups in the state.

It is a never-ending battle and at times she feels discouraged. But Donna is a fighter (a veteran who served in Vietnam) and was at one time police chief of the Penobscots. She doesn't give up easily and she has some extraordinary accomplishments to her credit—including the successful passage of a bill to require the study of Maine Indian history in our state's schools.

Having served sixteen years myself in the Maine House of Representatives, I have a keen knowledge of the effort it takes to be a good legislator, even when everything is structured in your favor. Donna greets every day in Augusta with the odds stacked against her—she cannot vote; she can only persuade. And, believe me, she does a super job.

This journal of hers is a frank and outspoken document and a highly valuable lesson to us non-Indians of how Indian people feel. It is also a good reflection of the flow of issues during a legislative session and the endless amount of work each legislator faces, while having to wrestle constantly with trying decisions, incomprehension, and political gamesmanship. Reading Donna's book brought back vivid memories of my own days in those legislative halls. She was (and still is) there—under special circumstances that make her job all the harder—and she tells it like it is.

A Brief History of Indian Legislative Representatives in the Maine Legislature

S. Glenn Starbird, Jr., 1983. Updated by Donald Soctomah, 1999, and by Donna M. Loring, 2001

The earliest Maine record of representatives being sent from the Penobscot Nation is in 1823, and from the Passamaquoddy Tribe, 1842. At that time there was no state law regarding election of Indian delegates or representatives to the legislature and the choice of this person or persons was determined by tribal law or custom only. Massachusetts records show that the practice of the two tribes sending representatives to the legislature was not new with the formation of the State of Maine in 1820, but probably had been going on since before the Revolutionary War.

The differences between the Old and New parties in the Penobscot Nation in the 1830s and 1840s caused such confusion that these two parties signed an agreement in 1850 which provided, among other things, that "an election should be held every year to choose one member of the tribe to represent the tribe before the legislature and the governor and council." This agreement governed the choice of representative until the legislature passed the so-called "Special Law" of 1866, which, with the tribe's agreement, finally settled the procedure of election for not only its representative but for governor and lieutenant governor as well.

A similar agreement setting forth the form of their tribal government was made between the two Passamaquoddy reservations in what is known as the "Treaty of Peace of 1852." The system of government established by this document has remained unchanged in its essential provisions ever since, although it was not enacted into state law until the Passamaquoddy Tribe petitioned the legislature to do so in 1927. Among the Passamaquoddy, the representative was to be elected alternately from each of the two reservations.

[A great deal more research must be done in regard to Indian representation in the Maine legislature, but our present meager knowledge of the subject shows that over the last half of the nineteenth century there was a gradual growth and development of the Indian representatives' status in the legislative halls.]

Only from the middle 1890s was there verbatim legislative record made, and not until 1907 was it provided with an index, but from that year on we can read clearly the record in session after session where the Indian representatives were seated, sometimes spoke, and were accorded other privileges.

This gradual improvement in the status of Indian representatives resulted in an effort during the 1939 legislature to place Indian representatives on a nearly equal footing with the others. This effort failed, however, and the 1941 session passed legislation that ousted the Indians entirely from the hall of the house, their status being reduced to little better than state-paid lobbyists. Since 1965, however, a gradual change for the better has occurred. Salaries and allowances have increased, and seating and speaking privileges were restored in 1975, after a lapse of thirty-four years.

The closest analogy to Indian representation in the Maine State Legislature now existing are probably the federal laws that allow the territories and the District of Columbia to seat delegates in the federal House of Representatives. Under federal law and House rule a delegate can do anything a regular House member can do except vote on pending legislation. He/she can sit on a committee and vote in committee, he/she receives the same salary and allowances, and for all practical purposes, except the House vote, does what any member of Congress can do.

Opinions by the Office of the Maine Attorney General over the years seem to support the position of Indian representatives in the Maine legislature as very similar to delegates of the territories in

Congress, under the law and house rules as they now stand. At any rate, it is to be hoped that improvements in status will continue, for with the settlement of the Maine Indian land claims in 1980 establishing an entirely new relationship with the state, the need for competent representation of the Indian tribes in the legislature is more vital than ever.

In 1996 the tribal representatives sponsored a Native bill for the first time ever, and in 1999 a rule change allowed the Passamaquoddy and Penobscot representatives to cosponsor *any* bill, statewide.

As of 2001 there were several provisions in statute and in the House Rules and Joint Rules related to the rights, privileges, and duties of the tribal representatives.[1] The provisions are these:

3 MRSA subsection 1

3 MRSA subsection 2

Rules of the House, Rule 525[2]

Joint Rules, Rule 206 (3)

Under these provisions tribal representatives:

- Must be granted seats in the house;
- Must be granted the privilege, by consent of the speaker, of speaking on pending legislation;
- Must be appointed to sit as nonvoting members of joint standing committees;
- May sponsor legislation specifically relating to Indians and Indian land claims,

cosponsor any other legislation, and either sponsor or cosponsor expressions of legislative sentiment;

- May be granted any other rights and privileges as voted by the house;
- May amend their own legislation from the floor of the house;[3]

Are entitled to per diem and expenses for each day's attendance during regular sessions and to the same allowances as other members during special sessions.

Tribal representatives are now working toward a vote in committee similar to what the territorial delegates have in Congress.

The Wisconsin, New Brunswick, and New Zealand legislatures have reviewed Passamaquoddy and Penobscot representative status to use as a possible model. The results of those studies are unknown at ths time.

Note: The above narrative concerning Indian representation in the legislature is based on information derived from the legislative record, federal and state rules, State Department reports, Maine public laws, resolves, private and special laws, federal laws, newspaper articles, and other published accounts.

[1]Final Report of the Committee to Address the Recognition of the Tribal Government Representatives of Maine's Sovereign Nations in the Legislature
[2] The Joint Standing Committee on Maine's Sovereign Nations Native Representation is the most recent in-depth study of the duties and history of the tribal representatives. It sets forth recommendations to both houses of the legislature, which to date have been ignored.
[3]This was the latest joint rule to be past during the 120th legislative session.

A final note: Since that horrific event on September 11, 2001, the legislative leadership has been working with security experts to develop a security and evacuation plan. One of the things the plan calls for is to be able to identify those legislators who are in attendance so that in the event of a catastrophic event (such as a bombing or an earthquake) they would know if anyone was missing. Legislator attendance is confirmed by a roll call. There are two big boards with all the legislators' names on them—with the exception of the two Indian representatives—and when the roll call is taken, the legislators push a button and a light next to their name lights up. It's a great way to know who is there and who is not.

The big problem for tribal representatives is that *our names are not on the board* although there are at least two blank spaces for more names. So in the event of the unthinkable, the tribal representatives are not recognized and there is no way to tell if they are in attendance or if they are missing. I have mentioned this situation to my fellow legislators and to the clerk of the house. Legislators are

Donald Soctomah, from Indian Township, representing the Passamaquoddy Tribe, and myself, representing the Penobscot Nation

surprised and say, "Wow, we never thought about that. We should do
something about that." The clerk said, "Yes, that needs to be looked
at but it has to go through the proper procedures." I have mentioned
this every session since the plan has come out, and there has still
been no move to include us on the board. Tribal representatives mirror their tribal governments' status in the legislature, but we are
both still marginalized on so many levels and are still struggling to
be visible and have a voice in our destiny, even at the cost of our own
well-being and personal safety.

—DL

Penobscot Legislative Representatives

(Names are spelled as they appeared in the legislative record, where they were often misspelled. Assistance correcting these errors was provided by Carol Binette and Donald Soctomah.)

1823	Francis Loran [Lolar] and John Neptune
1824	John Attean, John Neptune, and Francis Loran [Lolar]
1831	John Neptune and Joseph Soc Basin [Sockbasin]
1835	John Neptene [Neptune], Jo [Joseph] Sockbasin, Peol Malley [Molly]
1836	Joe [Joseph] Sockbasin, Joe [Joseph] Porus [aka Polis], John Peol Susop [Susep], Peol Tomer
1837	John Neptune, Peol Tomer, Nuil Luey [Newell Lewey]
1842	Joe [Joseph] Porus [aka Polis], Joe Socabeson [Joseph Sockbasin], Peol Newell
1844	Peol Porus [aka Polis], Joseph Socabasin [Sockbasin], John Neptune
1850	Attean Lola [Lolar], Joe [Joseph] Sockbasin, Joseph Porus [aka Polis]
1851	Attean Lolah [Lolar], Representative
1853	Peol [Peal] Sockis
1854	Peol [Peal] Sockis, Representative, Attean Orson, Special Agent of Tribe
1855	Peol [Peal] Sockis, Delegate
1856	Joseph Socabasin, Delegate
1857	Socabeson Swasson [Sockabesin Swassian] attending legislature; Peol [Peal] Sockis, Delegate
1858	Peol [Peal] Sockis, Representative
1859	Joseph Nicolar, Representative
1860	Joseph Nicolar, Representative
1861	Peol [Peal] Sockis, Representative
1862	Joseph Nichola [Nicolar], Representative
1863	Peol [Peal] Sockis, Representative, Joseph Sockbasin serves Commissioner of Indian Affairs

1864	Peol [Peal] Sockis, Representative
1865	Joseph Nicolar, Representative
1866	Joseph Lewis Orono, Representative; Peol [Peal] Sockis, before legislature for tribe
1867	Peol Mitchell Francis
1868	Sockabasin [Sockabesin] Swassian, Delegate
1869	Saul Neptune, before legislature
1870	Joseph N. Soccalexis [Joseph Mary Sockalexis], before the legislature
1871	Newel [Newell] Neptune, Representative
1872	Sockbesin Swassin [Sockabesin Swassian], Representative
1873	Joseph Necolar [Nicolar], Representative
1874	Joseph N. Socklexis [Joseph Mary Sockalexis], Delegate
1875	Mitchell Paul Susus [Peal Mitchell Susep], Delegate
1876	Joseph Francis, Representative
1877	Sebbatis [Sabattis] Dana, Representative
1878	Joseph N. Soccalexis [Joseph Mary Sockalexis], Representative
1879	Sabbatus [Sabbatis] Dana, Representative
1880	Lola Cola [Coley; actual surname is Nicola], Representative
1881	Joseph Nicolar, Representative

Two-year terms begin

1882	Lola Cola [Coley; actual surname is Nicola], Representative
1885	Joseph Nicolar, Representative
1887	Lola Cola [Coley; actual surname is Nicola], Representative
1889	Joseph Nicolar, Representative
1891	Lola Coly [Coley; actual surname is Nicola], Representative
1893	Joseph Nicolar, Representative
1895	Lola Coly [Coley; actual surname is Nicola], Representative

1897	Horace Nicola, Representative
1899	Sabatis Shay, Representative
1901	Thomas Dana, Representative
1903	Joseph Mitchell, Jr.
1905	Peter N. Nelson [Peter Mitchell Nelson]
1907	Nicholas Sockabasin [Nicola Sockbeson]
1909	Charles Daylight Mitchell
1911	Lola Coly [Coley; actual surname is Nicola]
1913	Peter Ranco
1915	Leo Shay (first time election)
1917	Peter W. Ranco (Old Party)
1919	Mitchell M. Nicolar
1921	Horace Nelson. First mention by speaker, who said, "The chair extends the welcome of the house of representatives to the representative of the Penobscot Tribe of Indians who is now seated in your body."
1923	Joseph P. Lewis ("Mr. Lewis is now in his seat with us in the rear of the hall." Applause.)
1925	Newall Gabriel, escorted to chair amid applause. Members rising.
1927	Lawrence Mitchell
1929	John Nelson, house messenger escorted him to his seat amid applause.
1931	James Patrick Lewis, asigned seat 150 by speaker.
1933	Elmer Attean, was seated. House order gave both Indian representatives stamps and telephone call credit cards.
1935	John Sebastian Nelson, seated Number 151 and conducted there by the sergeant-at-arms amid applause of the house.
1937	John Sebastian Nelson
1939	Leo Shay
1941[1]	Harold Polchies. A bill was introduced to change the words "Representative to the Legislature" to "Representative at the Legislature." Indian representatives were,

prior to this date, allowed to sit in the house hall and speak.

1943 James Lewis. He was conducted to the center aisle and greeted by the speaker, at which time he thanked the speaker for acknowledgment.

1945 Harold Polchies

1947 Harold Polchies

1949 Ernest Goslin

1951 John Sebastian Nelson

1953 John Mitchell

1955 Francis Ranco

1957 John Nelson was the tribal representative serving through 1957, 1959, 1961, 1965, and 1969 sessions.

1971 John Murray Mitchell, Sr., elected in December 1970 in a special election to succeed John S. Nelson

1973 Vivian F. Massey, ran on a write-in ticket in September 1972 and won by four votes after a recount. She was the first woman to ever be elected Indian representative.

1975[2] Ernest Goslin. On January 22, 1975, the Maine House of Representatives voted to seat the Indian representatives and give them speaking privileges by a vote of 107 to 40, thus ending a ten-year effort to restore the rights taken from Indian representatives by the 1941 legislature. Ernest was reelected in 1976 for the term 1977–78.

1979 Timothy Ray Love

1980 Reuben Elliot Phillips

1983 James Gabriel Sappier

1984 Priscilla Ann Attean, serving through the 1987, 1989, 1991, and 1993 sessions.

1995[3] Paul Joseph Biscula

1997 Paul Joseph Bisculea, served the first session and then resigned.

1997 Donna Marie Loring, elected in a special election.

1999 Donna Marie Loring, reelected and served in 2001, 2002, and 2004; ran for state senate in District 19 and lost.

2005 Michael Joseph Sockalexis, elected but ill for first three months of the session. Donna Marie Loring took over as alternate representative.

2007[4] Donna Marie Loring, reelected and presently serving.

Passamaquoddy Legislative Representatives

1842 Joseph Salmo [Selmore] and Sabbatus Neptune
1843 Joseph Salmo [Selmore] and Sabbatus [Sabattus] Neptune
1844 Joseph Lolar Salmo [Lola Selmore]
1845 Sabbatus Neptune
1852 John Gabriel, Attean Lewey, Joseph Lolar [Lola]
1854[5] Joe Lolar Selmore [Joseph Lola Selmore]
1855 John Newell
1856 John Francis
1857 John Gabriel
1858 Lewy Benauit
1859 Teol Tomah
1860 Peter sabattus [Sabattus]
1861 Peter Nicola sepsis [Susehp meaning Joseph]
1862 Joseph Lolar [Lola] Selmore
1864 Nicolar Andrew Dana
1865 Newall [Newell] Neptune
1866 Sapiel Gabriel
1867 Sabatus Ley [Sabattus Lewey]
1868 Peropole [Piemole] Sabattus
1869 Peol Tomah
1870 Louis Benewit
1871 John Gabriel
1872 Salmore [Selmore] Francis
1873 Peter Sepsis [Susehp]
1874 Peter Selmore
1875 John Dana
1876 Lewey Snow

1877	Tomah Peol Tomah
1878	Peter Selmore
1879	Newell Joseph
1880	Lewy [Lewis] Mitchell
1881	Newall [Newell] Joseph

Two-year terms begin

1883	Lewey [Lewis] Mitchell
1885	Mitchel [Mitchell] Lewey
1887	Peter Gabriel
1889	Peter Newell
1891	Newell Francis
1893	Joseph Sepsis [Susehp]
1895	Lewey [Lewis] Mitchell
1897	Atienne [Attean] Lewey
1899	Thomas Bailey
1901	Joseph Sepsis [Suschp]
1903	Lwewy [Lewis] Mitchell
1905	Peter Neptune
1907	Joseph Neptune
1909	Joseph Mitchell
1911	Louis [Lewis] Mitchell
1913	Peter Newall [Newell]
1915[6]	Frank Francis
1917	Wallace Lewey
1919	John Mitchell
1921	Wallace Lewey
1923	Samuel Dana
1925	Frank Socoby
1927	Simon Soctomah
1929	Newell Lewey
1931	Peter Moore
1933	George Stevens
1935	Samuel Dana
1937	William Sockbasan [Sockabasin]

1939	Samuel Dana
1941[7]	George Soctomah
1943	Samuel Dana
1945	Albert Dana
1947	William Neptune
1949	George Stevens, Jr.
1951	Joseph Nicholas
1953	Archie Lacoote
1955	Joseph Nicholas
1959	Newall Tomah
1961	George Stevens, Jr.
1963	Joseph Nicholas
1965	George Stevens, Jr.
1967	George Francis
1969	Albert Dana
1971	John Bailey
1973	Albert Dana
1975[8]	Joseph Nicolas [Nicholas]
1977	George Stevens, Jr.
1979	Ruben [Rueben] Cleaves

Four-year terms begin

1983	Wayne Newell
1987	Joseph Nicholas
1991	MaDonna Soctomah
1995[9]	Fred Moore
1999[10]	Donald Soctomah
2003	Fred Moore
2007	Donald Soctomah

1   No seating or speaking rights
2   Seating and speaking rights restored
3   Indian bills sponsorship
4   Tribal representative's position on bills in committees on which they serve to be noted in house and senate calendars.
5   Old Party, Pleasant Point
6   First election held
7   No seating or speaking rights
8   Seating and speaking rights restored
9   Indian bills sponsorship
10 All-bill cosponsorship

My swearing-in ceremony, January 8, 1998. Left to right, Ssipsis, a Penobscot Nation elder, activist, and writer; my partner, Deborah A. Bouchard; Governor Angus King; myself; and my sister, Elizabeth Sockbeson. Courtesy of the Governor's Office

INTRODUCTION: NOW IS THE TIME TO END OUR ONE-HUNDRED-AND-EIGHTY-YEAR SILENCE

Maine is the only state in the United States to have tribal representatives seated in its legislative body. The tribal governments represented are the Penobscot Nation and the Passamaquoddy Tribe. These legislators represent their tribal governments, not individuals or districts. They have seats in the house chamber, they may serve on legislative committees, but they do not have a vote. They have served in the legislature since the 1820s.

This book is a record of my experiences as the Penobscot Nation's representative to the Maine State Legislature. I wrote it in journal form because I was experiencing something unique and important every day. I wanted to be able to give an accurate account of my experiences and pass them on to my own people and the representatives who would follow me. I now believe that others would benefit from my record as well.

For people interested in First Nations political process and policy all over the world, here is a view of policymaking in the United States from a firsthand Native perspective. You will get a flavor of the day-to-day aspects of what it's like to be a Native American trying to influence policy on a state level, trying to be heard, trying to be visible within the halls of the most powerful and influential body in the state.

The two Indian representatives are treated cordially but when most bills are being discussed, they are discussed and decided upon in little groups and in small corners of the Statehouse. Indian representatives are not usually included in these discussions and are for the most part invisible bystanders. It has also been particularly difficult to influence any policy without a vote and without the same legislative standing that everyone else enjoys. One legislative leader likened the task to having one's arms tied behind one's back and still trying to function effectively. In the legislative rush the Indian representative must be able to gain the attention of legislators long enough and be articulate enough to convince them to back a policy that will help them, or to vote against a policy that will be hurtful to Native communities. Every bill passed by the Maine State Legislature has the same effect on Indian people as it does on Maine people. It has been a daunting task for me as a Native woman to protect my people and promote Native issues.

Indian representatives of the past chose not to write about their daily experiences, perhaps fearing some sort of repercussions against them personally or against their tribe. But I believe that now is the time to write about these experiences. Perhaps some will not like what I have written (and I know that the legislature has a long institutional memory), but I have decided to take the risk and let the chips fall where they may. Many in the white majority culture do not understand Native issues. In order for them to understand they must first be willing to listen and be educated.

I have learned many valuable lessons myself during my tenure in the legislature. One of the most important lessons is that politics are fluid. What might be of crucial importance to me one day may not be so important the next day or the next week or the next year. A legislator may be my worst enemy on one issue, but my biggest supporter on another. Representatives or senators that I did not like for one reason or another I later came to not only like but respect. There are some that I will most likely be at odds with on every issue, and those with whom I'll never be a friend, but for the most part they are reasonable and honorable people. I have found the house to be one huge family that unites in crises regardless of party affiliations. The senate is an entity unto itself, one that remains closed to Indian representation, though tribal representatives are working to break down this barrier.

I truly believe that now is the time to end our one-hundred-and-eighty-year silence. It is my hope that whoever reads this journal

Taking the oath as Governor King's aide de camp, February 14, 1999.
Governor King is on the left, and General Earl Adams is on the right.
Courtesy of the Governor's Office

will be enlightened and have a deeper sense of both the plight and
the contributions of Maine Indian people and their governments. It is
also my hope that, through communication and education, the State
of Maine will recognize and reconcile its past injustices and move
forward to develop a beneficial partnership with Maine tribal governments.

I chose to use the title *In the Shadow of the Eagle* as a result of
extraordinary events that happened in my personal life and the
world at large during my legislative career. The eagle is a symbol to
Native people of strength, dignity, respect, and power. It is sacred to
us. It is our belief that our ancestors see us through the eyes of the
eagle and guide us through the spirit of the eagle.

This is the story of my fight to be heard and to become visible
within the halls of the most powerful and influential body in the
State of Maine. At the end of the day I want my legacy to be that my
work has made a significant difference.

SETTING THE STAGE

Each tribe has its own election process. The Penobscot Nation's process is as follows:

There are no political parties—each person runs on his or her own merit and personal reputation.

A caucus is held on the first Tuesday in July. Tribal members may run for various open seats on committees and the Tribal Council, and for the offices of sub-chief, chief, and tribal representative to the state legislature. Tribal members cannot run for more than one seat or position. They must be present when nominated to accept or reject their nomination.

The primary election is held on the second Tuesday in August. The primary election is held if there are more then three people running for one opening. The two top contenders for each opening will run against each other in the general election held on the second Saturday in September. The chief, sub-chief, and tribal representative hold their offices for two years from October 1 through September 30 of the second year.

I was first elected to the legislature by special election in September 1997 after the former Penobscot legislator had resigned. I was sworn in by Governor Angus King in the governor's office at the same time as Representative Bruce Bryant of Dixfield; we had both been chosen by special election in mid-legislative term. We would have a lot of catching up to do, since the 118th legislative session was well underway.

I had to begin my legislative service without the formal orientation given to first-year legislators. But because my situation was unique and unlike any other in the legislature, it might not have been very helpful. I know now that I was fortunate to be elected at a time when Elizabeth (Libby) Mitchell, Maine's first woman speaker, presided over the house and Joseph (Joe) Mayo was clerk of the house. They, along with Passamaquoddy Representative Fred Moore, and Representative Joe Brooks, helped me a great deal. I will always be thankful to them for their words of wisdom and guidance. The 118th was the last session for Libby Mitchell, since she had reached the term limit set for representatives and senators; Representative Steven Rowe was elected as the speaker for the 119th session. Representative Fred Moore was also termed out.

The 118th proved to be a fast and exciting session. One of the bills that passed created a Maine Women Veterans Commission. I was very interested in participating on this commission, since I am a Vietnam veteran, so I requested an appointment to the newly created commission. General Earl Adams granted my request and I was later elected to chair the group.

The remainder of the second session of the 118th went by quickly, I put out two newsletters to the tribe, and before I knew it the 119th was to begin. It would be my first full two-year session and my first taste of political controversy over a Native issue.

The other tribal representative that term was Donald Soctomah. The Passamaquoddy have two communities, Indian Township and Pleasant Point. They elect a representative who serves four years, in turn, from each community. Representative Fred Moore (Pleasant Point) had served his term and Representative Donald Soctomah (Indian Township) had been elected to represent their tribe. Donald and I were to form a very strong partnership.

During the first two weeks of the first session of the 119th, I approached Representative Joe Brooks (D) from Winterport to submit a joint order for me. This order was to establish a joint (senate and house) legislative study committee on the history, duty, and voting rights of the tribal representatives. The joint order passed and the Committee to Address the Recognition of the Tribal Government Representatives of Maine's Sovereign Nations in the Legislature was established. The joint committee met throughout the summer and at the end of its study wrote an in-depth report that included recommendations to the speaker of the house, the president of the senate, and the Joint Rules Committee. Representative Soctomah and I were members of this joint study committee, and we were granted full participation and the option of writing our own minority report. We felt that we needed as close to a unanimous report as we could get, so we did not write a minority report. The fate of the final report will be told a bit later.

Also, during the second session of the 119th, Representative Soctomah submitted a bill titled "The Offensive Names Bill." We would find ourselves spending much time and energy on this bill, as it drew national and international attention from the media.

Come with me now into the halls of the Maine State Legislature and experience with me some of the day-to-day events—from a tribal representative's perspective.

A NATION IS NEVER CONQUERED UNTIL THE
HEARTS OF ITS WOMEN ARE ON THE GROUND.
—CHEYENNE PROVERB

January 4, 2000
Thursday
Yesterday, the 3rd of January, we had our first Joint Standing Committee on Judiciary meeting of the new year. The second session of
the 119th Legislature will start tomorrow. I arrived around 1:30 P.M.
at the meeting and saw most of the committee members for the first
time this year. I had received cards from a few of them, one in particular from Senator Benoit, who is a retired judge. I was told that he
was known during his time on the bench as "the hanging judge." I
suspect he has mellowed a bit since then. We do not always agree but
I like him a great deal. He had mailed me a copy of an editorial he
was going to send the *Franklin Journal* concerning the Offensive
Names Bill. He felt we needed to keep the word "Squaw" as used
in state place names; he felt the word was part of our heritage and
that we were throwing our heritage away by putting forth the bill. I
wrote him a letter explaining how I felt—that the word was abusive
and dehumanizing—and I sent him a copy of Representative Donald
Soctomah's editorial on the issue. I also sent him a humorous article
about the United Indian Nations buying California from a few
drunks off the street.

The letter I wrote is as follows:

Dear Senator Benoit:
Thank you for your card and the copy of the editorial you
submitted to the *Franklin Journal*. I always enjoy hearing from
you and am interested in your take on specific issues. I would
worry, as I know you would worry, if we both agreed on every-

thing. Your clientele and mine have very different interests and as a result we are not always on the same side (to say the least!).

I have enclosed a copy of Representative Soctomah's editorial on the word. Since it's his bill, I think it only fair that you should know his reasoning. I do have to agree with him on this one, as I am representing the Native women that this word degrades and dehumanizes.

Sorry, John; I would have to ask you not to help preserve a heritage that is abusive and treats my people as less than human.
Wiliwon
Best Wishes

The following is a copy of Donald's editorial in its entirety; it was cut quite a bit when it was published.

SQUAW: Its Dehumanizing Effect and Origins
By Passamaquoddy Representative Donald Soctomah
As we enter a new millennium, I have hope for a better relationship between the Native population and the State of Maine. In order for us to achieve this improved relationship, we must end 400 years of hurt and discrimination. We must learn to live together peacefully, by honoring and respecting each other. This hope was the motivating factor, when introducing legislation that would put an end to the use of a demoralizing and dehumanizing term within the State of Maine. This bill would remove the word *Squaw* from place names within the state. This is not an issue of political correctness. It is about basic human decency and respect for one's fellow citizens. This bill seeks to protect an underrepresented group within the state: Native women. Our women—grandmothers, mothers, and daughters—are all entitled to protection against basic human rights violations, such as the use of demoralizing language. The driving force behind this bill is hundreds of Native women, who are continually offended by the use of this slang word.

The *Thesaurus of Slang* identifies the term *squaw* as a synonym for prostitute, harlot, hussy, and floozy. The dictionary identifies this word as one that is used to offend Native females.

In order to understand the true origins of this word, we need to look at the history of the relationship between Native people and the early European settlers. Some settlers were unable to pronounce the correct word used for women and others refused to accept Native women as humans, so they chose to use a slang version of the correct word. The women weren't the only ones being referred to using dehumanizing words. Native men were also referred to as "bucks," as a hunter refers to a male deer.. The relations between the early settlers and the Natives quickly turned to warfare. It was during this time period (1650) when this corrupted word started being used to demoralize the Native population.

In addition to the physical violence that erupted, [there] came an equally destructive war of words. This was done in an attempt to dehumanize the opponent, in this case the Indian people. For the soldiers it was easier to kill if your enemy was not considered human. This tactic is still used in warfare around the world. As the line of settlements advanced, the Iroquois Nations were also seen as being in the way of the settlers and war broke out with them.

During this time the term squaw was also used as a corruption of a longer Native word, *otsikwaw,* which referred to a female body part. The early fur trappers used the squaw word to imply the crudest sexual connotations. The war continued in New England for 150 years, but the war of the words has continued for 400 years. The word became ingrained in the English language.

To the general public, after generations of exposure, the squaw word was seen as a neutral word, but to Native females this word continues to be a slanderous attack against them and their culture. Incidents occur more often near the Native communities, where the clash between cultures still exists.

When Native people name a geographic feature, such as a river or a mountain, the terms are used to describe a specific location for the ease of the traveler or to denote its spiritual significance. The name of the Kennebec River describes the contours of the river. Mount Katahdin was named to signify the spirits of the mountain and its geography. The term squaw was not originally used for place names because the word did not exist before the 1600s. It is not a linguist's definition of the original Native word that is of concern. It is the way that the term has been used to define Native women in its current context.

Through communication and education we can rid this state of offensive, derogatory words, so that Native women will have the right to define themselves. We need to grow and understand that the use of the term squaw shows a lack of compassion for human beings. It is hard for the general population to imagine how hurtful a word can be unless it is directed at them, their culture or racial background.

Representative Gerald Talbot of Portland worked hard in 1974 to remove the "N-word" from place names in Maine. He had to convince other representatives how hurtful and hateful this word is to Maine citizens and its visitors. During that floor debate the offensiveness of the word squaw was questioned and several representatives stated that, to the Maine Native population, it was offensive. So this is not a new issue to Maine—it is an issue 400 years old that needs to be put to an end.

Nationally, three other states have removed the word squaw from place names. In North Carolina the U.S. Justice Department was involved in the removal of the word squaw from a school system in March 1999. There is no other word used today that hurts Native women as much as the word squaw. It has been used as a slanderous assault in hate crimes. Last year a Native woman was brutally assaulted by two men who continually yelled "you dirty squaw" as they were kicking her. In 1998 there

Representative Donald Soctomah, Passamaquoddy Tribe, Indian Township (Princeton).
Courtesy of Donald Soctomah

was a high school fight that eventually turned into a racial incident. Native girls were called squaws, and this resulted in death threats being written on the walls. Being a Native man and the father of seven daughters, I do not want to see my daughters, or anyone else's daughter, have to carry verbal scars for the rest of their lives.

This bill sends, with such great effectiveness, a goodwill message of understanding to the Native people of this state, that the State of Maine will stop sanctioning the use of offensive words that dehumanize and exploit the Native people. The Native people and the Native communities of Maine ask for the passage of this bill to end the perpetuation of dehumanizing language that has been used to define our women.

It is never an aggressive act for a people to exercise their right to self-determination. It is an intrinsic right that is woven into the fiber of values that this country was supposed to have been founded upon. The following Cheyenne proverb summarizes the point of this bill concisely: "A nation is never conquered until the hearts of its women are on the ground." Every time this term is used the hearts of our women take another blow.

***

On the day of the first Judiciary Committee meeting Senator Benoit came up to me as soon as I walked into the room and said he enjoyed my letter and was glad I had written to him. He said, "You do understand that we have different interests we must represent?" I had said that in my letter to him and he appreciated my understanding this. He added that he would support my position on this offensive names issue. I find that rather hard to believe and will wait and see. I do like him and respect him as a person.

He also said that a little communication goes a long way and that he hoped we could keep on communicating. That was the highlight of my committee meeting.

WE FIGHT AND FIGHT AND FIGHT AND FIGHT FOR EVERY INCH OF RESPECT AND DIGNITY DUE US AS HUMAN BEINGS.

January 5, 2000
Wednesday

I always feel I can't participate much in a committee meeting, since I am not a voting member. I listen and only ask questions when I feel it is truly necessary or when a real injustice is about to happen. When I speak, most of the time the other members listen but won't give much weight to it unless it is on Indian matters—and then my word is golden, even better than any senator's or representative's. It is a good thing but it is not a vote. This past summer we have been attending meetings involved with study of the tribal representative in the legislature—the study that I requested Representative Joe Brooks to sponsor, since I cannot sponsor studies. He and I wrote it up and recommended a list of committee members. It was approved by the house and the senate and seems to be working well.

The study looked at what the roles of tribal representatives should be, whether we should have a vote, and what our exact duties in the house and senate should be, if any. It is a very complicated matter and we finally have a majority agreement from the committee on a draft proposal I brought to the committee at the last meeting. It allows us to vote in committee, to chair a committee, and also gives us a seat in the senate. It does not give us any rights on either the house or senate floor at this time. The senate seat will be a very difficult thing to achieve. The Democratic senators were at this last meeting but not the Republican senator. A Democratic senator, Anne Rand, was not much in favor of giving us anything. She finally reluctantly came around, but said, "I'm not voting for anyone who didn't get here the same way I got here." That statement (meaning by the elective process) bothered me for a few days but I wrote a note to myself and felt better about it.

How did you get here?

Whatever the answer is, I'm sure you're right, we did not get here the same way you got here. In our case, history dictated our role here. Our seats are a result of a debt owed to us by the Continental Congress. Massachusetts took over that debt and then the State of Maine took it over as part of an agreement with Massachusetts before Maine could become a state.

The debt owed to us by the Continental Congress was one resulting from our tribal governments agreeing to fight on the American side during the Revolutionary War. Without our participation, Maine as we know it would not have existed. General George Washington did not have the troops to hold this territory.

No, we did not follow the same path as you did to get here. We chose to become allies of America. We fought and died just like the Americans. They fought for freedom; we fought for the very survival of our culture. They fought for democracy; we fought for what we thought would be democracy. They fought for life, liberty, and the pursuit of happiness; we fought for fairness and equality.

We fought on the same side and even though our side won, we lost. We are still fighting. We fight and fight and fight and fight for every inch of respect and dignity due us as human beings. Since Maine became a state in 1820, it has tried to make us disappear—and, when that didn't happen, it chose to make us invisible. We are still fighting for fairness and for our dignity as a people. History gave us a seat in this body, and although the election process is similar, the dynamics are different.

Opening Session begins tomorrow at 10:00 A.M. I have a meeting with the deputy commissioner of education at 8:30 A.M. and a 1:30 P.M. work session with the Judiciary Committee. I also have a list for the Legislative Council to sign in order for my proposed bill to be allowed into this session. (The Legislative Council has to screen and approve any requests to introduce legislature after a session deadline, or for the second regular session and all special sessions.) I have to track them down and individually convince them to sign. It's a bill that would give the Penobscot Nation an extension to put our land into trust. I have been waiting to talk to the Tribal Council about having the bill eliminate the deadline altogether.

So the first day of session tomorrow will be a very busy one for me. I'm certain people will ask me about Donald's Offensive Names Bill.

January 6, 2000
Thursday
Yesterday, the 5th of January, 2000, we began the second session of the 119th. It was like old home week.

The newly elected speaker, Steven Rowe (D) from Portland, who was elected at the first session of the 119th, talked mostly about the many bills we have to deal with and the problem of having our committee hearing rooms located all over Augusta due to renovations to the capitol building and the state office building. He explained a lot of housekeeping details, etc. All we did for legislative business was approve a bunch of written communications between the house and the senate.

A few people spoke off the record. The most moving speaker was Representative Joanne Twomey (D) from Biddeford, who spoke about her husband's death from colon cancer a few weeks ago and how she appreciated the support of the house members and the speaker. She told how her husband, the love of her life, had died in her arms and that when she went home this summer she knew it was to prepare to say goodbye to him. She said she took care of him the whole time

Joint Standing Committee on Judiciary, 1999. Back row, L-R, Representatives G. Paul Waterhouse (R-Bridgton), myself, Charles C. LaVerdiere (D-Wilton), Charles E. Mitchell (D-Vassalboro), Peggy Reinsch (committee analyst), Susan "Soupy" Pinette (committee clerk), Debra D. Plowman (R-Hampden), William D. Norton (D-Portland), Thomas Bull (D-Freeport), David Madore (R-Augusta), and not shown, Patricia T. Jacobs (D-Turner). Front row, L-R, Senator John W. Benoit (R-Franklin), Senator Sharon A. Treat (D-Kennebec), Representative William J. Schneider (R-Durham), Senator Susan W. Longley (D-Waldo), and Representative Richard H. Thompson (D-Naples), chair.
Courtesy of Susan Pinette

and had him waked at home because that is where they lived, loved, and had their best times.

There is always someone who is going through a tough life experience in the house; it's like a huge, extended family. Members are very supportive and caring with each other.

The minority leader, Representative Tom Murphy (R) from Kennebunk, stood and praised the speaker for his work in preparing for the upcoming session and all its challenges. Tom said the speaker had done a terrific job and that got the speaker a standing ovation. We then heard some more housekeeping details and adjourned until next Wednesday.

I went in search of the Legislative Council members to get them to sign my ballot list. I needed to get my bill in to extend the time frame on putting Penobscot land into trust. To make a long story short, I got eight out of ten to say yes. The others would have also said yes but I couldn't find them, so I turned in what I had. I only needed six signatures, but I wanted to get everyone to sign that I could. It would make the bill look better and it was the politically smart thing to do. The Revisor's Office will now write a draft, and the bill will ask for a twenty-year extension.

I got home around 3:30 P.M., just in time to load the woodstove, since it has been very cold lately. I consider this first day a success.

"THE TOWN OF HOULTON BULLDOZED THE TRIBE'S TARPAPER SHACKS, WITHOUT WARNING AND IN THE MIDDLE OF WINTER." —CHIEF BRENDA COMMANDER, HOULTON BAND OF MALISEETS

January 20, 2000
Thursday

Tomorrow morning at 9:30 A.M., we—the Judiciary Committee—will hear the Maliseet Bill. It's being treated as a "concept bill"—an idea that gets brought before a committee, which can accept or amend it and turn it into a full bill, or kill it. This bill would give the Maliseets the same powers and rights as the Penobscot and Passamaquoddy tribes in the Maine Land Claims Settlement Act. The bill was not written as a concept bill to begin with but was changed to that status by its sponsor, Representative Roger Sherman (R) from Houlton. The Houlton Band of Maliseets had approached Representative Sherman with the bill and asked him to sponsor it. He agreed, but later decided to change it into a concept bill. He also decided to add "by request" onto the bill, thereby letting other legislators know that he did not craft the bill but was submitting it "by request" of his constituents. I tried to get him to allow me to sponsor the bill, after he told the Maliseets he did not support it, but he refused. Perhaps Representative Sherman simply planned to sabotage the bill from the beginning. A representative should never do that to a constituent—it's unfair and reprehensible!

To further complicate this bill, the state—through the person of Evan Richert, director of the State Planning Office and also a member of the Maine Indian Tribal–State Commission (MITSC)—has come out against the bill. Evan Richert feels that the state would be foolish to add another litigant to the equation, since the Penobscot and Passamaquoddy tribes are already at odds with the state as to

Chief Brenda Commander, Houlton Band of Maliseets, and myself, standing just outside the Judiciary Committee's hearing room with Legal and Vets in the background. Courtesy of Donald Soctomah

what certain aspects of the Land Claims Act mean. He wrote the Maliseets a letter asking them to answer questions that were being litigated or about to be litigated by the tribes and the state—which really puts the Maliseets between a rock and a hard place. I think it may even border on being unethical.

I will be meeting with the Maliseets tonight at the invitation of Brad Coffey, their attorney. I think Evan Richert has some questions to answer. It doesn't look good for the bill at this point, since the Maine Indian Tribal–State Commission is divided on the issue. (The MITSC is an intergovernmental organization with four members appointed by the state, two appointed by the Penobscots and two by the Passamaquoddy, and a chairman selected by these eight. It was set up to facilitate communication between the state and the tribes.) Evan Richert and two other state representatives on the MITSC are voting against the bill. I think Evan Richert and Paul Stern, who is from the attorney general's office, are in league on this one. Paul

Stern, a staff person from the Longley years, is famous for not giving an inch to any tribal issue. One would think that Mr. Stern's Jewish ancestry would help him understand issues of abuse and oppression.

I got back home tonight around 8:00 P.M. I met with Maliseet Chief Brenda Commander and the Maliseet attorney, as well as some Maliseet Council members. We met for dinner at the Ground Round in Augusta and did some strategizing for the hearing tomorrow. Chief Brenda Commander is not feeling well. She is also upset because she thinks her testimony isn't good enough. I read it and it seemed fine to me. The chief and her council members are revising some things based on my recommendations, such as having more than one person read the testimony that Fred Tomah, a Maliseet Council member, was supposed to read. I thought it would be better received if it was presented by more than one person. Senator Susan Longley will be chairing the meeting tomorrow. She has not been very cooperative on Indian issues lately, so I'll be surprised if the Maliseets get a positive outcome.

We prepared for the hearing as best we could and now all we have left is the hearing itself. I do not plan on testifying, since I really need to be able to ask questions. A comittee member who testifies at a public hearing for or against a bill is ordinarily prohibited from asking questions of other witnesses on that bill.

Governor King called me at home tonight. I, of course, was in Augusta. I had asked to be put on his call list to find out how he really views the Maliseet bill. *(I would learn later that Evan's view is usually the governor's view.)*

I guess we'll know more about the opposing view on this bill tomorrow. I wish the Maliseets well. I will do all I can to help them.

January 21, 2000
Friday
7:10 P.M.
This morning went better than I had anticipated. The biggest negative was the weather, blustery toward late afternoon and very cold—

the wind chill factor was -45 degrees.

Representative Roger Sherman introduced the bill by saying he was submitting it "by request." This is usually a death knell for any bill. He went on to say he was against it 70 percent and gave a history of the bill, saying it had been turned down by the Legislative Council a number of times and how he took over the bill with all good intentions. (I say "BULL!" to that. I think he took over the bill with every intention of sabotaging it.) He said he was willing to give the Maliseets the benefit of the doubt, but he just couldn't go along with their request to have the same powers and rights as the other two tribes.

Representative Sherman then referred to an editorial that had come out the day before in the *Bangor Daily News* (BDN). It favored Maliseets getting the same rights and powers, and he proceeded to pick it apart. Some of his objections were that he was afraid the Maliseets would keep the town and the state tied up in court just like the Penobscots and the Passamaquoddy. When I had a chance to question him, I asked him why he didn't allow me to sponsor the bill if he was so against it. He was trying to look sympathetic, but he didn't end up looking too good. I reminded him of how he had said to me that he referred to the Penobscot and Passamaquoddy tribes as P & P. I thought this showed disrespect. The scary thing to me is that he is a teacher! *(I must add here that Representative Sherman, now State Senator Sherman, has become friendlier on tribal issues.)*

After Representative Sherman's testimony I could see all of Senator Longley's negativity melt away. The representative from Houlton turned out to be our best ally.

Chief Brenda Commander gave a very stirring and emotional presentation. She mentioned how years ago her tribe had built shacks on the only land they were able to occupy, near the town dump. Then the town of Houlton bulldozed the tribe's tarpaper shacks, without warning and in the middle of winter. She was more detailed and emotional than I can convey here. Many of the Maliseets who were at the hearing were in tears, remembering how the town of Houlton had treated them and still treats them.

I think every single one of the committee members was won over, including Senator Benoit, who promptly put Representative Sherman in his place, saying he didn't care how the bill got before the committee, he was going to look at its merits. I know this doesn't sound like much, but Senator Benoit is usually one of our biggest foes.

Representative LaVerdiere (D) from Wilton told me that he would propose a solution at the work session. It will probably entail getting the MITSC and key players from the town of Houlton to work out language that will get the bill passed. I am very optimistic. I think it can happen. Even Evan Richert toned down his argument some and said he never intended to take away the tribe's management of internal tribal matters and would add the language back in the document.

Senator Longley asked me via a note if I would like to testify. I wrote back saying no, that I did not want to give up my right to ask questions. She didn't remember that the rules stated that, and asked the analyst to check it out. Sure enough, the rules stated exactly that.

I was able to interject questions and make clarifications, and this helped people understand certain points. Brad Coffey, the Maliseets' attorney, later told me he was glad I was able to ask questions, and Chief Brenda Commander said she was glad I made it clear that I had offered to sponsor the bill. A Maliseet elder came up to me and shook my hand and said it was wonderful to have another Native person in such a position. All in all, the Maliseets were happy with the hearing. They had stayed up until after midnight the previous night working on their testimony. Their hard work paid off. (So we thought.)

The work session for the bill will be next Friday. When a committee works a bill the committee members discuss the bill among themselves and decide how to vote on it. The meeting is open to the public, but the public can only participate if the chair allows it.

The voting choices are: Ought to pass (OTP); ought not to pass (ONTP); or ought to pass as amended (OTPA).

January 23, 2000
Sunday
12:05 P.M.
We have a session at 1:00 P.M. tomorrow, and at 7:00 P.M. the governor gives his State of the State Address in the well of the house chamber.

I read in the BDN editorial about the house chair of our Judiciary Committee, Representative Rich Thompson, working a $7 million package for the Baxter School for the Deaf students who had been abused and molested by state workers years ago. The article mentions that Senator Longley is only asking for $1 million in additional programs because she believes the statute of limitations has run out. The editorial makes Senator Longley look cold and heartless, but to be perfectly truthful, she's very compassionate on this issue. Without her push this would never have gotten before the committee. She has been a very strong advocate and is going to be upset when or if she reads the weekend paper.

Among other things that happened today, Passamaquoddy Representative Donald Soctomah forwarded me some e-mail. The e-mail states that Bill Green, a local television personality, is going to have an episode about Squaw Mountain on "My Hometown," his weekly television series, tomorrow night. I e-mailed Donald that I would call Bill and see if anything was going to be said about the offensive names legislation. I did call Bill and left a message on his machine. I stated that if something was mentioned, he should know the proposed bill does not try to change names of private businesses. I should hear from Bill tomorrow if he needs to talk to me.

...A PROGRAM THAT WAS DOING A GREAT SERVICE FOR MAINE'S PEOPLE OF COLOR AND MINORITY POPULATIONS

January 25, 2000
Tuesday
9:50 P.M.

I attended the State of the State Address on Monday evening. It was very positive. Governor King is an excellent speaker and he did a very good job, as always. It is a very formal affair, and one of those formalities is when the senators enter the house, the speaker strikes the gavel three times, we all rise, and the senators march down the aisle to the applause of the chamber. They walk past those of us in the front row, and some of them shake hands with us. We then exchange pleasantries and short greetings. When the speaker strikes the gavel once, we all sit down and the joint session begins. The house and the senate listen intently to what the governor has to say, and then the joint body as well as the media analyzes his every word. His speech usually sets the pace for the rest of the session.

This morning I drove to Indian Island with Representative Soctomah, since we had to attend a meeting on Indian Island about planning a workshop for the Baxter State Park Advisory Committee members and the Baxter Park commissioners. Of course, the first big northeaster had to hit us. Representative Soctomah has an all-wheel-drive vehicle, but we were still traveling at 35 or 40 mph. The island is about an hour and a half from Augusta on a good-weather day, and this turned out to be a hairy drive. After our meeting Representative Soctomah drove me back to Augusta and I drove the rest of the way home. Luckily, my VW Beetle actually does very well in snow, and I made it home without incident.

Tomorrow morning, if the storm has passed, I have a public

hearing with the Appropriations Committee. There's another public hearing tomorrow afternoon at our Judiciary Committee room at the Statehouse. Hopefully I won't forget my appointment with the AG. It's getting late, time to hit the hay.

One more thing I almost forgot to add. At the State of the State Address, State Planning Office Director Evan Richert approached Representative Soctomah and me saying that he and the Maliseets may have an agreement worked out by this Friday, which is when the work session is scheduled on the bill. I was going to Indian Island this Friday because of an Environmental Protection Agency hearing, but once I realized the Maliseet bill was being worked, I changed my plans. I wanted to make certain there were no last-minute changes or maneuvers by anyone. The Offensive Names Bill will be heard in the afternoon on Friday as well. Friday will be a very full and energy-draining day.

January 28, 2000
Friday
7:45 A.M.
Weather is cold, sunny, around 13 degrees
Wednesday we had public hearings; in the morning we sat with the Appropriations Committee to hear testimony from the AG's office and the chief justice on their budgets. Usually during these hearings I try not to say anything. However, the Maine Civil Rights Team project in the schools is no longer getting federal dollars. Attorney General Andrew (Drew) Ketterer wants to take money from the Victims' Compensation Fund to carry the civil rights program over the rest of the year.

Many legislators, myself included, don't want to hurt the Victims' Compensation Fund, so an in-depth discussion ensued. I did say something, and that was that the civil rights teams were sorely needed and helped students communicate and understand each other without violence. I felt this was a program that was doing a great service to Maine's people of color and minority populations. I hated to see victims lose any funding but hoped that there was a way to allow the civil rights teams to remain in place. Later the attorney general and Representative Richard Thompson thanked me for my comments.

In the afternoon the AG's special assistant, Oliver Wesson III, came to find me. Oliver is a new hire fresh out of law school. He is an African American, has a lot to learn about the Native American culture, and is usually the one that the AG sends to our meetings. I like Oliver and think that he usually gets it. Oliver reminded me of my scheduled meeting with Drew and we walked together to the AG's office. Drew was very cordial. I asked him if he would meet with the tribes to talk about the National Pollution Discharge Elimination System (NPDES) situation. He seemed reluctant at first but after a few minutes agreed *(though it never took place)*. I also mentioned that his staff member Paul Stern seemed entrenched on certain issues when he really should be a little more understanding. Drew agreed and cited the Baxter Park issue as an example. *(The Baxter Park issue was about Chief Dana's request to be allowed to enter the park without having to stand in line for hours to get a permit for the yearly sacred run. Paul Stern was against it. He would not change his mind. The details of this are discussed later.)*

I asked Drew about my Bill 2499 to extend the trust land purchase deadline for the Penobscot Nation. He said he would look into it.

I said, " If there's a problem please let me know. I don't want to see Paul Stern standing there ready to testify against it without my knowledge."

He said, "Don't worry, we'll give it to Bill Stokes to check over." I'm hoping that Bill Stokes will be assigned to work on most of our issues, since he is much more reasonable. I told Drew and Oliver that I found Paul Stern's strict stance toward the tribes puzzling—maybe if he remembered how the Jews were treated in Nazi Germany during the Holocaust, he would be a little more understanding. They found the comparison a bit extreme and that caused a little laughter.

I told them that even when the governor seems willing to compromise, the AG's office stands firm—probably because of Paul Stern. Evan Richert plays the same role as Stern in the governor's office. I suggested that Drew and Oliver must eat lunch with Paul and Evan often. This caused more laughter. All in all, I think Wednesday was a success.

...SHE WAS INSULTED BY THE WORD BUT HAD NEVER FELT EMPOWERED ENOUGH TO SAY ANYTHING.

January 29, 2000
Saturday
5:20 P.M.
Weather nice, in the high teens, low 20s

Yesterday was a very emotional day for many Indian women in Maine. Women from the Penobscot, Passamaquoddy, Micmac, and Maliseet tribes and one from St. Mary's, New Brunswick, testified before the committee working the Offensive Names Bill. My grand-niece, Maulian Dana, testified, as well as my niece, Rebecca Sockbeson. They both did a fantastic job! All the Native women gave powerful testimonies. The only opposing testimony came from residents of Greenville, who feared their economy would be affected. Greenville is the home of Squaw Mountain. The Greenville town manager testified that Indians in his town were not offended by the word. He said that Indians named those places themselves and he had Indian legends written in the 1930s to prove it. He proceeded to read these and was stopped by the chair, Representative Thompson. As a committee member I got to ask questions—and believe me, I did.

First of all I thanked the Greenville town manger for teaching me about my folklore and legends. I explained that Native people passed their legends and traditions orally—not in writing—and that I suspected white men wrote these rather unbelievable legends. He became very defensive and started talking over me. He was also very disrespectful to the committee members.

A woman from the Greenville area who was also a former representative testified against the bill. Her name was Sharon Libby Jones. She was concerned that if there was a name change it would hurt business, adding that Greenville used Native legends and history to attract tourists. I couldn't help it. I got a bit upset with that. I had just had the town manager try to teach me about legends of my people, and now this woman was standing there worried about the economic effect of not being able to sell my culture and history!

I said, "I have a very harsh question I'm going to ask, and it is this: Do you feel guilty earning money from a name that is abusive and dehumanizing to Native people?"

She seemed stunned and then said, "Could you repeat that question?"

I said, "Certainly. Do you feel guilty earning money from a name that is abusive and dehumanizing to Native people?" She responded that she certainly didn't think she was doing that. I did not want to prolong the discussion; I just wanted the committee to think about that possibility, and I'm certain they got the message. I also asked her if Native people got any of the economic benefit from the town using their history and legends.

She said, "No."

I said I had no more questions.

There were two others who spoke. One was Senator Paul Davis (R) from Sangerville. He started his testimony by saying he was confused and didn't think the word was offensive. He said he had Indian friends and one was a Penobscot state trooper who found no offense to the word and felt it was just people trying to be politically correct. A few others from the Greenville area had used this phrase. I asked him if he had heard the previous testimony of Native women and he said, "Yes, I have."

I said, "Are you still confused?"

He said yes, that he had never heard the word used in a bad way. He said if it was used in a bad way, then it was a well-kept secret. I asked him if he read the *Sun-Journal* or happened to read an article that mentioned a woman named Ann Wood. He said he had not. I told him that Ann Wood had said she was insulted by the word but had never felt empowered enough to say anything. She said she was

Rebecca Sockbeson (my niece) testifying in Augusta
Photograph by Roger Leisner, the Maine Paparazzi, Radio Free Maine

glad something was finally being done about it. Davis added during his testimony that he was afraid the history and culture of others would be destroyed. I asked him to clarify that statement. He said he meant the history and culture of the Greenville area.

Representative Thompson stated, "I find it hard to believe that never in your life have you heard this word used in an abusive manner." Senator Davis stuck to his story, and then Representative Thompson said, "Didn't you hear the testimony of these Native women who spoke about the abusiveness of this word?"

He answered, "Yes."

Representative Thompson then said, "Now you *have* heard about it."

The Native woman from St. Mary's, New Brunswick, was a very passionate and powerful speaker. I know she impressed the committee. After all was said and done, Senator Benoit came over to me and said, "I'm going to vote for this." (I'll believe that when I see it.)

We started the public hearing around 11:30 A.M. and it lasted until 3:30 P.M. I bought my niece Rebecca and my grandniece Maulian sandwiches and drinks for lunch, but I had to get back to committee since we had five or six more bills to do. The committee was exhausted but we made it through, then celebrated Senator Treat's (D) and Representative David Madore's (R) birthdays with brownies and ice cream. It was a rough day but a productive one.

The Maliseet bill got tabled for thirty days so that all parties could come to some sort of agreement.

"REPRESENTATIVE LORING, WOULD YOU LIKE TO SECOND THAT MOTION?" —SENATOR SUSAN LONGLEY

February 6, 2000
Sunday
6:40 A.M.
Cold

This past Friday, February 4, was a very special day for all of us. It turns out that "20/20," an ABC news program, was interested in filming the work session for the Offensive Names Bill and also in interviewing some of the women who testified on the bill. The producer called me and wanted to know if people would be there for her to interview. I said I would try to get the same people back who had testified before—and most of them did come back, with the exception of the woman from St. Mary's and Emma Nicola, who had to work at the tribal health center.

The "20/20" crew arrived on Thursday in Bangor and went to Greenville to interview the townspeople. When the producer called me, I tried to get her to have dinner with me so that I could fill her in on some historic background between the state and the tribes. She very nicely brushed me off by saying that was a good idea but she had to meet with her producers, etc. She did thank me for offering.

On Friday the first thing on the Judiciary Committee agenda was the re-appointment of Alan Bringham, who represented the state governor, to the MITSC. That took about a half hour; we were supposed to start at 9:00 but got started late. Alan was confirmed with no problem.

The "20/20" crew arrived and was trying to get set up in a hurry before we went into the Offensive Names Bill work session. They were a little late and the work session had begun, but it only took them a few minutes longer to set up. A motion was requested for purposes of discussion. Representative Thompson moved the bill be passed as amended and then a very unusual event occurred. Senator Longley said, "Representative Loring would you like to second that motion?" There I was, being filmed on national TV with my mouth hanging open in shock!

I calmly said, "Certainly, I second the motion." I sat there thinking, Wow! We just made history. An Indian representative actually made a motion during a committee session. Then, of course, I started to worry about the legal technicality of the action. When I was asked to second the final motion later on in the session, I declined. I said, "I would rather have someone else make the motion," and Senator Longley seconded it.

The deliberation process was a bit weird since Senator Longley and Senator Benoit seemed to be passing over the question of whether the name was offensive and getting right into process—how a new name would be processed by state government. Representative Jacobs (D) from North Turner asked if they weren't putting the "cart before the horse," and Senator Longley responded that she felt the majority of the committee had already decided that the name was offensive. (When she said that, I could see Representatives Plowman and Waterhouse look at each other as if to say, "You don't have our vote.") There were some present who would not vote in favor unless they were sure of the process, including Senator Benoit.

But then the precise meaning of the word in various Indian languages came up. We decided to stick with *squaw* and *squa* as a part of a word. Representative LaVerdiere (D) questioned the fact that making squa part of a word might inadvertently add many more names than we had intended. A long and complicated discussion followed. It was decided with my input that we keep the words squaw and squa as separate words. There was a tiny disagreement between Representative Soctomah and Esther Attean, a Passamaquoddy tribal member, about meaning, and this is what complicated things. I was afraid at one point we would lose whatever support we had gained. It's funny, but if Indian people don't agree on something 100 percent, then it is an excuse for legislators not to pass our bills. You don't see them using the same yardstick for measuring their own bills. The motion was made by Representative Richard Thompson, seconded by Senator Longley, and passed the committee 12 to 1. Senator Benoit (R) voted true to his word for the bill, and Representative Plowman (R) from Hampden also voted in favor of the bill.

The negative vote came from Representative Waterhouse (R) from Bridgton, who just prior to the first meeting at 9:00 A.M. approached me with two books in hand. One book was *Penobscot Man* by Frank Speck; the other was *Women of the Dawn* by my friend Bunny McBride. He said, "I noticed you have a comment on the inside cover of *Women of the Dawn*. Would you please sign the book before I vote on the bill? You may not like how I vote."

I replied, "Of course I'll sign it—we can't always agree on things."

After we broke for lunch he came over again and said, "I'm glad I got you to sign it before the vote."

I said, "Yeah, I signed it with disappearing ink." We both laughed.

"20/20" had filmed the whole work session. They now started interviewing the Native women who had attended. I really was glad my grandniece, Maulian Dana, (who is only fifteen years old) was there along with my niece Rebecca Sockbeson. The interviews took a while, and Representative Soctomah and I were the last two. We were interviewed separately and "20/20" was allowed to use the senate president's office for our interviews. I went in first and was grilled for about twenty minutes. I say *grilled* because the producer asked some really tough questions, but none that I hadn't heard before. Whenever she would ask a question, I would answer with what I thought was important.

For example she asked, "What about all the money the state is going to have to spend on new geographic listings and hearings for name changes?"

I replied, "The important issue here is the fact that an abusive term is being used to hurt Native women. The state needs to show some empathy in this matter."

Representative Soctomah came out five minutes after he went in. He was concerned that he didn't do a good job answering the questions. Knowing Donald, I'm sure he did do a good job. Donald told me he got stuck trying to answer the questions with a direct response to the question itself. I explained to him that after a while you learn not to respond the way the media wants you to. They have their agenda and most of the time it's not the same as yours.

It was indeed quite a day for all of us. Now we wait to see how much of what we said actually made it into the show. The local newspaper reporters got their interviews, too, and the story would come out in the Friday papers.

I returned to the hearing room (most everyone had gone) to pick up my briefcase and some paperwork. Senator Longley was still there reading some material. I walked over to her and said, "Thank you for asking me to symbolically second the motion."

She looked as if she was going to say something about the symbolic description but said, "You're welcome. I was glad to do it. You know the public hearing on this bill really enlightened me. I never realized there was still so much hatred and prejudice left in the state. " She reached out, shook my hand, and said, "Peace?"

I said, "Peace."

I went home exhausted but exhilarated. It had been one hell of a day.

February 1, 2000
Monday
10:30 P.M., cold and windy
Tonight I learned that the Passamaquoddy lost their court case with Albany Township. Now it will be more difficult for my bill—asking for a twenty-year extension on buying Penobscot trust land—to pass on Wednesday.

Here's some background: Our tribes hold land in several different ways. Our reservation lands are original homelands that we have never given up. They are protected by the federal government. We don't pay taxes in any form on our reservation land or land that we have placed in trust (both known as Indian Territory). Reservation land and trust land can't be sold outside of the tribe or alienated in any way from the tribe. In addition, the tribes have acquired land bought with the Land Claims Settlement Act money or other funds, and unless it is converted to trust land, the tribes pay state taxes on it and often municipal taxes, too. This is land they can sell, unless they put it into trust.

In 1988 the Passamaquoddy Tribe bought some land in Albany Township from a tribal member. Because this land wasn't listed in the Settlement Act as land the paper companies were willing to sell to the tribes, the Maine Indian Tribal–State Commission approved a bill introduced to the legislature that amended the Settlement Act to include the Albany parcel among the listed lands that could potentially become Passamaquoddy territory. The bill was passed and signed into law on March 22, 1992.

In 1998, believing the land had been approved to be Indian territory by the Maine State Legislature, the Passamaquoddy Tribe requested that the Land Use Regulatory Commision (LURC) approve its rezoning request that would allow it to build a high-stakes bingo facililty on the rezoned Albany land. (The tribes are allowed to have high-stakes bingo on their land.) Area residents requested a public hearing, and LURC held a two-day hearing. LURC granted both the rezoning request and the redevelopment permit, but Albany Township filed motions against the decision in superior court. Superior Court Justice Humphrey held that LURC had erred and the Albany parcel was not Indian territory under Section 6205 of the Land Claims Settlement Act. All parties appealed to the Maine Surpreme Judicial Court.

The matter in question was the legislature's failure at the same time it added the Albany land to the list of eligible trust lands to change the date within the Land Claims Settlement Act for the required acceptance of new trust land by the U.S. secretary of the Interior. Normally this oversight would have been corrected in a technical housekeeping bill by the Judiciary Committee, but it took on a life of its own. I don't think this should have gone to court—it should have been sent back to the legislature's Judiciary Committee to be included within the errors bill. The full legislature had passed the bill authorizing adding Albany to the trust lands and the governor had signed it. The problem was a simple oversight of not extending the authorization deadline within which that was permitted to happen. I believe the legislative intent was clear.

I also believe the state courts overstepped their authority and reached out for this one. This is a clear example of a breach of the Settlement Act.

I'll speak to Donald in the morning and find out what they are going to do.

(Little did I know that this Albany Township issue would play a big role in my lobbying efforts in the very near future.)

February 8, 2000
Tuesday
7:00 P.M.

We had a session today, and the highlight of the session was a tribute to Chuck Cianchette, who passed away in a plane crash.

There was also a joint resolution honoring Nelson Mandela. This went well until after I got up to speak. Representative Kasperzsak (R) then got up and said she was voting against the resolution because the Mandela regime was responsible for murdering her friend, a woman who had been tied up and gagged and killed. Well—that sort of put the kibosh on testimony. I was horrified that that kind of racist thinking is on record. How many African women were killed by De Klerk and others? I did not dignify her remarks with a comment. We voted and the resolution passed easily.

THE "CORRECTION" BILL WILL NEED ACTIVE SUPPORT...IF THE LEGISLATURE IS GOING TO SALVAGE THE INTEGRITY OF ITS OWN PROCESS....

February 9, 2000
Wednesday

I had to go to Indian Island for an emergency meeting on my trust land extension bill. The Passamaquoddy lost their case in the Maine Supreme Judicial Court. Somehow the law court's ruling was that the land was trust land but not Indian territory. That puzzles me; I have to read the case and have asked for it to be faxed to me.

The Passamaquoddy are having a council meeting tonight. They will decide what they want to do. I hope they won't be asking to tag onto our bill, which would mean certain death for it. I'll write more tomorrow after the hearing on my trust land bill.

February 10, 2000
Thursday
Warmer, low 20s

The meeting went surprisingly well. I spoke with Donald Soctomah and Greg Sample and told them I would prefer not adding their amendment to my bill. I told them the trust land extension was too important an issue for us to play with. I said I would support them if they chose to submit a separate bill to address the technical legal problem. Greg didn't like it; he would rather have tagged on to my bill and taken everyone by surprise, but I didn't want to risk my bill. I felt that the law court decision was so technical that it should be addressed separately and have the legislature's full attention. If the legislature realized that the law court had rendered a legislative policy moot—then some legislative egos would kick in. He made the comment that my own ego must be just as big as everyone else's because I was a member of the legislature as well. He laughed and then told me my face was turning red. I replied I didn't think so.

Greg and Donald went directly to the Revisor's Office to get the new bill going. I went to the hearing, where there were two bills to be heard before ours. The first one up, and the one getting the most publicity, was an act to remove the statute of limitations on sexual assault. (This was a direct result of the sexual abuse that took place at the Baxter School for the Deaf over a decade ago.) Penobscot Nation Council members and some staff were waiting for the public hearing on my bill, and they had to listen to some pretty rough testimony while they waited. It gave them a glimpse of some of the horror stories we hear in our committee every day. At one point during a young man's testimony Senator Longley started to cry, as did a few others on the committee.

Our turn to be heard finally came and the sub-chief, Ann Pardilla, read her testimony after I presented the bill. Mark Chevaree, the Penobscot Nation's "in-house" attorney; Diana Scully, the executive director of the Maine Indian Tribal–State Commission; and the town manager of Carrabassett Valley testified in favor. No one testified against the bill.

Representative Waterhouse suggested that it might be a good idea to remove the twenty-year deadline altogether, and I indicated that I would welcome that as an amendment. Senators Longley, Benoit, and Treat, along with Representative Thompson, were absent from the hearing. They all sit on other committees, too. It looks good so far—we'll have to be prepared at the work session next Monday.

Now I will also be working with Donald to get his bill passed. The Passamaquoddy had a joint council meeting last night to discuss the situation. Donald won't be around until tomorrow. I told him I'd help him talk to the Republicans.

Greg Sample, the attorney for the Passamaquoddy tribe, e-mailed me that the Albany Township bill was being drafted in the Revisor's Office. Donald had the ballot for Legislative Council signatures. He needed a majority of Legislative Council members' approval to allow the bill in during the second session. The second session usually hears only new bills of an emergency nature. Greg said that Democratic leadership had signed off on this one, but so far no Republicans had been spoken to. Greg thought my active support would be critical, and that the "correction" bill will need active support from Judiciary Committee members and a number of other influential legislators if the legislature is going to salvage the integrity of its own process and the Implementing Act process.

On another subject, I had a Maine Women Veterans Oral History Group meeting this morning. Pauleena MacDougall, a professor at the University of Maine, couldn't make it, so that left me and Chris Beam, a professor at Bates. We are trying to get the project off the ground. It's slow going, but I think we made a little bit of progress. I think I'll try to combine the oral history project and the first-ever Women Veterans Conference into one package and look for funding. This would be a really great thing for Maine's women veterans if the Women Veterans Commission can pull it off.

I MUST BE HONEST AND SAY I DO NOT SEE A BRIGHT FUTURE FOR THIS BILL. THE GAMING IS GOING TO KILL IT.

February 16, 2000
Wednesday
7:55 A.M.

I took Donald's ballot around yesterday during session to get enough signatures to get it in this session. I got each member of the Legislative Council to allow the bill in except Senator Bennett (R), so it has been approved to be in this session. I must be honest and say I do not see a bright future for this bill. The gaming is going to kill it. I did promise I would do what I could to help, and I will. The ball is now in Donald's court to lobby for the bill this week.

We had a Maine Indian Tribal–State Commission meeting yesterday. It was not a very good meeting. For one thing, a woman showed up who is adamantly against the Albany Township bill. She's one of the attorneys for Albany Township. Also, Mike Hastings, a state representative on the commission who has been an ally in the past, gave us a very hard time. The Penobscot Nation had asked MITSC to be a cosponsor of the Katahdin workshop on April 13. The workshop was scheduled as an educational meeting for the Katahdin Advisory Committee. Mike Hastings wanted to involve MITSC as a negotiator and wanted MITSC to set part of the agenda. I finally got mad and said the Penobscot Nation would take care of this itself. So now we will have to find the money to bring in a speaker ourselves.

To top it all off, Deb DuBrule, the *Indian Country Today* reporter, was sitting in on the meeting; she laughed out loud when Diana Scully mentioned some national organization wanted input from the committee on how well the state and tribes could cooperate.

February 22, 2000
Tuesday
Today was a session day, nothing of importance except that one of the Albany Township attorneys wrote a letter to the Judiciary Committee asking it to vote down my bill to extend the deadline for the Penobscot Nation to buy trust land. This individual thinks the Passamaquoddy are not going to give up on the gaming issue, and that the Penobscot bill will extend Passamaquoddy deadlines, as well. This is, in fact, not the case, and I think the committee will see this.

Something else came up. Senator Judy Paradis (D) is introducing a bill to fund Native students who attend technical colleges. I expressed my concern that we might lose whatever tuition waivers we now have with the state university system if she pushes her bill. It's a bill that is estimated to cost close to $4 million. I spoke with Representative John Martin (D) this afternoon, and he said he'd speak with her and try to work something out.

One last thing. A reporter from the *Bangor Daily News* (BDN) caught up with me in the hall and asked about the mascot issue. I've been trying not to talk about this issue all year because I did not want it to be confused with the Offensive Names Bill. I told him what I thought—that the mascot issue could and should be taken care of in the schools through education and communication with Native people. Mascot names should be changed at the request of the students, not the legislature. It might be in the paper tomorrow.

February 24, 2000
Thursday
Warm day, around 45 degrees
My bill to extend the Penobscot deadline on trust lands came before the Judiciary Committee yesterday for a work session. The Albany Township attorney was there, which didn't surprise me. I noticed her talking to Representative Thomas Bull (D). Tom is unpredictable in some respects, so I made a point of speaking to him before the committee started its work. I told Tom in no uncertain terms that I did

not want any amendments whatsoever from this attorney! When we got to my bill, Tom asked if any members had seen the letter from the attorney and if there was any interest in discussing it. There was dead silence, and Tom said, "I guess not."

Then Representative Paul Waterhouse made a motion to accept the bill with an amendment, the amendment being to remove the deadline from the bill. Discussion followed. Most people felt it wasn't a good idea to remove the deadline, simply because of the title of the section of law that reads, "Date by which trust land can be acquired." They also felt that there might be some federal implications and did not want any legal complications. Representative Bill Norton (D) felt that a deadline was good because it would give the feds a time limit, but his argument carried the least weight. Senator Longley came out against eliminating the date, and Representative Waterhouse and Representative Plowman (both Republicans) were the only two that voted in favor of the amendment. Then there was a vote on the original bill itself, which asked for another twenty years, and that bill passed with a unanimous vote. The Albany Township attorney's face got redder and redder as things progressed to the final vote, and she left rather abruptly.

Beth Sockbeson, my sister and a tribal council member, just called and told me that the town manager of Greenville, the same guy who tried to teach me about my heritage, has been recruited by the town of Carrabassett to be its new town manager. That may put a crimp in the tribe's relationship with Carrabassett. The tribe owns most of Carrabassett Valley, and there has been a problem with people in the resort area respecting our land, a situation that has received some media hype. We had a joint meeting with the town a few months ago and resolved to work on our issues together. Beth is trying to find out more about this new development. I told Beth we should have another meeting with the town and make sure we are going to be able to work with this new guy.

"THEY DON'T EVEN CELEBRATE COLUMBUS DAY!"
—BARBARA WALTERS, ABC "20/20"

February 26, 2000
Saturday

Got a call from ABC last night asking me to go to New York to be interviewed. They had reviewed the tapes from the past interviews and decided to make it a longer show. They thought I would be the best representative for the offensive names issue. I asked for some time to think about it and make arrangements to stay with some friends. I then called Donald, since he is the sponsor of the bill. I didn't want to go on national TV to talk about Donald's bill without his consent.

Donald said, "Of course you should go. We need national exposure." He was hoping this program would air before the floor debate in the legislature. I told Donald it's a two-edged sword—it could help us or hurt us. It might make it a more popular subject, so I'm hoping it *doesn't* air before the debate. I called ABC back and told them I would do it and wanted to leave on Monday and come back on Tuesday. A guy named James will call me sometime today to make the flight arrangements.

I am a bit concerned that the interviewer, John Stossel, might try to make me angry so that I lose my temper. I understand he does that sort of thing with a smile. We'll see what happens. Regardless of the outcome, I hope this will make Native people and tribal governments visible. Maybe this can be the mustard seed, so to speak.

March 3, 2000
Friday

It's been one long and crazy week, starting with my trip to New York. I left Monday morning and it was windy and foggy. I thought my plane might be delayed or canceled, but we took off in a lot of wind gusts and fog and it was a very turbulent takeoff and landing.

I had trouble finding the car that was supposed to be waiting for me, but after forty-five minutes or so, with a lot of cell-phone talk back and forth with one of the "20/20" producers, I finally found the car parked a half-mile down the street with my name in very small letters (I'm not joking) on a sign. I had packed a suit and thought perhaps there would be a dressing room where I could change, but I had to change in a bathroom. The set was not very impressive, but I really didn't think it would be. I figured it would be a lot like the one where we filmed our Women's Commission PSA—a small space with cameras and wiring all over. There were two director's chairs in the middle of the room.

They put the microphone on me and wired me, and shortly after that John Stossel came in. He introduced himself, said he hoped I had a good trip, and asked if they were putting me up in a nice hotel. He then said, "This shouldn't take long, depending on how well you do." He was right—it didn't take long, probably all of fifteen or twenty minutes. I don't think I answered his questions the way he expected. For instance, he had a pile of pages he was holding and claimed they were place names across the country that included the "S-word." He asked me if I thought they should all be changed.

I said I was only interested in changing the names in Maine.

He said, "Come on, tell me what you think."

So I said, "Yes, I think they should all be changed."

He said, "Well, if all these names are changed, isn't that changing history?"

I said, "I hope so—someone should change history and start telling the truth!" He looked like he had been totally surprised by my answer. He then started talking about the mascot issue, the dictionary meaning of the word, and also the effect it would have on language. I basically said those were all moot points and the only thing that was relevant was how the word was used to hurt and abuse Native women, and how Native women felt abused and dehumanized by its usage. After Stossel left the room his crew placed an 8 x 10 color photo of him in his chair. I walked over and turned it around. Everyone cracked up.

I left for home the next morning and arrived back around 2:30 P.M. I had all kinds of messages waiting for me. They were mostly from Indian Island and people concerned with the Indian scholarship bill that Senator Paradis had submitted. The concern is that by creating a scholarship program at the technical college, we might lose the tuition waver program we have within the University of Maine System. The bill would likely result in the waiver program being cut out of the system and the scholarship program put on the legislative appropriations table. We'd have to fight every year to get anything. I had spoken to Senator Paradis about my concerns before I left for New York, and she had indicated that she was willing to rework the bill. It was clear from all the calls that she now wanted to kill the bill.

On Thursday, by chance, I ran into her at the Senator Inn. I was there to attend a Legislative Women's breakfast, but it had been cancelled. Since I was there, I decided to attend another breakfast, a Manufactured Housing Association breakfast for legislators. Senator Paradis was there and we had breakfast together and discussed the implications of her bill. She told me she was going to withdraw the bill on Monday. I will attend the hearing to make sure that is what happens.

March 4, 2000
Saturday
The sub-chief called me yesterday and gave me a hard time about not being able to be reached on Monday. She had read about Senator Paradis's bill and was going nuts! She must have called and written letters to every council member, including the Passamaquoddy, as well as the tribal governor and anyone else she could think of. She said she was going to the hearing on Monday. I asked her to keep a low profile, since there are those who would love to take our scholarship monies away from us. She said she would go just to monitor

the situation and might not even speak.

As if that was not enough, yesterday morning a DJ came on the air stating that he had gone to dinner with his wife the night before and they discussed the Sacajewea dollar. The DJ then proceeded to tell the public that they had decided to name it the "S—— Buck" and wanted everyone to call it that. The weatherman tried to stop him from saying this but to no avail. I think it was the weatherman who said, "If you say that, you'll have the Penobscot Nation sitting on our doorstep." Well, sure enough, Penobscot people heard it and started calling each other and a van full of people picketed the station. I haven't heard from any TV stations or newspaper reporters yet, but that's just a matter of time.

The problem with this whole mess is that finally the federal government does something to honor Native women and then some idiot or bigot—whichever the case may be—says something like this over the public airwaves. The S-word directly denigrates this symbol. Native women are really upset. I'm not sure where this is going but I will talk to the AG's office on Monday. This is Saturday morning and I have received a phone call already from a Penobscot woman mad as hell and wanting something to be done. I sure hope this does not complicate the debate on the floor over Donald's Offensive Names Bill. I don't think the bill will hit the floor until next Friday.

March 17, 2000
Friday
Winter storm today, 6 to 10 inches expected. Happy St. Paddy's Day! "20/20" aired on March 10 and the debate hit the floor of the house on March 15. Not many legislators saw the program, thank goodness! Stossel put a negative spin on everything I said—that is, everything they didn't cut. To make a long story short, Stossel decided to make it part of his "Give Me a Break" segment. I did very well, since I was calm and reserved and came off looking a heck of a lot better than Stossel and Walters! But the segment compared the S-word to mascots on football teams, Bessy the cow in Canada, and some sort

of fish in Colorado. They missed the whole point that this word is abusive to Native women. They made a joke out of the issue on national TV, and at the end of the piece Walters said, "Now I'm not sure; what do we call them—Native Americans or what?" She went on to say, "They don't even celebrate Columbus Day!" and Stossel said something about giving us the land back!

I expected something like this, but not such a negative from Barbara Walters. I must say I was really disappointed and surprised at her ignorance and total disrespect for Indian issues. I'm just glad it's over, but I think it probably started some dialogue across the country. I know I received some concerned calls from members of the Vietnam Women Veterans Organization. They said they e-mailed the station. I am certain that had this been an African-American organization or group targeted by those insensitive comments, they both would be apologizing profusely and maybe even looking for another job! How could they get away with such disrespect toward Native people on national television?

As for the tuition waiver bill, the vice chancellor of academic affairs for the University of Maine System and a lady from their finance department got together with me the morning the bill was to go to public hearing. We strategized on how to kill it. After many questions from Senator Michaud, the chair of the Appropriations Committee, the bill was officially killed (a great relief to many others and me). It was a good thing this happened, because for many years Native people have been afraid to say anything about the waiver program for fear we would lose it. I'm not so worried about that anymore. I found out through the course of all the questions that the university has a total waiver program of over $11 million and only $1 million is used for Native students. The rest goes to other entitlement programs, such as foster children, widows and children of firefighters who died on duty, as well as veteran's survivors, etc. So if they do away with or try to cap our program, then they have to do the same to these others—and believe me, there are some powerful groups here!

On the same afternoon that this was before the Appropriations Committee, I was told by General Adams, at the last minute, that I should stay and answer some questions. The committee wanted to know about the Women Veterans Commission and how it was spending the money allocated last session. They asked, "Was this money a one-time allocation?" I explained that it was less than what I had asked for and that last session they had said they would review it at a later date to see if we needed more money. They seemed to be satisfied with that answer and asked for a breakdown. General Adams informed them that they had a breakdown in their packets.

That was it for a while, anyway.

We needed to win this one for them.

March 18, 2000

Saturday

Donald and I were starting to gear up for the debate we knew would come in the house over the Offensive Names Bill. Donald said he was getting nervous, and the day before we knew it was to hit the floor he said, "I'm going to go home, take an aspirin, and go to bed." We both laughed, but we were both nervous because we knew not only would the public be watching us debate this, but most important of all, our people. We needed to win this one for them.

When we walked into the house chamber the next day, on March 15, there were close to twenty Native women and a few Native men in the hallway with some huge signs and a lot of round yellow stickers that said, "Vote yes on L.D. 2418." Diana Scully, the executive director of MITSC, was there and told me she'd heard they were not going to debate the issue today. I went directly to the speaker's office and asked what was going on. After talking with Representative Richard Thompson, the chair of the Judiciary Committee, and Nancy Kelleher, the speaker's chief of staff, they agreed that they would help to get the debate on the floor—which they did, and Speaker Rowe was very willing to allow this to happen. The debate started around 11:30 A.M. and ended around 1:30 P.M.

The representatives speaking against the bill were Paul Waterhouse (R) from Bridgton, John T. Buck (R) from Yarmouth, Stavros Mendros (R) from Lewiston, Thomas F. Shields (R) from Auburn, Zachary Matthews (D) from Winslow, and Earl E. Richardson (R) from Greenville. That's all I remember. For our side, Representative Donald Soctomah spoke, Richard Thompson (D), William R. Cote (D) from Lewiston, Linda Rodgers McKee (D) from Wayne, Harry G. True (R) from Fryeburg, Matthew Dunlap (D) from Old Town, and others. Representative Wendy Pieh (D) from Bremen spoke and said, "If I could, I would give my vote to Representative Loring." I was glad she said that on the record. It called attention to the fact that tribal representatives cannot vote even on an issue that affects them so directly, such as this one.

Anyway, we were finally ready to vote and the final house vote was 129 to 17 in favor of the bill! The Native women in the balcony broke out in applause. The house truly made history by that overwhelming vote. They sent the message that this word is an offensive name and they did something about it. They actually empathized with us!

The day was not over for Donald and me. We met and talked with the press and media and knew the next day it would be in all the newspapers. We were euphoric! We had finally won a victory!

We had one more public hearing to attend before we went home for the day. It was the hearing on the newest Passamaquoddy bill, Representative Soctomah and Greg Sample's bill that would correct a mistake by the legislature, overrule the law court decision, and make Albany Township Indian territory.

We went downstairs to the first floor. Our committee had to shift to a bigger room because of all the interest this was generating from Albany Township and the surrounding towns. When we got there, there was no room for Native people to sit, since the people from Albany Township and others were already there. You could feel the tension in the room as we entered.

The Passamaquoddy Tribe presented its case first, and then the Albany people. Albany is so afraid of the casino issue that its people could see nothing else. Donald and I tried to focus our arguments on the mistake that the legislature had made. Others from Albany said there was no mistake, and that the court never mentions a mistake in its decision. One guy testified that Albany and the surrounding towns were getting together and had formed an economic development committee. I found this strange, since they had used development as an argument *against* the Passamaquoddy Tribe. They were afraid of what it would do to their pristine land, etc.

The owner of the Bethel newspaper testified that "The state had better watch out because the tribes have sovereign powers that the state can't touch, and if they get in partnership with a foreign country who knows what could happen!"

Would you believe that these people from Albany and Bethel brought their children with them into this atmosphere? The sub-chief had sung a song for the committee when she testified at the beginning. She felt the negativity in the room and knew it was not a good atmosphere for children. During her traditional song the Albany people were starting to grin. Some of the Native people sensed this and were ready to jump in and start a riot right there. *(I found this out later—a good thing I didn't know it then.)* I didn't stay for all of Albany's testimony. I had had enough for one day. I went home, kicked my dog, and had a beer. (Just kidding.)

"THE GOVERNOR AND THE LEGISLATURE GOT AMBUSHED BY A SMALL GROUP OF INDIANS." —QUOTED IN THE BDN

March 18, 2000—continued

I forgot about the work session on the Albany Township bill today. Donald called and told me that after they had talked about it for an hour or so, they tabled it until next Friday. Donald said Senator Longley was all for passing the bill if the Land Use Regulatory Commission (LURC) could rehear the issues. Donald said the Passamaquoddy Tribe would agree to this. I hope we can get a divided report; then we can debate it on the floor with some effect. If it comes out unanimous ONTP, then we're just speaking on the record, which I will do.

I was worried about the senate vote on March 16 on the Offensive Names Bill because we have no presence in that chamber and they are usually more conservative than in the house. I woke up at 3:00 A.M. and couldn't get back to sleep. When I got to the senate chamber later in the morning, many of the same Native women were there for the senate vote who had been in the house hall the day before, and this time there were some younger Native students, too. I went into the chamber and took a seat. The senate majority leader, Chellie Pingree (D) from North Haven, came over and told me they were going to try to pass it under the gavel. I waited, holding my breath. When the item came up, I saw the assistant minority leader, Senator Richard Bennett (R) from Norway, start to rise then change his mind. The moment passed. It had gone under the gavel with no opposition in the senate! I was amazed. Not only did the Offensive Names Bill pass that day, but my bill for the Penobscot deadline extension passed in the house and the senate without debate.

March 19, 2000

Sunday

Nice warm day, around 40 degrees

The *Maine Sunday Telegram*, the weekend edition of the *Portland Press Herald*, printed a very nice article about Donald. It was a profile and went into detail about his personality, etc. I thought it was great—it's about time Donald got some recognition!

Tomorrow the week starts and Monday is a very busy day. The Women Veterans Commission group meets at 8:00 A.M. and the session starts at 9:00 A.M. At noon I meet with James Andrew Mitchell from Camden, who has asked to talk with me. He is writing a book profiling a number of independent Maine women and asked if I would be one. I'm thinking about that. At 2:00 P.M. Donald and I will be in Senator Pingree's office being interviewed by phone by Boston Public Radio. Donald is afraid that there will be a lot of questions about linguistics pertaining to the Offensive Names Bill. I told him I didn't think so, but now that I think about it, who knows? At least the issue is starting a national dialogue on Native issues. We are becoming more visible every day.

March 20, 2000

Monday

First day of spring—nice day, around 50 degrees

I thought we were to have session today but we did not. I met with James Mitchell and we had a pleasant lunch at the Senator Inn. I decided to do the profile and we will meet again after session closes at the end of April.

Donald and I did two radio interviews today on the Offensive Names Bill, one for Boston Public Radio and the other for New Hampshire; the New Hampshire guy said he also covered CBS News events as well as Massachusetts and the lower part of Maine. He told Donald he was going to give this national coverage. Tomorrow, first thing in the morning, I have an Arizona interview. This will be live over their radio station.

We have a session tomorrow, and hopefully the Offensive Names Bill will pass the final stages in the house and senate and go to the governor for his signature. In the afternoon I have a meeting scheduled at Indian Island. I may or may not attend, depending on where the bill is. I also have a meeting in the afternoon sponsored by the English Department at UMO. The reason I am attending this particular meeting is because my good friend Tony Brinkley, chair of the department, asked me to.

March 21, 2000
Tuesday
A very nice day, around 50 degrees
The Offensive Names Bill had a second reading in the senate this morning and will be engrossed (presented in final form) in the senate tomorrow and go to the house for enactment. It will then be sent to the governor's office. Donald and I stopped by and talked with David Wilby, one of the governor's staff, and everything seems to be in order. The governor is still willing to sign the bill, as far as we all know. Tomorrow will be a double legislative session, meaning we will have a session in the morning and another in the afternoon.

This morning I got up at 5:30 A.M. to be ready when radio station KAKY called from Arizona. They called around 7:10 A.M. eastern time and I talked to them for about ten minutes. It was a live talk show and listeners could call in. They got about three calls while I was on the air—all of them negative. No one could understand why Maine would change the names of places. They gave the same old, worn-out arguments about the meaning of the word, and they thought if they didn't mean it in a bad way then it was all right. One caller compared it to being called a "cracker" when he was younger.

The last caller was a woman who thought the whole thing was about being PC and that people should learn to live with it and accept it and just become stronger people because of it.

Ridiculous! I was stressed out before I left the house!

When I arrived at the Statehouse and bought a cup of coffee and the *Bangor Daily News*, I noticed the headline "Owner Won't Rename Resort"—a big banner front-page headline! I was taken a bit by surprise that the BDN would print such garbage on the front page and on the day the bill goes in front of the senate for the second time. The article quoted the resort owner, who is from Florida, complaining that Maine people did not get a fair say in the vote and this should all have gone to referendum! He said, "The govenor and the legislature got ambushed by a small group of Indians." I showed the article to Representative Thompson, who was shocked and bemused all at the same time.

Donald and I waited in the senate and watched Senator Davis, one of the senators from the Greenville area, pass notes and confer with Senator Bennett, who is the assistant minority leader in the senate. We were sure they were planning something—an amendment or an objection of some sort. We waited, holding our breaths.

Needless to say, when the senate passed the bill this morning for the second time, Donald and I were greatly relieved. Because the newspaper article had made it sound as if the governor had doubts, we felt we should talk with someone from the governor's office, but his staff person assured us everything was fine. I was emotionally drained.

The session ended around noon and I decided to forego my meetings in Orono and just go home and take a nap. Hopefully this will be over tomorrow, the bill will be enacted in both the house and senate, and it will then go to the governor to be signed into law.

Can we trust the legislative process to work the way we intended it to in the Land Claims Settlement Act?

March 26, 2000
Sunday
A very nice day, mid 50s
Friday morning we had judicial appointments to confirm at the Judiciary Committee. The first appointment to be confirmed was Rick Lawrence, who would be the first black person to be appointed to the bench in Maine history. His presentation was the best I had heard to date, his credentials impeccable, and he had done his research! He impressed me like no other candidate I had heard before, and I was proud that he was a person of color and had accomplished the things he had, especially in the field of education. He was a Yale undergraduate and a Harvard law school graduate. The committee asked quite a few questions and he answered them with no hesitation. His confirmation was a well-deserved one, and I got up and gladly shook the man's hand.

The next one was an attorney from up north; he was much less impressive, but everyone seemed to know him and admire him. I looked through his paperwork and found he had been convicted of OUI when he was the district attorney. He had been divorced twice. I wondered how a man with such a past would even be considered for the bench. His undergraduate education was at the University of Maine, followed by Maine law school. I did have a little discussion with my seatmates about the comparison between the two candidates—I couldn't help myself and I couldn't let it pass. I also noted that the committee never asked him about his OUI conviction and how that might influence his decisions on the bench.

Afterwards, I spoke with Senator Benoit, who was a judge in his previous work. He explained that one cannot be narrowly focused—one has to consider everything, including accomplishment, etc., and then decide. I owned up that I may have been too narrowly focused and said I would try to be a bit more broad-minded in the future.

Friday afternoon the Passamaquoddy bill that would correct the oversight made by both the Passamaquoddy Tribe and the legislature went before the Judiciary Committee for a work session. This is where we debate the issue and a committee vote is taken. I knew this one was going to be tough and that all I could hope for would be one vote against the Ought Not to Pass motion that I knew would be coming. I debated the bill as strongly as I could, using the government-to-government relationship and not arguing the gaming issue. The vote was 8 to 2 in favor of the ONTP motion. Among the reasons given were that they felt it should be redone right this time, since times have changed, and because Albany Township has a bigger interest.

My argument was that it was a treaty that all parties had agreed to, and that they should fix the oversight to conform to the original intent, which was to place this land into territory status. I argued it would be a breach of good faith not to do so and it was their duty to the tribes to make this right. I said we—meaning the Penobscot Nation as well as the Passamaquoddy Tribe—expect them to honor the treaty.

Senator Longley and Representative Mitchell voted to amend the bill by removing the retroactive clause and just changing the date in Part 1 to allow the Passamaquoddy to buy trust land. Senator Longley said they could fight about the meaning in court. That was the best I could get out of them. (The room was full of Albany Township people.) After the work session was over, Representative LaVerdiere came over to me and said, "Let's talk later about this."

I said, "Fine." We will get together next week when not so many Albany people are around. They had ambushed Senator Treat as she was leaving, and she had not been there to vote. I heard her say, "My vote doesn't count that much, anyway." I think she will vote with

Longley and Mitchell. She has always done right by us. I am preparing a scathing speech on this. Although I do not agree with gaming, there is a bigger issue here and it is one that could make or break the Land Claims Settlement Act. The issue is: Can we trust the legislative process to work the way we intended it to in the Land Claims Settlement? The key elements are trust and reliability. The other piece to this is that the federal government is a third party to this Settlement Act and it has already recognized the land as trust land and placed it in trust. Can a state court overrule that federal action?

Representative Thompson took me aside and said, "The biggest reason I voted against this was because I do not trust the Passamaquoddy; they tried to pull a fast one on us in 1992 by putting this in for trust status and at the same time put in a separate bill to allow high-stakes bingo on Indian territory. It is not so much that I don't trust Donald, as it is that I don't trust their attorney. I really do feel bad about voting against this."

I responded by saying that I thought he was being too narrow in his focus. I was remembering what I'd been told by Senator Benoit and others when I asked why they would appoint a district court judge to the bench who had been convicted of an OUI—that we shouldn't be so focused on just one issue. I reminded Representative Thompson of that policy lesson I had so recently learned. He said, "Well, maybe you're right, but I still don't feel I can support this."

TODAY WE MADE HISTORY.

April 3, 2000
Monday
Rainy day, 45-50 degrees
Today we made history. Governor King signed the Offensive Names
Bill in his office with media all over the place. There must have been
twenty or thirty people present. He made a two- or three-minute
speech and asked me if I wanted to say something. I had already told
Donald he would be speaking first and the governor took me by surprise, but I did okay. Donald did well also. Sherry Mitchell also spoke
on a mascot question the press asked about. I was glad to see Emma
Nichola there; I had her stand next to me but later on TV, I noticed
she was standing behind me and no one could see her. She was glad
to be there and thanked me. Brenda Commander was there and so
was Esther Attean with some of her students. Donald and I and every
other Native person were interviewed by at least three or four different stations as well as by various newspaper reporters. I got a chance
to mention the study committee on Native representatives and our
hopes to be able to at least vote in committee.

A few days ago I had breakfast at the Blaine House with the governor, along with other legislators, and Senator Benoit brought his
wife with him; she seems to be a very nice lady and I think Senator
Benoit is a decent person, as well. He's an old softy—he grows on
you. Anyway, this was before the governor signed the bill, and the
governor asked me if I was nervous that he wouldn't sign it. When I
said yes, he said, "Stop worrying about it." After he said that to me, I
did stop worrying and it seemed like it was signed before I knew it.

It's the last week of session, and Donald and I have one more bill
to debate on the floor the day after tomorrow. It's a loser and we
both know it. I need to start thinking seriously about my speech.

WHEN THE SMOKE HAD SETTLED, IT WAS YET ANOTHER INDIAN MASSACRE.

April 6, 2000
Thursday
Cold day, around 35 or 40
Well, today the loser bill hit the floor for debate. Donald and I had been preparing our speeches for the floor all week. I worked on mine the night before last until ten o'clock, and I worked even more on it last night until around midnight. We didn't get out of the session last night until ten o'clock.

Representative Thompson introduced the bill we call the Albany Township Bill to the house and gave a detailed explanation without really trying to truly convince them to vote for the majority report. I think only one person argued against it, and he did a bad job. Representative Charles Mitchell (D) did one heck of a job for the bill and seems to have taken it on as if it were his own. Representative John Martin also came out on our side, as well as Representatives McKee and Tracy. We were all very persuasive on the floor. We got a vote we did not expect—78 to 68 in our favor! Later there was another attempt by Republican leadership to kill the bill, and that was foiled by a vote of 74 to 71.

The bill is now in the senate for action tomorrow. Representatives John Martin and Charlie Mitchell are lobbying hard for us. I am also doing my share. It has turned into a party issue mainly because of Senator Bennett, the assistant minority leader in the senate. I figured that he got lobbied by the attorney from Albany Township, but I later found out that he lives in Albany Township! She was there all day sending legislators notes if they were from her area and telling them how to vote, etc. She has been a real thorn in our side. I'm sure she fully intends to be. I got home tonight at

9:30 P.M. because I had an interview scheduled with a London radio station interested in the Offensive Names Bill. (Donald and I are being called about this bill two or three times a week by the media). The interview lasted about five minutes. I think the guy didn't know what questions to ask—it was kind of awkward. But maybe someone over there heard it and now understands what's really happening over here.

This afternoon Donald and I were interviewed by FOX News again about the Offensive Names Bill. FOX is a TV station that shows national news out of Boston. I hope they treat the story with the respect it deserves. We'll see.

April 8, 2000
Saturday

Today was the day from hell. The bill turned into a party issue all right, but our party didn't support us. We lost the Albany Township Bill in the senate. The *Bangor Daily News* weekend edition came out with at least two stories that hurt the Passamaquoddy. One was a story about fishermen being angry because they had to pay to fish on the Passamaquoddy side of certain lakes and rivers. The tribe had claimed its jurisdiction and the locals were not pleased. The second article was about Indian Township governor Richard Doyle being suspended from the payroll for sexual harassment. These stories certainly did not help our cause.

It was the hardest thing I have ever done to have to sit there helpless and listen to these self-righteous, pompous senators talk so degradingly about Indians and gambling in the same breath. Senator Benoit was the first one to speak, and he went into how Albany Township had been denied due process and that was just plain unacceptable and shouldn't happen in this country! He went on and on. Senator Bennett, with great emotion and close to tears, begged the other senators not to make his home into a casino. He was so convincing I would have changed my vote. "Please don't take away my family's home," he pleaded. Of course this was after he told all the other senators he loved them and said they were all honest and good people (as opposed to those *Indians* who just want to gamble and ruin his home). Senator Peter Mills took the high holier-than-thou road. He talked about how gambling was so terrible that we shouldn't allow it in this state and that the tribes were being used by people out of New York for their own gain. He went on and on about how horrible gambling was, especially when Indians were involved.

I was so mad I couldn't think or see straight! None of these pompous, self-righteous, expletives-deleteted individuals had ever proposed a bill to remove gambling from the state! Yet they had the audacity to stand and speak so outrageously against Native people.

Albany Township people, most of whom were retired and well off, just sat there grinning from ear to ear. They knew they had the vote. We knew they had the vote, and it all had to do with gambling. I'm sick and tired of gambling being an issue with Indian bills! The senators who spoke against us knew they had the vote but kept rubbing salt into the wounds. When the smoke had settled it was yet another Indian massacre. White men win and Indians lose again, with no regard whatsoever for a government-to-government relationship and no effort at all to honor the 1980 treaty process and thelegislative vote in favor of this change in 1992.

Someday they are going to realize that they are dealing with governments and not regular towns. The obligation they have to a government-to-government relationship is far greater than to Albany Township. Since when did a disorganized town—or any town—have the power to turn around a treaty agreement between governments? The only question I heard in reference to the Maine Land Claims Settlement Act was from a senator during caucus prior to the senate debate. He asked what would happen if they ignored the treaty obligations? (He was referring to the Land Claims Settlement Act.) The answer the senator received was, "Probably nothing."

We are not getting the respect and honor due us as a people—people slandered, used, cheated, abused, and murdered us for our resources and our lands. What about *our* lands that were stolen from *us*? What about our way of life and the very resources we depended on to survive? What about when we cried and begged and pleaded in those very halls and in those chambers? Our pleas fell on deaf ears. No one would listen.

Yet when Senator Bennett cries in the senate it's worth more than all our generations of grief and mourning combined. They heard him, they honored him, and we are left with nothing yet again. Senators Longley and Cathcart did the best they could but gave up when Senator Bennett stood up and gave his emotional teary-eyed speech. I am truly disgusted and discouraged. It's not that I'm for gambling. But I am not for making Native people look like criminals just because we are desperate to find something that works for us economically.

Has Maine helped us to find other ways to survive economically? As a matter of fact, when the Penobscot Nation approached the Taxation Committee last year for a tax break on bingo to help us finance emergency services for our tribal government, the very same senators—including senators Mills, Bennett, Benoit, and Ferguson—refused to give us a tax break. When we, as the Penobscot and Passamaquoddy representatives, put in a bill that would allow us to be part of the Homestead Exemption Act, we were voted down because we did not pay property taxes.

We may not pay property taxes per se but we pay plenty to the state in what is termed PILOT taxes (Payment in Lieu of Taxes). Every attempt we have made to be economically self-sufficient has been shot down with excuses and bogus reasons. It is easy to sit in judgment of "those Indians" when you're doing well yourself. Who cares about what generations before you did to us; who cares about what we have to do to survive as long as it doesn't bother you or yours, or as long as you don't have to share the wealth? That's it, isn't it—share the wealth? Sorry if I sound like I'm ranting, but pompous self-righteous senators have that effect on me.

My last word on the subject is this: I heard a lot of mean-spirited negative words during that senate debate and they were calculated to hurt and to criminalize Native people. I left the senate chamber feeling personally attacked and wondering, "Where is the integrity of this process? Will the people of Maine ever get it? Will they ever open their ears and hearts and decide to allow us in on some of the wealth?" Don't criticize us; don't criminalize us for just trying to survive.

On the 14th the *Bangor Daily News* came out with yet another article on the Passamaquoddy fishing dispute. The title was "Passamaquoddy Fishing Rules Plan Angers Anglers." The first sentence reads: "Fishermen are stocking up on ammunition rather than fishing gear, Baileyville resident Danny McPhee warned the Town Council on Monday night." Next to that huge article was another article about two Perry men indicted in a firebombing. This was also a negative Passamaquoddy article. I was very concerned with the message the fishing article was sending—it was inflammatory and could ignite a very volatile situation. I brought this to the attention of other legislators and the governor's office. I called Mark Woodward, the paper's manager, and complained.

April 19, 2000
Wednesday
I stewed all weekend about what had happened in the senate. I even sat down and wrote an article about it. I figured when the bill went back to the house, it would easily be killed with one simple motion to recede and concur. I was totally prepared for that outcome.

When I walked into the house chamber on Monday morning, I saw the female attorney for Albany Township sitting there, and sure enough, the first item on the calendar was the Passamaquoddy bill. I'll be damned if Representative Paul Waterhouse didn't stand up and start debating the issue. He said some of the same things that were said in the senate. I just could not let it pass. At least in the house I have a voice. (Donald wasn't there—he had no idea it was going to hit the floor.)

So I stood up and began to read part of my legislative diary, the part about what happened to the bill in the senate. When I got to Senator Bennett and his crying, the speaker banged his gavel and stopped me, since I was out of order—house rules forbid us to speak of what happens in the senate. I knew I was going to be stopped, but it's one of those ploys every attorney makes when she/he wants the jury to know something. I did it for the record. I finished by reading the last paragraph in my diary. When I sat down, all of a sudden all I could think of was my ancestors and how pained they must have been to have to beg for their lands and their lives in these very halls and in this very chamber. All the stress of the media attention, interviews, etc., came to a head and I lost it—I cried. (The assistant clerk of the house, Millie MacFarland, sent me a small manila evnvelope with a bunch of tissues in it. This, of course, only made me cry more. I thanked her the next day.)

After I had spoken, two or three more representatives got up and spoke against the bill. I could not let this be the last word. I stood one more time and said, "I remind you that the issue here is a government-to-government relationship, not gambling. Please vote against this motion." The vote was taken and we lost by about thirty votes. If I had any doubts about sending my article to the papers they were gone. I immediately left the chamber and started to call the newspapers to see if they would print the article I'd written about the bill. I have yet to see it appear. I've been told that *Maine Sunday Telegram* is planning to print it this Sunday. Good timing, as this coming Sunday is Easter.

I've been relaxing this week and getting ready to go back next Monday. Oh, yes, on Friday, April 14, 2000, the senate and the house passed a resolution declaring 2000 the Year of the Native American Woman! It was sponsored and signed by all the leadership in the house and the senate. This was something that was initiated by MITSC after the radio commentator made his remarks over the airwaves about the "Squaw Buck." No one spoke on this resolution except me. I felt I was forcing this down their throats, but it was an acknowledgment of the strength and the worth of Native women, and I felt proud that we had been recognized. After all how could they have refused?

The resolution read as follows:

Joint Resolution, (4-5) On motion by President LAWRENCE of York (Cosponsored by Speaker ROWE of Portland and Senators: AMERO of Cumberland, BENNETT of Oxford, PINGREE of Knox, RAND of Cumberland, Representatives: CAMPBELL of Holden, MURPHY Of Kennebunk, SAXL of Portland, SHIAR of Bowdoinham, the following Joint Resolution:
S.P. 1086
Joint Resolution Declaring 2000 the Year of the Native American Woman:
WHEREAS, Maine's Wabanaki peoples have proclaimed 2000 as the Year of the Native American Woman; and
WHEREAS, we recognize the strength of the Native American Woman and we acknowledge that the Native American Woman is the cohesive force that is the foundation of her family and community alliances; and
WHEREAS, the Native American Woman is the giver of life and her mental, physical, emotional and spiritual well-being determines the direction of the next seven generations; and
WHEREAS, the Members of the One Hundred and Nineteenth Legislature enacted Public Law 613, "An Act Concerning Offensive Names," and sent their best wishes to Maine Native American women; now, therefore, be it
RESOLVED: That we, the Members of the One Hundred and Nineteenth Legislature now assembled in the Second Regular Session, join Maine's Wabanaki peoples in declaring 2000 the Year of the Native American Woman; and be it further
RESOLVED: That suitable copies of this resolution, duly authenticated by the Secretary of State, be transmitted to each of Maine's Tribal Communities.

"DONNA, YOU KICKED ASS!"

April 21, 2000
Thursday
Cloudy
This past Sunday the *Maine Sunday Telegram* and the Lewiston *Sun-Journal* printed my article in its entirety. When I arrived at the house on Monday all the Democrats and some of the Republicans told me it was a great article. Representative Harry True came up to me and put his arm around me and said, "Donna, that took real courage to do that. I'm proud of you." I just said, "Thank you, Harry, it had to be said. I'm going to miss you at the next session." Harry was one of the representatives who is being termed out. I also ran into Drew Ketterer, the AG, who said, "Donna, that was a great piece on Sunday, very powerful, I almost gave you a call at home. I had the phone in my hand and realized it was Sunday afternoon and that I could see you here on Monday." I just said, "Thanks, Drew, you should have called. I would have liked that." Representative Nancy Chizmar (D) of Lisbon Falls said, "My husband saw the article first and got so excited he woke me up and started reading it to me in bed." She said it was all true and it was about time someone said so.

My friend Rachel Talbot Ross told me her father, Gerry Talbot, a former representative from Portland and the first African American in the legislature, saw the article and that it's pretty much what they talked about at Easter dinner. Rachel said they all loved it and thought I told it like it was. She added, "Donna, you kicked ass."

My sister also read it and thought it was right on and about time it was said. That was pretty much everyone's sentiment on Indian Island who read or heard about it. I'm glad I did what I did, but I know that article most likely has created some diehard enemies for me in the senate.

Rachel Talbot Ross, my good friend and president
of the Portland branch of the NAACP
Courtesy of Rachel Talbot Ross

I'm speaking of senators Richard Bennett and Peter Mills. I know Mills will be there next session. I'm not sure about Bennett, since he is running for office at a higher level. But these guys have never been friends to Indian issues, so I guess I'm not losing too much.

The reaction that really bothers me is the one from Senator Longley. She said, "I didn't agree with a lot that you said and you were probably trying to make a political case about Native presence in the senate. Well, I think you can consider that's not going to happen now." I told her I didn't do it for any political strategic reason, I did it because it needed to be said.

It's going to be an interesting next session. There will be over twenty-five new house members. Some of the house members are running for senate seats. Rumor has it that Mike Saxl will be the next speaker, but I'm not sure about the rest of the house leadership team. I've got to figure out who to give copies of the Sovereign Nations Representation Study that was done on tribal representatives, so that we can generate support for our voting on committees, etc.

I had dinner with Representative Jane Saxl (D) from Bangor and a few others. Jane is termed out in the house but is running for a senate seat. I gave her a copy of the study. She said she will be talking to her son Mike, the future speaker, about the study and some of the other things we discussed, such as the relationship between the state and the tribes and why there is such mistrust between the two. We talked about my summer projects and the fact that our little entrepreneurial group, through Rachel Talbot Ross, got Secretary of Transportation Rodney Slater to agree to visit Maine this year. Jane was very interested in meeting him. She says the east-west highway project was her idea to begin with, and that Tim Woodcock, former Bangor mayor, was the mover and shaker.

It looks like one more session this afternoon until whenever, and hopefully we're done for a few weeks until so-called Veto Day, the day the legislature reconvenes to take up any bills the governor has vetoed since it adjourned—usually about two weeks after adjournment. Got to run for now and start the woodstove, it's cold!

I'M NOT SURE HOW THIS WILL PLAY OUT, BUT I AM SURE THAT MITSC WILL NEVER BE THE SAME.

April 29, 2000
Saturday

The night of the 27th was the last session for a few weeks until the May 11th Veto Day. I went home around 8:00 P.M., but everyone else stayed to try to finish. It was a losing battle. They ended up staying until 3:30 A.M. and still have a lot to get through. As I was leaving the house, Representative Harry True (R) asked if I was leaving and gave me a great big hug. I kissed him on the cheek and told him I would miss him next session, and he invited me to stop by and visit if I'm ever in his area. If I am, I'll do that. I truly like and respect Harry.

I'll see everyone one more time this session, since I am going for veto day. Clerk of the House Joe Mayo asked if I was coming back on Veto Day, and I told him I was. He said something about hoping both Donald and I would come back for that day. Joe will be leaving his position as clerk and will be sorely missed by the whole house. He has been diagnosed with Lou Gehrig's disease.

Yesterday I had a Maine Indian Tribal–State Commission meeting to attend. Donald had called me up the night before to let me know that he was going to walk out after he read a statement of protest about how the state members of the commission, by writing a separate letter to the Judiciary Committee, had undermined the process of getting the Passamaquoddy bill passed. Senator Benoit had later used the letter against the bill on the floor of the senate. I arrived around 9:30 A.M., just on time.

Eric Altavator, the Passamaquoddy member of MITSC, read a very stinging letter describing what his tribe felt about the letter and the actions of the four state members. He submitted his resignation

68

effective immediately, and he walked out. Representative Donald Soctomah then read his statement and walked out. John Banks, the Penobscot member, then asked Evan Richert (director of the State Planning Office and a state member on the commission) if he was happy, and went on to say that he had better things to do than waste his time with this commission, and he left. Evan was clearly upset and so were the other state members. Evan said, "Seeing we no longer have a quorum, I think we should close the meeting."

An elderly man who comes to all the meetings as an observer for the Quakers said, "Don't you think members of the public should be allowed to say what they think about this?"

The chair of the commission, Cush Anthony, said, "Yes, I do, but I'd like to hear from the members first."

The state members spoke, basically saying they felt they did the right thing and had no regrets. The one Penobscot member, Mark Chevaree, had just arrived and had missed the initial fireworks but said he felt that what the state members did was not right. He compared it to when the tribal council heard from the commission on the land use issues. He said he and John never wrote a separate letter to the council to change its members' minds.

I sat and listened to this argument go on with no one giving in. Evan Richert suggested that perhaps the Maine Indian Tribal–State Commission should disband or start talking about how to do away with the Land Claims Settlement Act, since that seemed to be what all the tribes want anyway. The other state members complained about being called names and spoken to abusively. (When they were asked when this happened, they couldn't provide specifics.) Mark Chevaree said he had the utmost respect for them, even though they didn't agree on much, and said he didn't think he'd offended them.

Finally Cush Anthony asked, "Representative Loring, we know you have strong feelings on this issue [I think he was referring to my Albany Township editorial]. What do you think?" I said I thought the disagreement went back far beyond the Land Claims Act, back to when Maine became a state and basically treated us like prisoners of war. The State of Maine kept total control over us and treated us like sub-humans. The fact is, we do not trust the state. But the problem is on a higher level than the commission. Commission members only represent the policies of their governments. Perhaps we need to have meetings that would include policymakers from both governments. We talked for a long time along those lines and agreed to continue talking about this and perhaps submit an amendment to the Settlement Act creating a policy level of MITSC. I had to leave at noon but I did ask them to go ahead with the education networking meeting they had sponsored, since I was planning to submit a bill that would mandate the teaching of Maine Indian history for grades K-12.

I'm not sure how this will play out, but I am sure that MITSC will never be the same.

May 15, 2000
Monday

It seems that the Maine Indian Tribal–State Commission will meet to discuss the issues on June 12. Donald told me he does not intend to be there. He feels that they just don't get it. But he said that Wayne Newall, the Passamaquoddy representative on the commission from Indian Township, would be there. Donald also thinks that if MITSC dissolves, so will the Land Claims Settlement Act. I don't think MITSC will dissolve; it will just get new members. MITSC is a creature of the Land Claims Act and the Land Claims Act would have to dissolve first, not vice versa.

"WOULDN'T YOU BE BETTER OFF IF YOU BECAME ONE WITH THE MAJORITY?"

We had Veto Day on May 11, and Governor King's vetoes were all sustained. A two-thirds vote in both houses was impossible. I thought it was ironic and a bit hypocritical that the house passed by the proper margin the harness-racing bill to allow bets to be taken over the phone. Some of the same people who voted against the Albany Township bill because of their concerns about Indian gaming voted for this bill.

The senate killed the harness-racing bill, since it did not have the two-thirds requirement. I kept a copy of the house roll call vote on the bill. I also went to the Revisor's Office and put in two new bills: One was to mandate Maine Indian history be taught in all of grades K-12. The other was a resubmitted bill that a former Penobscot Nation representative put in, which would allow the tribes to operate bingo without paying equipment taxes or prize taxes. I think I'll go a step further and put in an amendment to the Land Claims Settlement Act that would allow the tribes to operate bingo without paying taxes in any form to the state.

I'm so mad—I found out the State of Maine makes an estimated $38 million a year on gambling, which includes the state lottery and harness racing, plus the taxes the tribes pay. We might as well shine some light on this issue (and it should prove to be a hot-button topic next year).

Just this second I got a call from Representative Michael Quint (D) from Portland who asked if Donald and I would speak to a Palestinian delegation from the West Bank on May 25. I said we would be happy to. Mike wants us to give them something that would be unique to our cultures.

June 1, 2000
Wednesday

Donald couldn't make the meeting on the 25th so I met with the delegation. I spoke to them in the well of the house. I was straightforward with them and very candid. I told them the tribes' relationship with the state was not a good one. I mentioned the EPA license situation, and they couldn't understand why the State of Maine had no laws to protect Native people from this exploitation. One delegate even asked the AG that question at the Stone Center, while we all sat around the huge granite table. Chief Justice Wathen was there as well. I think Drew Ketterer, the attorney general, was at a loss for words for a few seconds. All he could do was refer them to the Maine Civil Rights Act.

The Palestinians clearly identified with us and seemed to want to know more about us. They were also interested in our positions in the state legislature. They asked if I thought we had any influence. I told them we did. One of them also asked, "Wouldn't you be better off if you just became one with the majority? Wouldn't you get better treatment and be better off, all the way around?" I responded by saying that if we assimilated, our cultural identity would disappear along with our traditions, our beliefs, and our self-identity. We would lose our self-respect and dignity—and we would never do that!

They all stood and applauded.

Since that meeting with the Palestinians, relations with the state have worsened for us. The U.S. Department of Interior has come out with an opinion to the U.S. EPA saying that a state has no jurisdiction in Indian Country—and that includes all the Maine tribes! The paper companies are sweating bullets and the governor is very upset. The *Penobscot Times* came out with an article about this possible finding and mentioned a "secret" agreement signed between the U.S. EPA and the Penobscot Nation. The agreement recognizes that a government-to-government relationship exists and states that the EPA will honor that agreement and work with the tribes to clean up their environment and protect their health and welfare.

HOW IRONIC—NATIVE PRESENCE IS SO PROMINENT IN THE POLITICAL SYSTEM OF THIS COUNTRY AND YET WE ARE MADE INVISIBLE BY IT.

June 15, 2000
Thursday

Yesterday I met with Governor King. I tried to contact Drew Ketterer but was not successful. Our meeting went very well. Governor King is hung up on the nation-within-a-nation scenario that bothered former Governor Longley, but I pointed out that the very fact that we have a Settlement Act proves that we are a government and that Maine has recognized us as such. Angus feels that the Settlement Act clarifies the fact that we are a municipality and received $81 million for that status. I told Angus that the State of Maine never paid the tribes one penny. In fact, the state had refused to negotiate unless the federal government paid all the costs. I explained that I was around when the Land Claims Settlement Act was being negotiated, and that the way it was presented to us was that municipal status was given us only to allow us to get state grant monies when they were available. For us to accept total municipal status as the state wants us to would mean our assimilation into the state and our termination as a tribal government. This is totally unacceptable to us.

Angus said he did not understand why we didn't just join the majority and accept the laws and regulations like any other Maine citizen. I explained that we are not just any other Maine citizen. We are tribal governments and we have special status and special rights. Angus, of course, feels that this in itself is a threat to the state's jurisdiction. I told Angus this reminded me of when I was presenting to the Palestinian delegation and they asked me, "Why not just become one with the majority?" I told him how I had responded "We would lose our culture, our heritage, our traditions along with our dignity and self-respect, and we would never do that!"

He replied that we would not, *could* not last much longer as a separate government. I mentioned to him that Thoreau thought the same thing back in the late 1800s and wanted to visit the North Country before the Indians disappeared.

"And you're still here," he interjected. I think he was starting to get it. He needs some processing time. He did agree to meet with the tribal chiefs to talk about our differences. He felt we may not be able to agree but at least we could start communicating and open some dialogue.

It is my hope that we can find some compromise position where neither side has to give away the store. I urged a meeting as soon as he could do it. He was thinking of a meeting in the fall or when the MITSC meets. I felt a separate meeting would be better and also stated we needed to meet sooner. He said, "Let me handle it," and asked me if I really believe compromise is possible. I said yes, as long as one person and maybe a few others feel that way, I think there's always hope. His last words to me were, "Don't leave thinking that we won't go to court on the National Pollution Discharge Elimination System (NPDES) issue."

I said, "I won't, what I really wanted to get out of this meeting was your willingness to communicate to the tribal chiefs about policy issues."

He said, "You got it." With that we shook hands and the meeting ended. I left feeling that we might yet avoid a court battle. Even if we go to court, we will have at least a better understanding and respect for each other's positions.

Some other issues we had talked about in our meeting were the paper companies and the possible loss of jobs if Lincoln Pulp and Paper should be made to shut down. Angus felt that we wanted Lincoln to close. My response to that was we did not want even one Maine citizen to lose his or her job. I asked if the state, the paper company, and the tribe had ever sat down to discuss this matter. Angus said he didn't know. I said if I project in my own mind how you will react or think about something without talking to you, the message will always be negative and blown out of proportion. I think that's what's happening in this case. We also talked about the NPDES. I explained to Angus our position on chemical dumping in our waters—how it threatens our very survival. I did agree that the state has cleaned up its act in the past few years. My concern and the Penobscot Nation's concern is about the toxic waste that was dumped in the water prior to that, and this is why we want the Superfund to investigate. We want that mess cleaned up. There must be a way to do it without closing Lincoln.

Angus did start to discuss gambling, but I said I no longer could buy his arguments and that we should discuss that topic at length later. I preferred to talk about the NPDES, since that was the most immediate issue and we had very little time to talk. He agreed.

July 6, 2000
Thursday
Yesterday was the night of the Penobscot Nation's caucus, when we find out who is running for what office and who will be running against who. Representative Mathew Dunlap (D) from Old Town is a history buff and told me that he looked up the origin of the word caucus and found it was originally an Algonquian word used to describe council meetings. I thought, "How ironic—Native presence is so prominent in the political system of this country and yet we are made invisible by it."

I woke up thinking about the caucus and wondering who I would be running against. Jim Pardilla had mentioned to me at one point that he would like to run for tribal representative, and Francis Mitchell, the Penobscot chief, said he thought someone would be and should be running against me this year. Francis said this at the beginning of the year. Francis and I disagreed on a very controversial issue and have not talked for a long time.

I usually go for a two-mile loop walk in the town of Richmond where I live. I walk two or three times during the week. This morning I headed out and got about two-thirds of the way home when a hound dog came running at me and barking from across the road. I turned and told the dog to go home, and it turned and started going in the opposite direction. I started walking again but I could hear it running at me from behind. I turned and again told it to go home. I thought it had retreated, but when I turned to leave, the dog bit the back of my right leg! Then it ran off. I limped home and then went to the police station to report the incident, and from there to the health clinic, where I cleaned the wound and they checked my blood pressure and temperature and gave me a tetanus shot. Before I allowed them to give me the shot, I made sure that I would be able to make the hour-and-a-half drive to Indian Island. I was not about to let anything stop me from attending the caucus. Caucus rules state you have to be present in order to be nominated for an office. I just hoped the dog bite wasn't indicative of the rest of my day. Luckily it was not.

The caucus took place a little after six o'clock and there were lots of nominations for land committee, school committee, census committee, and finally representative. I had asked Erlene Paul, director of human services for the tribe, to nominate me when I first arrived. Erlene, holding her grandchild, slowly walked up to the microphone and officially nominated me, somebody seconded, and I consented to the nomination. Steve Paul went to the mike and nominated David Sapiel, who promply said he did not want the nomination. Everyone laughed and a motion was made that nominations for representative cease. I breathed a sigh of relief, glad that I did not have an opponent. With the work I had done this past year and since I was the incumbent, I felt I had an excellent chance of winning, regardless. But running unopposed was just a lot less nerve-wracking. More than one person reminded me that there was always a chance for someone to run as a write-in. I knew this was their way of telling me not to get too overly confident. They were absolutely right.

July 17, 2000
Monday

As a follow-up to that comment, just the other day I read in the paper that a candidate for the Green party was running unopposed in a primary and he lost! He didn't get one single vote. Not even his own. I'm certainly going to vote for myself!!

I've set up a meeting to speak with Steven Rowe, since he is running against Drew Ketterer for attorney general in January. The AG gets elected by a majority vote of the legislature. I think he has the election wrapped. I'm making it a point to fill him in on Indian issues.

Another interesting thing has happened. Evan Richert, director of the State Planning Office and the governor's appointee to the Maine Indian State–Tribal Commission, has sent Governor Doyle, the Passamaquoddy governor from Pleasant Point, a letter of apology for the way the state delegates handled the Albany Township issue. I wonder if that's in any way related to my meeting with the governor. It seems that after my e-mail to him a couple of weeks ago reminding him of what he said about maintaining communication with the tribes, he may have spoken to Evan and had him do this in order to put MITSC back on track. Who knows?

"IF SUCH A SITE WERE CREATED WE COULD HAVE THE PENOBSCOT THERE ONE WEEKEND AND THE KKK DEMONSTRATING THE NEXT." —PAUL STERN, DEPUTY ATTORNEY GENERAL

On the weekend of July 9, Jeannine Guttman, editor and VP of the *Portland Press Herald/Maine Sunday Telegram* wrote a very long column stating that she was creating a new policy for the paper that would not allow them to print the word Redskins when describing a sports team and that they would also do everything possible to avoid using the word squaw. I thought that was very "gutsy" of Guttman— she is certainly sticking her neck out there. I do admire and respect a person who has the conviction and fortitude to do something even when it may not be the popular thing to do. I wrote her a thank-you letter.

But I did not fail to note that her column was printed just opposite a huge sketch of a chimpanzee with the headline, "One Species Away." Perhaps I should not be so sensitive. I'm sure they'd say nothing was meant by it. (A picture is worth a thousand words.) Maybe a staff person did it as a way to make the point that one need not use words to be racist. (Very subtle message.) In fact we spoke of just such usage of media at the National Conference of Race and Ethnicity (NCORE) meeting in Santa Fe.

This weekend there was also an article in the *Maine Sunday Telegram* titled "Chapels in the Wilderness: American Indians Struggle to Preserve Sacred Sites from Modern-Day Interests." It was an excellent article written about the Sioux Tribe in Pine Ridge, South Dakota. The *Sunday Telegram* must not realize that Wabanaki people here in Maine have the same problem. Instead of a site in South Dakota called Devil's Tower, we have a very sacred site here in Maine we call Katahdin. The Baxter State Park Authority is

Katahdin, our sacred mountain. Photograph by Martin Neptune

reviewing the question of allowing Penobscot runners—who have held a 100-mile run and ceremony in the park for almost twenty years—into the park. The purpose of the run is spiritual, to honor the sacredness of the mountain and our ancestors and to renew spiritual energy.

Katahdin plays a prominent role in our culture and traditions. Our ancestors passed stories of Katahdin down to us generation after generation. Gluskabe our creator sleeps within the mountain and one day will wake up and come to our rescue. One of the very first things the state legislature did when Maine became a state was to take four townships from the Penobscots. One of those townships held Katahdin. Neither the Penobscot nor any other tribe would have sold their sacred and spiritual center. The state bought these townships without our consent. It is still the Penobscot Nation's belief that Katahdin was stolen from us. The fact that we have to petition the Baxter State Park Authority or any other entity to hold sacred ceremonies at our place of worship is unconscionable.

The attorney general's office was asked by the Baxter State Park Authority to write an opinion on whether or not the Penobscot people should be allowed access to the park to practice their religious ceremonies. Here is what the attorney general's office wrote:

STATE OF MAINE
DEPARTMENT OF ATTORNEY GENERAL
MEMORANDUM
TO: Irvin C. Caverly, Jr., Director, Baxter State Park
FROM: Paul Stern, Deputy Attorney General
DATE: December 9, 1999
SUBJECT: Penobscot Proposal

Inquiry was made regarding the legality of a proposal to create a site for the Penobscots to engage in religious and cultural ceremonies within the park. It is my understanding that this will entail the expenditure of funds and resources to build a road approximately 1,800 to 2,000 feet, as well as the clearing of a site. As discussed in more detail below, it would appear that there are problems with such a proposal from the standpoint not only of the trust created by Governor Baxter, but due to constitutional considerations as well.

Trust Issues

As we are all by now well aware, Governor Baxter created the 200,000-acre wilderness enclave primarily to be kept "forever wild" and secondarily to allow access and recreation. *Normand v. Baxter State Park Authority* 509 A.2d 640 (Me. 1986) The Baxter State Park Authority "must administer the Trust like any private trustee of a charitable trust, exercising their best judgment...." *FitzGerald v. Baxter State Park Authority,* 385 A.2d 189,202 (Me. 1978).

Although I have not reviewed every document Governor Baxter has written regarding the park with an eye towards the issue of the Indian sites, I am unaware of any suggestion that the Governor intended that there be a special location for Indian ceremonies, in addition, this site would require the creation of a road 1,800 to 2,000 feet long. As you are aware, Governor Baxter made clear, most notable in a May 20, 1960, letter to Governor John H. Reed and Executive Council:

As to roads within the park. This must be left to the discretion of the Park Authority but I request that no additional roads for automobiles be constructed therein, that no additional camps be erected.... In light of this, this proposal appears to exceed the limits of the Trust as Governor Baxter intended.

Constitutional Considerations

It is fundamental constitutional law that public funds cannot be used to promote or prohibit the exercise of a religion and, generally speaking, public property cannot be dedicated to the exclusive exercise of a particular religious group. The proposal here would appear to violate both those basic structures.

At best, without violating the constitution, a site could be created within the park for use by any and all groups for any sort of ceremony—religious, political, or secular. Up until now, the park has not had to broach this issue, but in discussions we have opened that if someone requested to engage in some sort of political, religious, or public demonstration, the site of the old sporting camp at Togue Pond would be made available. That site, of course, is not within the original confines of the park and likewise is more manageable and interferes less with the park experience.

Creating such a site well within the park, of course, opens the location to be used often and by any group. For example, if such a site were created, we could have the Penobscots there one weekend, and the KKK demonstrating there the next. Therefore, in considering the creation of a site, from a constitutional standpoint we must be content-neutral with respect to its use and make it available to all organizations.

Conclusion

For the reasons discussed above, the proposal is problematic, and any recommendation you do make to the authority should include these considerations.

If I can be of further assistance please call me.

Luckily, Attorney General Ketterer and the commissioner of Natural Resources voted to allow the tribe one more year to have its sacred Katahdin run and to negotiate with the Baxter State Park Authority in the meantime to come up with an acceptable solution.

August 2, 2000
Tuesday
Yesterday I met with the present speaker of the house and soon-to-be new AG. Steve Rowe is a very nice, open-minded person. He's the one person I think would really give the tribes a fair deal. He said he would be more than happy to meet with me or tribal officials on any topic and asked me to continue to educate him on tribal issues. He advised me to have luncheons with some of the legislators, since he feels I am a very effective communicator one on one. I think that might be a good idea. I don't have a budget at this time to pay for lunches. I'll have to work on that.

I think it was a very successful lunch and Steve did agree to advocate for tribal representatives to vote on committees. I gave him a copy of the Sovereign Nations Representation Study. He promised he'd at least read the executive summary.

August 9, 2000
Wednesday
Yesterday was the runoff election for candidates for tribal governor. I had knee surgery on the 7th but felt well enough to go and be with my sister Beth, who is one of the candidates. I stayed until 9:30 P.M. and got home at 11:00 P.M. Beth did not make the cut.

The race is between Francis Mitchell and Barry Dana. I think

Barry has a lot to learn, but he's quite capable and has the ability to speak well in public. We need someone who can communicate. We'll see what happens. Right now—at this moment in time—I feel that I do not want to run as tribal representative for another two years. I may not even stay this two-year term. Tribal politics are tough, downright vicious sometimes. I think that's too bad. We should all be on the same side. But some people are less concerned with the tribe than they are with their own personal and family gains. The tribe will never move forward until it gets good professional people in office who want to serve the common good of the tribe.

I truly feel Beth wanted to serve the common good. There is talk that she lost because the tribe is not ready for a woman governor. That may be, and hopefully the time will come when a woman does become governor.

THE WHOLE SITUATION WAS ONE OF MANY POLITICAL INSULTS WE SUFFER IN THE WHITE MAN'S WORLD.

August 23, 2000
Wednesday

Yesterday we had judicial confirmations. We considered gubernatorial nominations in the Joint Standing Committee on Judiciary until around 5:00. Most were judicial nominations; one was for the Human Rights Commission. Nothing extraordinary happened. Two of the judges had a person testify against them.

I saw Steve Rowe, who had come down to talk with Representative Thompson. I asked Steve when the Joint Rules Committee would be meeting. He told me sometime in December. I mentioned to Representative Thompson that I'd like to see who was on the Joint Rules Committee. A short time later Representative Thompson handed me the list.

Now I have to talk to all of them about the Sovereign Nations Representation Study and recommendations. I really want to see us have a vote on committees. It would be a tremendous improvement. I'm not sure how strongly Senator Bennett will oppose any of these recommendations. I'm sure he will, though. I didn't make a friend when I named him in my senate article. He's on the Joint Rules Committee. I have to concentrate on getting a majority vote. I'm talking to Representative Tom Murphy, the house minority leader, sometime next week. I will meet with Mike Saxl, as well. Mike will be the next speaker of the house.

This past weekend Roberta Scruggs from the *Maine Sunday Telegram* published her article. It was on the Land Claims Settlement Act twenty years later. Roberta came to interview me two months ago. She knew nothing about Maine tribes or any of our issues, and was fascinated by all she had learned. She found the tribal-state relationship depressing. After talking to state and tribal officials, she feels that there's no hope of reaching mutual agreement on any of our issues. The article itself was excellent. The paper did a very good job in getting the stories out. They featured people and used separate sections to describe how these people felt. I think they couldn't have done justice to the subject and all of Roberta's research using any other format. The article was printed in the *Maine Sunday Telegram* on August 22, 2000. It was on the front page and was titled "An Unsettled/Settlement," and it covered most of the front page and three full pages inside.

September 15, 2000
Friday

On or about September 4, I received a letter from the chairs of the Joint Select Committee on Rules-Schedule. This is the committee that will decide whether or not it will endorse the recommendations of the Sovereign Nations Study Committee. The study committee recommended a number of rule changes. The most important was that tribal representatives be allowed to vote in committee. Other recommendations were that the tribal representatives could sponsor legislation on any subject (unanimous), that tribal representatives serve as members of the joint standing committee, and that authority be granted to vote in committee on any matter except gubernatorial nominations (supported by a majority of the committee). The letter stated that the first meeting was to be held on September 7. I had only three days to muster support and make sure the committee placed us on the agenda. I had already gotten Speaker Rowe's support. He was very helpful with calling the two chairs of the committee to get me on the agenda for the meeting on the 7th.

But that meeting turned out to be very preliminary. I gave a brief description of the committee's findings and recommendations. The Rules Committee chairs were Representative Mike Saxl (D) from Portland for the house and Senator Lloyd P. LaFountain III (D) from Biddeford for the senate. The members of the committee are as follows: senators Michael Michaud (D), Millinocket; Beverly Daggett (D), Augusta; Richard Bennett (R), Norway; and Joel Abromson (D), Portland; and representatives David Etnier (D), Harpswell; Christopher O'Neil (D), Saco; David Madore (R), Augusta; and Janice Labrecque (R), Gorham. They are a tough crowd. I really don't know how they will be voting.

The chairs had scheduled the complete presentation for September 13 but because of Vice President Al Gore's appearance in Maine, they canceled that and rescheduled for the 19th. None of my supporters could attend that day, and I requested to be put on the September 28th agenda. The powers-that-be granted my request. I have spent most of the morning making phone calls and garnering people who would be willing to speak in our favor. So far that looks good.

On August 31 I attended the Sagadahoc bridge dedication ceremony in Bath. The tribal chiefs and representatives were sent special invitations (at my request) by the chair of the organizing committee, John Brill. Representative Donald Soctomah and Governor Richard Stevens, Passamaquoddy, both of Indian Township, myself and Governor Barry Dana, Penobscot, of Indian Island, attended. Barry played the Welcome Song on his drum and sang. He got a huge round of applause and verbal recognition from Senator Susan Collins. This was more than what the rest of us got. Governor Stevens and Donald had traveled all the way from Indian Township and did not even get official recognition.

The official commemorative coin and artist were recognized. The coin had the symbol of a Wabanaki chief on it—Joseph Francis. The artist had called me and wanted to know if I thought it would be okay to use the figure of a chief on the coin. I told him yes, if he put a name to it. Too many times Native people are used as symbols without names. He agreed, and the coin has the likeness of Penobscot Chief Joseph Francis and bears his name, as well. I considered this one of my best accomplishments. (None of us received an official

Sagadahoc Bridge commemorative coin

coin. I later ordered five from a local Bath store.)

The whole situation was one of many political insults we suffer in the white man's world. Speaking of those insults, I will mention the Al Gore rally that the chiefs and I attended in Lewiston. First things first though.

WE TRIED TO EXPLAIN WE HAD BEEN CLEARED, BUT HE INSISTED, AND EVEN THREATENED TO HAVE THE SECRET SERVICE REMOVE US!

In August a person from the Democratic campaign office called and asked if I wanted to see Senator Liberman. I said yes, that would be great. I invited my niece Rebecca Sockbeson to go with me. We had our names placed on a list. I was also asked if I'd be interested in *meeting* the senator. Of course I said yes. The rally went well and I went to the Northeast Airport to meet him.

When I arrived it was sweltering hot, around 90 degrees. A small group of us were escorted into the air terminal and later to the tarmac, where we got to stand in line and shake his hand. I was able to give him a video on the environmental issues in the Native communities. All in all it was very nice.

A few days later I was called and asked if I would like to attend a Gore rally at Lewiston High School, and it was mentioned that a meeting might be arranged with Gore and the tribal officials. I asked if my aunt might be able to get her picture taken with him. I was told they would work on that. The big day came on September 13, and everything turned out to be one big mess.

Only five of us were allowed to go up front in a roped area where there were hundreds of people standing penned in like sardines and sweating like pigs. I was asked who to send up, and I chose Passamaquoddy Representative Donald Soctomah; Brenda Commander, the chief of the Maliseets; Richard Doyle, one of the Passamaquoddy chiefs; William Phillips, chief of the Aroostook Band of Micmacs, and Barry Dana, Penobscot governor-elect. I chose to stay in the back with my aunt, Aleta Levesque. We were assured that Al Gore was going to walk right past us on his way out. This never happened, and my aunt was very disappointed. She lives in Massa-

Top: Chief Barry Dana of the Penobscot Nation, with my aunt Aleta. Above: Standing in the back are Chief Richard Doyle of the Passamaquoddy Tribe, Pleasant Point (left) and Chief William (Billy) Phillips, Aroostook Band of Micmacs. Seated in the front row are Chief Brenda Commander (left), Aleta, and myself. Courtesy of the author

chusetts and had traveled from visiting her sister on Indian Island to Lewiston, which is a two-hour drive. This would not be that significant except that she is recovering from a double lung operation where they removed one third of each of her lungs. She is also disabled with osteoporosis.

We all were treated poorly by one of Gore's advance people. He had approached us where my aunt sat in a wheelchair and the chiefs were waiting in the front of the stadium by the bleachers, and told us we would have to go to the back of the building. We tried to explain we had been cleared to be where we were but he insisted, and even threatened to have the Secret Service remove us! This took place in front of hundreds of people and a section of empty bleachers. We left and went to the back, since we had no choice. I walked up to Qwethelyn Phillips, the executive director of the Democratic party in Maine, and said that the chiefs were being forced to go to the back, which wasn't a good thing. Another big political insult. The rally ended without any of us even shaking Al Gore's hand! I felt the worst about my aunt, who was so excited about meeting Al Gore but never even got to see him. She did, however, get to meet newly elected Chief Barry Dana and the other chiefs; she was thrilled to have her picture taken with them.

The mayor of Lewiston, Kaileigh Tara, publicly acknowledged each of the five tribal officials by name, title, and tribe from the podium, which I believe was the first time in Maine history that tribal officials were recognized during a presidential rally. It was worth it for me just to have that accomplishment. Later that night the individual from the Democratic party who handled our appearance at this rally called me to say that she was going to resign because of the way they insulted the chiefs. I told her not to resign, that we need all the Native people on the inside that we can get. I pointed out the one real positive and powerful thing: we had finally been recognized at a national political event. She felt better, and I think she will stay on and fight the good fight.

WE ARE TRIBAL CITIZENS, BUT WE ARE ALSO MAINE CITIZENS WITHOUT A VOTE OR A VOICE FOR OUR TRIBES.

September 25, 2000
Monday
This week will be a very important one for me. The Joint Rules Committee will be hearing the recommendations of the Sovereign Nations Study Committee. The recommendation that I am most interested in passing is the right to vote in committee. If we get the backing of the Rules Committee it would be a piece of cake, but if we don't, chances are it will not happen.

I find it degrading and frustrating to sit on committees and watch others raise their hands to vote with the public watching, and have to sit there like a nonperson. That action itself sends a strong message to the public and to fellow legislators—that Indian people are not as good as everyone else, that we are less valued. It is historical fact that we have been treated as less than human and considered by some to be on the same level as animals. One only has to read the Proctor Report of 1942 and the floor debate in January of 1975 to understand the mindset the state legislature and the state government had toward Indian people and their government.

September 26, 2000
Tuesday
I testified before the Joint Rules Committee. My testimony was as follows:

The Penobscot Nation has had a representative present in the house of representatives since Maine became a state. The earliest documentation of that presence was in 1823. The State of Maine, the Penobscot Nation, and the Passamaquoddy Tribe have a unique relationship—a relationship like no other in the United States. Two tribal representatives represent their respective tribal governments in the Maine State Legislature. Legislators have wondered about our presence in this body, our powers and duties, and our voting rights. The 119th Legislature passed a joint order to establish a committee to study these questions, the Committee to Address the Recognition of the Tribal Government Representatives of Maine's Sovereign Nations in the Legislature.

The committee met seven times and reviewed many historical documents and interviewed numerous individuals with expertise in the law, Native tradition and culture, and looked at international aboriginal models.

Historically the Wabanaki tribes were asked by General George Washington to fight on the American side during the Revolution. The Wabanaki Confederacy fought on the side of the Americans and helped to secure the borders of what is now called the State of Maine. Without our help Maine may very well be a part of Canada right now.

As a reward for our support, the Continental Congress allowed our representatives to attend their sessions. This practice carried over to the Massachusetts General Court and continued when Maine took over the treaty obligations from Massachusetts. Wabanaki people have continued to serve in the military and fight for the United States. We have never fought against the United States.

In 1924 the United States declared all Native Americans to be citizens. They had the right to vote in federal elections, but it was not until 1967, well after the Civil Rights Act, that Maine Indians were fully franchised to vote in state elections. Maine was the last state in the Union to allow its Native American population to vote in state elections.

Native people have been the invisible population. Yes we have held a place in the state legislature for almost two hundred years. We have kept our place here simply by being persistent and staying. In 1941 the tribal representatives were unseated from the house. Yet they remained. In 1975 they were reinstated after a long and exhaustive debate on the floor. The 1975 debate is a prime example of racism and prejudice that still existed at that time even after civil rights were won for the African Americans in this country.

The history between the tribes and the state is not a good one. It is one of distrust, abuse, and neglect. This state has benefited from our natural resources as well as our human resources. We have been the most heavily state-regulated tribes in the country. There was a state law for every day of the year. The tribes were under the control of Indian agents who sometimes didn't care about the sick and elderly and even allowed some to go without food and firewood for long periods of time. The living conditions of the tribal communities were dreadful, no sewer or running water, and no electricity.

One day an old treaty was found in the attic of a Passamaquoddy elder and the tribes began a process of litigation that led to federal recognition and improvements in housing, health, and a higher standard of living.

On October 10, 1980, the Maine Indian Land Claims Settlement Act was signed into law. Much has improved since 1980 including the standing of the tribal representatives. Tribal representatives now have the ability to speak on the floor of the house, cosponsor any legislation, sponsor sentiments, and serve on committees. We have no voting rights either in committee or on the floor.

After reviewing the history and hearing testimony from a number of individuals the study committee has recommended two joint rules changes. The first is a unanimous recommendation that the tribal representatives be allowed to sponsor any legislation. The second is a recommendation by a majority of the committee that tribal representatives be allowed to make motions and vote in committee. It was determined that tribal representatives should not vote on gubernatorial nominations. The majority of the committee felt that tribal representatives' votes in committee did not affect the outcome of the legislative process. (However, a floor vote would clearly affect that process.) Therefore it could withstand a constitutional challenge.

I feel strongly on this issue. I sit in committee day after day and watch as votes are taken and it is as if I am invisible, a non-person. I can see it in the faces of my fellow legislators and on the faces of the general public. There is heaviness in the air, and I know people feel this is not right. The message this sends to everyone in the room is that this person is less important and less valued than everyone else.

This committee has an opportunity to take the lead in recognizing and treating Indian people as equals. Allowing us to participate fully in committees would give us a small voice in the policymaking process that has had such a tremendous effect on our tribal governments, our everyday life, and our very survival. It is simply a question of human decency. I urge you to support a rule change that would allow us to be equal participants on committees.

Thank you.

October 3, 2000
Tuesday
Today the Rules Committee voted on the recommendations. The bottom line is that they were not ready to allow Indians to vote on any level, including in committees. They even refused to pass the unanimous Sovereign Nations Joint Study Committee recommendation that would allow us to sponsor any legislation. Why would somebody vote that way?

The committee had submitted an in-depth analysis. This joint committee researched voluminous historical documents and did extensive interviews with an assistant attorney general, tribal attorneys, and even officials from the federal level. The assistant attorney general stood before the Joint Rules Committee on October 3 and stated that he saw no problem with allowing us to sponsor any legislation. He said he saw a clear constitutional problem with tribal representatives voting on the floor and with them voting on gubernatorial nominations. As a result of the assistant attorney general's testimony, the committee did not recommend voting on the floor. They did recommend that tribal representatives be allowed to vote in committee but not vote on gubernatorial nominations. The assistant attorney general had further stated that a committee vote could be defended, since the legislature may create any committee it sees fit to carry out its process. It could even create committees with no legislators on them!

It was clear after his presentation to the Rules Committee that if these members wanted to—and the key words here are "wanted to"—they could indeed give the tribes a small voice in the policymaking that affects them so tremendously. Senators Michaud, Daggett, and Abromson, along with representatives Madore and Labrecque, chose not to allow the tribal representatives to have a voice. What was their reasoning?

Well, Senator Daggett's reason was that she couldn't get beyond the constitution. In her opinion tribal members are not elected according to constitutional requirements and therefore should not have the same powers as the constitutionally elected senators and representatives. She chose to ignore the assistant attorney general's presentation. Obviously Senator Daggett did not consider the tribes' unique political status. The senator did allow that we were special and that we were sovereign. But this counted against us in her reasoning.

Senator Michaud had a very interesting perspective, which was that because tribal governments elected their own representatives and because there was no tribal law stating that only Maine citizens could be representatives, then we could very well have a New Brunswick Indian on our Utilities Committee voting for foreign electricity.

(A bit of a reach.) When Representative Saxl suggested that the house and senate could make it a rule that only tribal representatives who were Maine citizens would be allowed on committees, Senator Michaud then defended the tribes' sovereignty stating, "We would not want to tell the tribes what to do. [Since when?] They would not want us messing with their internal tribal matters."

I was asked by Representative Saxl what I thought, and I simply stated the obvious to the committee members, not once but two or three times. The obvious is this: the house and the senate can set their own rules, and those rules could say that only a tribal representative who is a Maine citizen would be allowed to serve on a committee. That rule would be a rule. It would not be a law that the tribes would have to follow. Simply put, if the tribes thought it important to have a vote on committees, they would make sure their elected representatives were Maine citizens. Some committee members refused to get it.

The concern about citizenship expressed by Senator Michaud goes to show you what creative thinking you can have when you're reaching and searching for ways to continue to subjugate and deny a special people a voice in their own destiny. The truth of the matter is that certain committee members had closed their minds and hearts and were not open to compromise. It is my hope that in the near future Maine people will contact their legislative representatives and let them know how they feel about this issue. I know Maine people are fair. Maine tribes are unique and special; we are tribal citizens but we are also Maine citizens without a vote or a voice for our tribes.

On October 26 I spoke to students at the USM Law School. The Native American law students have a lunch program where they invite various speakers to talk with them over a few sandwiches—very informal. My topic was the voting rights of tribal representatives in the legislature. I did not expect to have many students attend, and there were only two who showed up to meet me and my niece Rebecca. As we waited another ten minutes or so, students and others started to arrive. I was surprised to see representatives Charlie

Mitchell, Douglas Ahearn, and former senator and mayor of Lewiston John Jenkins, as well as my friend, former chancellor of the University of Maine, Bob Woodbury. There were about twenty-five or so. I spoke to them about the history of the tribal representatives from the time of George Washington to the present and the issues surrounding our voting rights. They found it very interesting and wanted to do something to help. I left them newspaper articles and the Sovereign Nations Joint-Study Committee Report.

I had a great time talking to them and they were a very intelligent audience.

IT IS TIME FOR MAINE STATE GOVERNMENT TO TAKE A FRESH LOOK AT MAINE TRIBAL GOVERNMENTS.

November 4, 2000
Saturday
The tribal chief's inauguration is very traditional to the tribe. The ceremony is hundreds of years old. My sister, Beth Sockbeson, a member of the tribal council, along with Butch Phillips, a Penobscot tribal member and former representative to the legislature, spent many hours planning and coordinating this event. This was only the second time members of the public were invited in such high numbers. I provided the guest list for legislators and VIPs, as I had done for the inauguration of our former governor, Richard Hamilton. We had a very special guest at the last inauguration and that was consul general of South Africa, Sheila Sisulu. Sheila is the former ambassador from South Africa to the United States. Consul General Sisulu commented to me how impressed she was that our culture and traditions remain. She made this comment after visiting the Indian Island Elementary School. She was also impressed with the Claymation video *Frog Monster,* created by the 5th, 6th, 7th, and 8th grade students. The video was about our traditional hero Gluskabe. It was a winner at the 1994 Maine Student Film and Video Festival.

Unfortunately, we had no guests of Ambassador Sisulu's caliber at this inauguration. We did however have Max Kennedy, the nephew of former President John F. Kennedy and son of Robert Kennedy.

Here is my speech at the inauguration of Governor Barry Dana at Indian Island, November 5, 2000:

Tribal chiefs, Tribal Council members, tribal members, and honorable guests:

It is an honor to have you all here on Indian Island at the inauguration ceremony of our tribal governor and chief.

As representative of the Penobscot Nation to the Maine State Legislature, I represent a political bridge between the State of Maine and our tribal government. It is not an easy task. We have many contentious issues in areas such as sovereignty, economic development, environmental protection, and natural resources. Sovereignty and jurisdictional concerns are always at the top of the issues list. The issues become compounded when we find legislators know little or nothing about tribal history or background. Education, communication, and understanding are needed in order to develop an equitable solution to these issues. The keys to a successful state and tribal relationship are recognition, respect, trust, and equality.

The state has traditionally viewed tribal governments as being liabilities and not assets. The challenges tribes face in order to overcome this paradigm are great. The state government has not considered that tribal governments have become more sophisticated. Since the land claims, we have strengthened our own governmental infrastructures such as police and safety, health services, tribal courts, our school systems, as well as human services. We have a greater pool of college graduates who have come back to the tribes in various fields of expertise.

Maine tribes have been successful in some business endeavors and have contributed economically to their surrounding towns and municipalities. These contributions have gone unnoticed.

The Penobscot Nation has developed its own land management plans and regulations. It has a GIS system that is second to none. Tribes across Maine are experiencing their own successes.

It is time for Maine state government to take a fresh look at Maine tribal governments and recognize their contributions to the state and their full partnership potential. There needs to be reconciliation in this state between its tribal and state governments. We need to reconcile the past and move up to the present so that we can lay a permanent foundation of trust and mutual respect.

The world is changing and a highly competitive global market is emerging. The State of Maine will need all of its natural and human resources to compete. The tribes and the State of Maine have an opportunity to take the lead in this country and redefine tribal and state relations in a positive manner—one of partnership and equality, one of growth and opportunity, one of vision and creativity. We look forward to working with the State of Maine towards reconciliation and redefining the paradigm to include one of respect, recognition, and equality.

Thank you.

JUDGE CROWLEY ORDERS CHIEFS TO JAIL FOR CONTEMPT

November 9, 2000
Thursday

Today I sat in the Androscoggin courthouse and heard Judge Crowley of the Maine Superior Court render a ruling of contempt of court against Chief Barry Dana, Penobscot Nation; Governor Richard Doyle, Pleasant Point, Passamaquoddy Tribe; and Governor Richard Stevens, Indian Township, Passamaquoddy Tribe.

Great Northern Paper, et al. v. the Penobscot Nation, et al. involved the paper companies' request through the state Freedom of Access Act for documents that would allow the paper companies access to our tribal council minutes. But the minutes of a tribal government conducting its business is clearly an internal tribal government matter and not subject to state law, according to the Maine Indian Land Claims Settlement Act. The paper companies have also requested documents that are private between the Penobscot Nation, the Passamaquoddy Tribe, and the U.S. Department of the Interior and the Environmental Protection Agency. They filed this action because they want the tribes to yield and allow the State of Maine to be the sole issuer of permits to discharge toxic waste into our rivers.

Judge Crowley had no regard whatsoever for the positions of our tribal chiefs or for the tribal governments they represented. He overstepped his jurisdiction by hearing the case in the first place, and then, in an unbelievable decision, he further overstepped his judicial authority by ordering them to jail for contempt! I had to pinch myself to see that I was awake and not dreaming.

As I listened to this judge I knew what it must have been like for African Americans in the South during the early sixties. It was a tremendous feeling of inferiority and loss of power.

These are heads of governments and not subject to a district court judge, no matter how much his judicial ego has been inflated. I sat and listened to tribal attorneys argue the tribes' case without any tools. The judge had refused to consider our tribal laws, culture, or traditions. He barely listened to our attorneys' arguments. The state judge refused to see us as tribal governments, but instead referred to us continually as "sub-state entities." He refused to acknowledge the laws of our tribal government and council. Council minutes have never been released to the public.

The paper company attorneys, on the other hand, didn't seem to have to do too much debating, since they knew their case was already won. The judge listened intently to every word they said.

The tribes see allowing the state to have sole control over certification in this area as a threat to our very survival, since the state has failed to monitor the paper companies and has allowed the paper companies to do their own testing. The Penobscot Nation hired its own scientist and found that one paper company was not even doing the testing, but was sending in a false weekly test result stating that toxins were at safe levels.

The tribe brought the results of its own scientific test to the state DEP, and the paper company was hit with a fine of $800,000 dollars—a small fine, considering the eight years this company had been turning in false reports to the state.

This case was filed against us in state court as a result of our protests to the federal government. We had asked the federal EPA not to allow the state to be the sole issuer of permits. The paper companies, of course, are scared that we will want to issue our own permits, as some other tribes have the right to do in other states. But our sole purpose at this point is to keep EPA in the permit issuing process.

I find the paper companies' request for council minutes ludicrous. The state Freedom of Access Act was written to make information available to the public. It was created to allow the public access to governmental documents created by publicly elected government officials. But the public has no right to vote to elect Indian officials, nor is our government an electorate of the general public. This is why I find it outrageous that this law could by any stretch apply to tribal governments.

Only Penobscot tribal members are allowed in council chambers. The exception is when nontribal individuals have business before our council, and then we allow them to appear only for that one issue and afterwards they are asked to leave. This same procedure is followed by other tribes throughout the country. Our tribal council is the heart of our government, and the decisions our tribal government makes are internal matters.

If the judge and the paper companies get their way, they will have ignored tribal law and interfered with internal tribal matters. I view this as yet another breach of the Land Claims Settlement Act. We hope that we can get some sort of intervention from the federal government, since it is clear the state government is not going to intervene on our behalf in this. *(The state did intervene, but on the side of the paper companies.)*

It's the same old story, big corporations being allowed to come in and destroy the environment at the cost of poor people or people who do not have the same power in government as the majority. I couldn't believe it when I heard that judge say, "For the purposes of this hearing I will not consider your tribal laws or customs.... You are a 'sub state entity.'" He gave no recognition whatsoever to our relationship with the federal government or even our government-to-government relationship with this state.

Judge Crowley's ruling stated that unless we chose to appeal in the state court system, our tribal chiefs would go to jail until we decided to comply with his order! When he announced "jail," there was a collective exclamation of shock and disbelief.

The courtroom was full of tribal members and supporters numbering fifty or more. Then the judge left the bench and the court security officer came to take the tribal chiefs into custody. They had

Chief Barry Dana and me on the steps of the Androscoggin court-house shortly after he and chiefs Doyle and Stevens were placed under arrest. Photograph by Jose Levia, Lewiston *Sun-Journal*

been placed under arrest by Judge Crowley. There was mass confusion, since the tribes' attorneys quickly took the chiefs into the judge's chambers to plead for time.

The judge reconvened and allowed until Monday at 9:00 A.M. to receive the documents and appeals, or the tribal chiefs would be in the Androscoggin jail. He asked the chiefs if they would turn themselves in. Each chief agreed. I think they were under duress when they promised to return; if they had said no, the judge would have had them in custody then and there.

As I sat in that courtroom, I saw two years of trying to build a trusting relationship with the state go down the drain. I fear this has caused irreparable damage in tribal-state relations. I just could not believe this was happening in the year 2000 in Maine. I felt like I had traveled back in time to the late fifties and early sixties in the South. Unbelievable.

THE TRIBES WERE IN FULL AGREEMENT.

November 14, 2000

Tuesday

We had a Tri-council meeting on Saturday evening which began around 4:30 P.M. and lasted until around 8:30 P.M. I was certain that all three tribal councils would not agree on one way of doing things. The Passamaquoddy are usually pretty aggressive when it comes to their rights and sovereignty issues. The Penobscot are a bit more laid back and calmer. Maybe it's because we've been closer to the majority population or maybe it's because we are the more abused. I don't know.

We had a very spirited debate with Governor Richard Doyle of the Passamaquoddy Tribe at Pleasant Point, who wanted to tell the state to go to you-know-where and was more than willing to go straight to jail himself to make a statement. Marvin Francis, an elder of the Passamaquoddy Tribe, and Jim Sappier, a former governor and former Penobscot Nation representative to the legislature, were pushing civil disobedience as well. I spoke against it and against anyone going to jail, since it would prove nothing. I mentioned Wounded Knee and Alcatraz. Where are those people today? What good did that disobedience do them? Representative Donald Soctomah backed me up but said nothing during the Tri-council meeting. Lieutenant Governor Ed Bassett from the Passamaquoddy Tribe agreed with me, as did Lorraine Dana (Barry's mother) and Barry himself.

We split up into two separate rooms with each council. The Passamaquoddy stayed in one room and the Penobscots went to the governor's office. We decided to appeal on the jurisdiction matter only, and to hire a PR firm out of D.C., as well as have me speak to Governor King to see what he suggests. (He had called me the night before, offering to look at mediation or some other way to make relations between the tribes and state better.) We went back and joined the Passamaquoddy council to see what they had decided. I fully expected them to vote not to comply, but Governor Doyle made the announcement that the Passamaquoddy Tribe was in full agreement to appeal and had come to the same conclusions that we did.

We were of one mind and one voice, ready to face the reporters outside, but we decided we would get better media coverage if we did not make any announcement until Monday morning, when we were to appear at the Androscoggin courthouse. We wanted to maximize our publicity.

Monday morning came and we did one heck of a job. Barry did very well in front of the cameras, especially with his bottle of Penobscot River water. We had been in contact with Rex Hackler, the former PR person for former Secretary of the Interior Kevin Grover. We hired Rex as our PR firm for some advice and some talking points for the chiefs. We had given some thought to asking for a nationwide boycott on the paper products these companies produced, but Rex advised us not to say anything at this time about a boycott. If we wanted a boycott we should be better organized about it beforehand, and he said boycotts usually don't work well, anyway. We all decided to go along with his advice so no boycott was announced.

I had a one-on-one meeting with Governor King last night at 5:30 P.M., and we talked for about an hour. The governor was very cooperative about everything. He has agreed to look at possible mediation between the tribes and state on various issues to see if we can't start working together on some level. He has changed his mind on sovereignty, since his thinking now is that it is possible to be sovereign on different levels. In the past he had felt that you were either sovereign or not and there was no in-between. He changed his mind after we talked and I used the example of law enforcement and how they get along on all various levels—municipal, county, state, and federal. He said the ball was in his court now and that he would consider various options and talk to the chiefs about them at the December 1 meeting. I left this meeting feeling that we may be headed in the right direction, finally.

I got home and got a call from Rex. He was at the annual meeting of the National Congress of American Indians (NCAI) on Monday and would be there for the week. He is going to try to get NCAI's support for us. Jerry Pardilla, a former Penobscot Nation tribal governor, is out there and Barry will fly out on Thursday to make a big PR move for the national media at the NCAI conference.

I will be speaking at the Great Falls Forum in Lewiston on Thursday, November 16. The forum is sponsored by the *Sun-Journal*, St. Mary's Hospital, and the Lewiston Public Library. The *Sun-Journal* has had a lot about me in the paper. They had the advertisement for the forum as well as a preliminary piece about my background. Today they had Barry's picture, with me next to him, that covered half the front page. I sure hope I can give a decent talk after all this publicity! This is a talk I agreed to give four or five months ago. The topic will be "Educational Apartheid in Maine." I haven't had much time to get ready for it, since I waited until the last two weeks and then all this other stuff broke. But I will spend tomorrow afternoon and night working on my presentation. I sure hope that's enough time.

I will be attending a half day of a housing conference tomorrow morning at the Ramada in Lewiston. It seems like I've spent a great deal of time in Lewiston this week.

Did I also mention the statewide, first-ever Women Veterans Conference this Friday and Saturday? I will be hosting both the opening of the convention and the banquet on Friday evening, as well as hosting the next day, all day. (I am the chair of the commission.)

"WHEN YOU MAKE A PEOPLE INVISIBLE, YOU DON'T WANT TO TALK ABOUT THEIR HISTORY."

November 11, 2000
Saturday

The forum went very well. I gave my half-hour speech and got many good questions afterwards. When I went to sit down, I had to stand back up again because there was a line of people waiting to shake my hand and talk to me! The *Sun-Journal* printed a story about my speech the next day. It is as follows:

Speaker Says Indians Just Want Justice
By Lisa Chemlecki, staff writer
LEWISTON. At the start of the American Revolution, George Washington asked Maine's Indians for a favor. He wanted their help in defeating the British. In return, he promised to take care of them.

The Indians agreed to the deal.

Centuries later, Donna Loring, a representative for the Penobscot Nation in the legislature, wants people to know their end of the deal was never upheld. Instead, she said, the State of Maine tried to make her ancestors—and their history—disappear.

"There we were, we had just helped win a war and we were put in what many might consider concentration camps," dependent on the State of Maine for everything from heating oil to shoes, said Loring while speaking at the Great Falls Forum in Lewiston Thursday.

Still, Loring told the audience of about 100, many people believe that the Indians of Maine survived as a result of the goodness of the state.

It's a misconception that she and other American Indians are fighting to overturn. But they face a difficult challenge—a challenge that Loring refers to as educational apartheid.

"When you want to make a people invisible, you don't want to talk about their history," she said.

"When I was in school, I learned about Columbus, George Washington, and the American Revolution. I never remember being taught anything about Maine's tribal history."

Missing History

Apartheid is most commonly used to define the segregation of nonwhites in South Africa. Although Loring believes American Indians have been forced to endure some of the same abuses, she had to ask herself an important question: "Do we really have apartheid here in Maine, in any form?"

After careful consideration, she realized that apartheid does exist. It exists in classrooms throughout the state where students are studying from textbooks that exclude the true history of her people.

"The Europeans wanted our land and our resources, and they wanted them at any cost," said Loring before reading a proclamation that was written by the first European settlers offering rewards to anyone who killed or kidnapped a Penobscot Indian. The scalp of a young male Penobscot Indian, for example was worth 25 pounds.

"That's genocide," said Loring as some people in the audience shook their heads in disbelief. "When the Europeans came, the world as we knew it disappeared."

Although American Indians disappeared completely from many states, those in Maine managed to survive. The state currently is home to four Indian tribes: the Penobscot in Penobscot County, Passamaquoddy in Washington County, and the Micmacs and Maliseets in Aroostook County.

Of those four tribes, two have representatives in the legislature. Loring represents the Penobscots and Donald Soctomah represents the Passamaquoddy, though neither of them has voting privileges due to confines outlined in the constitution.

Voting Rights

Loring, fifty-two, the former police chief of the Penobscot Nation and a Vietnam War veteran, pointed out that Maine is the only state in the nation that allows representatives from tribal governments to sit on the legislature. Although she enjoys having the opportunity to bring concerns of her tribe to the state's lawmakers, she said her people's opinions and ideas haven't always been welcomed.

Nationwide, American Indians earned the right to vote in federal elections in 1924. Maine, however, didn't allow Indians to cast ballots in state elections until 1967, making Maine the last state in the nation to do so.

It's that type of history that Loring believes should be included in classroom textbooks. The truth must be taught, she said, in order for people to earn the respect they deserve.

"I hope that I've made Maine tribes real to you today," she said. "We ask for nothing less than equality and respect."

(Article reprinted with permission of the *Sun-Journal*.)

INDIAN GOVERNMENTS NEED TO BE TREATED AS SUCH AND LOOKED UPON AS ASSETS, NOT LIABILITIES.

November 25, 2000
Saturday

The next evening after I spoke at the Great Falls Forum, I opened the Women Veterans Conference. There were around thirty-five or so women veterans attending. Congressmen Baldacci and Allen were there at different times. I talked to Congressman Baldacci for about twenty minutes. The opening ceremonies went well, with the 195th Army Band and the Army National Guard doing the posting of the colors. The next day we had about sixty-five attending and it was a very successful event. I got home around 5:00 P.M. Saturday evening and breathed a deep sigh of relief. Many women veterans had thanked me and said they learned a lot about medical services and other types of benefits that were available to them. They wanted more conferences and newsletters.

On the homefront, we have managed to keep the tribes in the news now at least every other day since the announcement on the Androscoggin courthouse steps.

The National Congress of American Indians announcement went well. Chief Barry Dana didn't go to Minneapolis but Chief Richard Doyle of the Passamaquoddy Tribe went instead, and they had a tele-conference with the president of NCAI and Barry, with the media from Maine in Barry's office listening. It made *Bangor Daily* head-lines and also the AP picked it up, as well as the *Post* and the *Globe*.

December 1, 2000
Friday

We had opening/swearing-in ceremonies at the Statehouse on the

6th. It was very interesting and very emotional at times. The most emotional event for me was when Clerk of the House Joe Mayo left his podium in the front of the house for the last time as clerk. He loves his job but because of his physical condition can no longer carry out the duties of clerk. He drove his wheelchair down the aisle with tears rolling down his face. I don't think there was a dry eye in the house. The other touching event was when the newly elected speaker, Mike Saxl, recognized his mother, who had served with him in the house and was his mentor. She had run for the senate and had lost that race. I, for one, will miss Jane Saxl this year. It was bittersweet for Mike to be speaker and not be serving with his mother.

The very interesting situation of seventeen Democrats, seventeen Republicans, and one Independent in the senate will play out. Senator Jill Goldthwait, the Independent, will be chairing the Appropriations Committee and senators Michael Michaud and Rick Bennett will take turns at the senate presidency. This year Michaud will be president with Bennett president pro tem, and next year the roles will be reversed. Neither Senator Michaud nor Senator Bennett have been pro-Native. Neither has Jill.

These three have taken positions that other senators were in line to have. Senator Rand was in line for the presidency and Senator Cathcart was in line for the chairmanship of the Appropriations Committee. They are not happy campers.

The road in the legislature for Native issues will be a tough one this year. But there was one bright light in all this, and that was when the newly elected speaker recognized the tribal representatives and asked us to stand and receive the congratulations of the house on being newly elected. It was a sign, at least to me, that Speaker Saxl was going to recognize us and take us seriously in the upcoming sessions. *(At least I thought so at the time.)* There was one more highlight, and that was the election of Secretary of the Treasury Dale McCormick. I was amazed that the new majority whip, Representative Pat Colwell (D) from Gardiner, mentioned her activism and the fact that she was his mentor and a gay rights advocate in his nomination speech. I thought how far Maine has come to be able to openly speak about being gay during a nomination for a state constitutional office. Hopefully someday that liberalism will include the tribes.

Now I must prepare a couple of bills to be submitted. One is a bingo bill that would allow games to be played on New Year's Eve and New Year's Day and would allow certain items such as prizes and inventory to be tax-free. The other is a bill that would make Maine Indian history mandatory in the Maine Learning Results. The biggest push I'm going to make is an amendment to the Joint Rules Committee giving Maine tribal representatives a vote in committees. I've decided to narrow the focus of the vote to only issues that directly affect Indian tribes. This would include any of the legislative bills submitted by me or Donald, or bills that are submitted by other legislators on Indian issues. If this joint rules amendment does not pass, then the people of the State of Maine will know who is against it and why.

December 12, 2000
Tuesday
I have called my partner in crime, Representative Joe Brooks from Winterport, and have asked him to make amendments for me in the Joint Rules Committee, since I cannot submit amendments for anything yet. I will be in Houston, Texas, on January 4, the first day of session, remaining there until the 7th. This is the first time I have been granted a fellowship for anything, and this fellowship seems quite important. It focuses on innovative and creative legislators and states' issues. I really hope that I can network with some other state legislators and begin a dialogue on tribal-state relations. There needs to be a new paradigm on the part of the states and the federal government. The focus needs to be on positive partnerships as opposed to oppressive and sometimes abusive relationships. Indian governments need to be treated as such, with respect and dignity, and looked at as assets, not liabilities. I hope some headway can be made there that would have a national impact.

THIS COMMITTEE WOULD RECOGNIZE THE UNIQUE RELATIONSHIP THAT EXISTS BETWEEN THE TRIBES AND THE STATE, AS WELL AS FACILITATE KNOWING EACH OTHER AND EACH OTHER'S GOVERNMENTAL RESPONSIBILITIES.

December 28, 2000
Thursday

I'd like to propose a committee that could be called the Joint Standing Committee on Tribal–State Relations. The committee would hear any bills relating to Indians or the Indian land claims. It would develop a certain expertise in Indian-state relations and would meet with tribal councils to talk about current issues. It could meet two or three times a year. The creation of this committee would recognize the unique relationship that exists between the tribes and the state, as well as facilitate knowing each other and each other's governmental responsibilities. The Maine Indian Tribal–State Commission could be used as the committee's resource.

Why is it needed? Tribal representatives are in the legislature representing our tribal governments, but Maine Indians have no say in laws that affect them. It is only fair and right that we get to have a vote in committee on those issues that directly affect us.
Indian representatives would sit on this committee only and have full voting and committee rights, including being able to chair or co-chair.

I feel this would clarify tribal representatives' duties and powers as well as make clear the government-to-government relationship that exists between the tribes and the state. The formation of such a committee would show a respect and recognition never before given the tribes by the state.

I'M NOT GIVING UP, BUT I CAN SEE IT'S GOING TO TAKE ANOTHER TWO YEARS, MINIMUM.

January 10, 2001
Wednesday
First day back we had a half-day session and I found out the Joint Rules Committee was going ahead with the joint rules change to allow tribal representatives to amend their own legislation on the floor. That's a good thing, but it doesn't go far enough.

I'm asking Representative Brooks to submit two amendments to the Joint Rules Committee that would allow the tribal representatives to vote in committee on their own bills. He's submitting a second amendment that would allow tribal representatives to vote in committee on other legislative bills that deal with Indian or Indian land claims issues.

The joint rules will be voted on tomorrow morning; hopefully they will pass in the house but the senate is the big question. I met with Senator Bennett (R) yesterday. After the scathing article I wrote about his emotional presentation in the senate on the Albany Township issue, I wasn't sure if we could ever work together. He seemed a bit upset about the article but understood where I was coming from and even said it gave him a perspective that he had never considered before. I agreed to talk to him in the future before I wrote another one of those articles. I told him I got overly emotional over an issue I never expected to, and he admitted he did the same. We'll try to be more professional next time. I left feeling that maybe he would be fair.

January 11, 2001
Thursday
The amendments from the Joint Rules Committee hit the floor this

morning. Leadership decided to support the committee's unanimous recommendation to allow us to amend our own legislation, but told Representative Brooks and me that they were not officially supporting us with a caucus vote. *(This, I later learned, was a red flag.)* The Democratic house leadership said each legislator should vote his or her conscience. I thought that was fine, but we lost 68 to 74. Some Democrats voted against us.

Representative Elizabeth Watson (D) of Farmingdale was fit to be tied. She had her finger in Representative Pat Colwell's face. He is the majority leader of the house. She saw how everyone in the majority Democratic leadership, the whip, and chairs of committees voted against us. She was very upset. She told Representative Colwell that she thought we were supposed to vote our conscience and not be playing political games. The fact that our own Democratic leadership voted against us was telling. They must have decided to do that in their chairs meeting this morning.

Representative Colwell felt attacked by Representative Watson. I stepped between them and told them both not to point fingers or assign blame, since it's not productive. I tried to soothe tempers, but Representative Colwell said that unless we could get senate support he was not going to vote for it.

Representative Brooks and I were both shocked and discouraged that we lost. We thought we could at least win this one in the house. We will try to present this in our caucus and get caucus support.

The media had a heyday with it. They approached me as soon as I was outside the chambers. I put a positive spin on it and said I thought it was a promising sign that we at least got 68 votes and that this was basically a "dry run," something educate people and make them discuss the issue. I did say I didn't hold much hope for the rule to pass in the senate.

Maybe someday they will allow us to vote on our own issues in committee—it seems like such a simple thing. I hope I get to vote in committee during my time as a legislator. I'd hate to leave without accomplishing that goal. I spoke with Representative Paul Waterhouse (R) from Bridgton and Representative Bill Schneider (R) about their negative votes. They both said they were on the edge and it wasn't that much of a big deal to them. I almost think if we can get the rule up for a revote, they may change their votes.

The senate is another story. I don't know about senators Rand (D), Treat (D), Longley (D), Daggett (D), etc. I think the Democrats in the senate are just plain insensitive to our position.

If those Democrats had truly voted their conscience and they voted no, then maybe I am in the wrong party and the Democrats are not the party of social justice I thought they were.

January 17, 2001
Wednesday

Yesterday's session started with an announcement by the speaker that Representative Rosaire J. Sirois of Caribou had passed away. I felt upset that I wouldn't get to go to his funeral because of committee testimony I had to present, but I know Rosie would have understood. Rosie felt that the French and the Indians had a lot in common. I was fine until the house pages tossed a peppermint on everyone's desk. I picked mine up and knew instantly it was in memory of Rosie, because peppermints were his trademark. I couldn't help but shed a few tears. They will be eulogizing him during tomorrow's session and his whole family will be there. I'm bringing some tissues for sure.

Representative Benjamin Dudley (D) of Portland brought our joint rule back onto the floor for reconsideration; since he voted against it the first time, he could make a motion to bring in back. Representative Watson had asked him to. He then tabled it and we will take it up most likely tomorrow. The speaker said we would not be debating anything and our closing would be in honor of Rosie.

Representative Colwell asked to speak to me, Representative Brooks, and also Representative Dudley in his office after the session. He wanted to talk further about the joint rule change. He told me he had problems with it but was willing to listen. After the session,

Representative Brooks left the house floor (later I found out he was in the speaker's office), so I asked Representative Bill Norbert of Portland, the majority whip, to come with me to talk to Representative Colwell. Bill was also against our rule, and I wanted to understand why.

During our discussion Bill and Pat both felt that allowing tribal representatives to vote in committee was unconstitutional. Bill felt strongly on the subject of one person, one vote. I responded that voting in committee was not the same as voting on the floor. A committee is an advisory body only and does not have the same weight under the constitution as a house vote. Bill couldn't understand why I would want a vote in committee and not a vote on the floor. I explained, "A floor vote is against the constitution and I stipulate to that. Tribal governments are not covered under the constitution. A vote in committee on legislation we submit would not be interfering with the process. We would only vote on our own legislation."

Bill then asked about the fact that one vote could cause a minority report to be made and the legislation would go to the floor on our vote only. I replied that that's the way it is now for everyone else. We discussed changing the requirement in committee to two votes for something to go to the floor for debate, but the caucus had turned that down in their last meeting, reasoning that allowing a bill to get to the floor because of one lone vote was the true democratic process. (I still felt we were truly being left out of this democratic process.) I said I would agree to the two-vote requirement if everyone else on the committee was held to the same standard.

We went back and forth and Bill said, "Isn't getting a vote on the floor the same as voting in committee? What's so different? Why would you be satisfied with a committee vote only?"

I responded that as a representative of tribal government, I would not want to vote on the floor because that would make me like all the other towns and districts of Maine. We are not a political subdivision of Maine. We are a separate government. (This, of course, made him even more confused.) I said, "We are in a very unique situation. We are dual citizens. I want to vote in committee because committees are advisory bodies only. I want to have as much impact on policy that directly affects my tribal government as I can.

The key here is that Maine, because of the Land Claims Settlement Act, is unlike other states. Maine makes laws that directly affect our tribal governments. I'm trying to represent my tribal government to the fullest extent possible." He began to soften at this point, said he would think about it, and added that he was not so dead against it as he once was—but he didn't know if he would change his mind.

Representative Colwell then brought up the idea of asking the Maine Supreme Judicial Court for its opinion under the "solemn occasion" provision of the Maine Constitution, to give the legislature its opinion on the constitutionality of the bill.

My first thought was no way. I have no confidence in the state court system, especially since the fiasco of Superior Court Justice Crowley ordering the tribal chiefs to jail! I kept thinking that this rule was not going anywhere and maybe this was where it would end, especially since I was certain it would be killed in the senate. But I told Representative Colwell I would consider the option and made an appointment to see him today at 2:00 P.M. to talk about the wording and procedure of submitting a "solemn occasion."

I had an appointment to see the new senate president, Michael Michaud. I wanted to hear his argument in opposition to our committee vote. I didn't get in to see him until after four o'clock. I began our conversation by saying I knew he was not in favor of Indian representatives voting on committees, but I wanted to tell him about my new idea and see what he thought. I explained that Indian representatives would only vote on Indian legislation they bring to committee and on Land Claims issues, that we would vote on nothing else, and that we had no interest in voting on the floor.

He smiled and said, "You know my objection was only that someone who is not a U.S. citizen would be voting on Maine issues. [Some Penobscot Nation tribal members live in other states and in other countries. All Penobscot Nation members are allowed to vote in tribal elections, the same as U.S citizens who live abroad are allowed to vote in U.S elections.] Your idea sounds logical and sounds okay to me."

My mouth must have hit the floor. I said, "Am I to understand that you will support this?"

He said "Yes, why not? Isn't the Joint Standing Committee only advisory, anyway?" He looked at his aide, who had been listening and taking notes.

His aide said, "Yes, that's right."

I then said, "So I can tell other senators you support this?"

He said, "Yes." He stood and held out his hand and said, "That wasn't so bad now, was it?"

I said, "No, and thank you so much."

I left the president's office and saw one of my old nemeses, Senator Norman Ferguson. I was feeling so good that I asked Norm if he had a few minutes. Norm said sure. I explained my position on tribal representatives voting in committees only on our legislation and he said, "I don't see anything wrong with that but I'm worried about the Albany Township issue." I told Norm that was over and it wouldn't come back. He said, "I have to watch out for that."

I said, "Norm, the tribe has moved on and it's not coming back."

He said, "We'll see."

I said, "Norm, do you think you can support this?"

He said he'd have to think about it. That was the best I was going to do with him; when someone says they'll "think about it," that usually means no.

I left for the speaker's office to tell him I was not interested in a "solemn occasion." I don't know if the rule change will pass in the house, but we can at least caucus on it and I can say I have the senate president's support. Senator Bennett (R), the senate president pro tem, was not against it, either. I'm willing to talk to a lot of senators now. Maybe there is a slight chance.

I got home around six-thirty last night but didn't really mind because I thought I had made some positive headway. Rosie would have been proud.

January 18, 2001
Thursday
Rosie would not have been so proud today.

When I got to the Statehouse, leadership had decided just to go with it and not allow us to present to the caucus. This wasn't good, because questions from our own caucus would remain unanswered. When the vote came and the debate hit the floor, I used the following argument: "A similar situation exists on the federal level in Congress with the U.S. territorial delegates. Territorial delegates have the right to vote in committees. For several years they were granted the right to vote in the committee of the whole; the latter situation was challenged and upheld by both the D.C. District Court and the D.C. Court of Appeals. When the legislative body is taking a non-final action through its committees, including a committee of the whole, it is not legislating, and therefore the 'one person, one vote' principle is not applicable. Rather, the relevant constitutional provision is the one giving the separate houses of the legislature the authority to adopt their own procedures for considering legislation. (See Maine Constitution, Article 1v, Part 3, Section 4.) Actions by committees are advisory, rather than final, and legislative rules could allow voting participation by tribal representatives." This language was taken from a draft that tribal attorneys prepared for Donald and me to use while we were on the Sovereign Nations Study Committee.

Representative Joseph Bruno (R) from Raymond was adamant that we needed to go through the process and be heard by the Joint Rules Committee. The other argument was that we would have two representatives from the same district adding up to more than one person, one vote. They just didn't get the fact that we are not representatives of another municipality but representatives of a different government. The dual citizenship thing confused them as well. They argued we could run for a district seat if we wanted to vote.

We stopped debate and the vote was taken. We lost again, only this time by ten votes, 66 to 76, instead of six! Speaker Mike Saxl waited until the very last second to cast his vote, I'm sure it was because he didn't want to signal others to follow his lead. I think leadership stuck with their decision not to support us. He stopped the voting just seconds after he cast his yes vote.

We clearly did not have leadership behind us, at least officially. I would like to think it was only because of the failure to follow the procedural process. This was the major objection by Representative Bruno. I don't think that was it, totally. Representative Norbert did vote yes and so did Representative Colwell. I was interviewed once more on the failed vote and said the same things, stating this was an educational process and I was not giving up.

I'm not giving up, but I can see it's going to take another two years, minimum. I need to get past the Joint Rules Committee and get leadership and the caucus behind me. The request for voting in committee never made it to the senate because of the house vote and manipulation by leadership.

Tribal seats contemplated in other states.

January 24, 2001
Wednesday
Last Thursday I attended a Flemming Fellows Leadership retreat for legislators (countrywide) held by the Flemming Leadership Institute of the Center for Policy Alternatives. The retreat was held in Houston, Texas, over a four-day period. It was very intensive. We worked all day, followed by a four-hour break, and then came back until ten or eleven at night. I met many good people there and actually got to educate them on Indian issues. They were very receptive and interested in learning more. I even got Indian rights into our make-believe Constitution of the State of Flemming.

This was a class of 35 chosen out of approximately 4,000 legislators. It is very competitive; I was lucky to have been chosen, and I consider it an honor. Coincidently, the day after I arrived back in Maine I got two calls, one from the National Council of State Legislators asking me to speak at a seminar on the fact that Maine is the only state that has tribal representatives and how it is working, etc. The State of Wisconsin is considering allowing a seat in its legislature for a nonvoting tribal member. The council will pay my expenses and I understand they will be contacting Representative Bill Schneider, the assistant minority leader in the house, to go as well. Bill is a very nice person, and I'd enjoy attending this seminar with him.

The other call I received was from Minnesota Public Radio about the South Dakota legislation to create a tribal seat. I spoke to that reporter in depth about tribal representatives' rights and duties in Maine and how effective Donald and I believe we are. I think it was a really positive interview. She will send me the on-air tape.

WHEN THE CHAIR ASKED IF THERE WOULD BE ANYONE SPEAKING AGAINST MY EDUCATION BILL, ONE MALE VOICE SAID, "NOT ON YOUR LIFE, LADY!"

February 1, 2001

Thursday

I got back from D.C. yesterday, but before I left, Chief Barry Dana, a delegation from tribal council, and I visited Senator Susan Collins and Representative Tom Allen on Tuesday. Senator Collins was a bit reserved with us and her staff aide was not at ease. Neither she nor her aide wanted to talk about the National Pollution Discharge Elimination System (NPDES) situation. Susan felt the courts would decide it. We agreed. She was willing to do other things for us, such as trying to get the Bureau of Indian Affairs (BIA) to move on our trust land designations and writing a letter to the Administration of Native Americans (ANA) in support of our business project (Olamon Industries). Tom Allen and his staff were much friendlier but just as reluctant to discuss the NPDES issue. Tom was willing to discuss our needs with the Native American caucus and be an advocate with them for our other issues.

The tribal governor and chiefs presented their case to the United South and Eastern Tribes board of directors (made up of tribal chiefs) earlier in the day. USET board members had approached Chief Dana with offers of support and asked what they could do. At least two of the board members were from casino tribes, with some money to back us up. The federal case will be argued in Boston on February 9 and the Maine Supreme Judicial Court case will be argued in Portland on the 12th. I've heard that the paper companies want to meet with the tribal governors and chiefs before the hearing in Portland. It is for sure that we cannot back down now, since Judge Crowley's decision would stand and set precedence. We must move on up the legal ladder to get that decision dissolved or abrogated.

February 12, 2001
Monday
I've just finished writing my testimony on my education bill, L.D. 291, for this Thursday. Here it is:

> Good Afternoon Senator Mitchell, Representative Richard, and members of the Joint Standing Committee on Education and Cultural Affairs.
> I am Donna M. Loring, the representative of the Penobscot Nation to the Maine State Legislature.
> I am here to present L.D. 291, An Act to Require Teaching of Maine Native American History and Culture in Maine's schools.
> Maine history and Maine Indian history are interwoven. You cannot teach one without the other. Make no mistake, we are unlike any other ethnic group and to compare us to minority groups and groups such as the Boy Scouts shows a tremendous lack of knowledge. Wabanaki tribes were here long before the Europeans came to this continent. We had our own governments, our own traditions, languages, and culture. We have left our mark on the State of Maine with names of Wabanaki origin such as Allagash, Androscoggin, Aroostook, Caribou, Carrabassett, Katahdin, Kenduskeag, Kennebunk, Norridgewock, Ogunquit, Olamon, Penobscot, Passamaquoddy, Piscataquis, Sebago, Skow-hegan, and Wiscasset (just to name a few).
> The Penobscot, Passamaquoddy, Micmac, and Maliseet tribes played a prominent role during the Revolutionary War in securing the boundaries of the state we now call Maine. When Maine requested to be separated from Massachusetts, one of the conditions of its statehood was to honor the obligations that Massachusetts had with the Maine tribes. Since 1820, when Maine became a state one hundred and eighty-one years ago, it has had

a constant relationship with the tribes. That one-hundred-and-eighty-one-year relationship has gone unnoticed in the history books as well as in the classrooms. Only recently has it started to come to light.

When I was elected to the state legislature in October of 1997, I came into the legislative process in midstream. I had no idea of the 180-year history of my position as a tribal representative or the fact that Maine is the only state that has tribal representatives seated in its legislative body. In April of 1999, the legislature passed a joint study order establishing a Committee to Study the Recognition of Soversign Nations in the Legislature. It was through this study committee and the research that I learned more about the history of my position and my people.

I was never taught one word about my tribal history in Maine schools. I realized that the average Maine citizen knew nothing about Maine Indian history, let alone current Indian issues. I also found that I was spending much of my time educating and reeducating my legislative colleagues. I came to the conclusion that Maine Indian history needs to be taught in the Maine schools.

The state of Maine and the Wabanaki tribes have a history together and this needs to be recognized through education. It is only through education and communication that we can build a foundation of trust and partnership.

The relationship that exists between the state and the tribes is like no other nationally or internationally. In fact, within the past two years other countries and states have looked to Maine as a model for representation of their indigenous peoples. New South Wales, Australia, sent a delegation to Maine in 1997, and New Brunswick, Canada, showed interest in 1998.

Representative Schneider and I just returned from a trip to Wisconsin. That state and its eleven tribes are looking for models of tribal-state relations and requested our participation through a presentation. They compared models from Oregon, Washington, and Arizona but were most impressed with ours. Maine, as a result of its historic relationship with the tribes, has become a national and international model.

I ask you to vote this bill out of committee as Ought to Pass.

It is time we started to educate our children about our historically unique partnership. Let understanding and communication through education be the building blocks of a new tribal-state relationship, one that recognizes and honors the struggles and contributions of its Native people.

Thank you

February 16, 2001
Friday
First of all, I should start by saying that the oral arguments on the Freedom of Access Act case brought against us by the paper companies before the Maine Supreme Judicial Court went well. At least the justices asked the right questions. They showed a certain knowledge of the subject. Justice Saufley seemed to be the most in tune with the law. Chief Justice Wathen made some good comments as well. I'm cautiously optimistic, as they say. One can never tell how a court decision will come out.

At one point during the argument, when the woman attorney for the paper companies was being very overly aggressive about being allowed into tribal council meetings, Justice Wathen snapped, "It's none of your business," and everyone laughed.

The state court security director had called me at home the night before, wanting to know how many people might show up. I gave him my best guess. There must have been about two hundred or a little less. They put the overflow into another room with speakers, so they could at least hear the proceedings. After the arguments were heard, everyone went outside to talk and listen to the drummers, as well as be interviewed. All three TV stations were there, and some USM students were making a documentary. I had dressed casually on purpose because I didn't want to be interviewed by the media, but the USM kids found me. There was a law school event later at 7:00 P.M., but I was too tired to attend.

Yesterday, February 15, the Education Committee had a public hearing for my education bill L.D. 291. The turnout was beyond my expectations.

First, I want to mention what happened to me on the way home the afternoon before the hearing: I was driving home thinking and wondering if the hearing was going to go well and if my education bill was going to make it through the process. I noticed the fluttering of wings and looked up. It was a bald eagle, landing about two and a half car lengths in front of me! It touched the road and slowly flew up to the closest tree. It sat there and as I drove past, our eyes locked. It was the closest I had ever come to a bald eagle. It was a good sign. The ancestors were with me. I felt much better about my bill after that.

When I arrived at the hearing room, it was already filled to capacity and people were still trying to get in. The testimony lasted from 1:00 P.M. until after 4:00 P.M., more than three hours!

Not one person rose to speak against the bill. When the chair, Representative Shirley Richard (D) from Madison, asked if there would be anyone speaking against the bill, one male voice said, "Not on your life, lady!" Everyone laughed. The committee was totally amazed that so many people showed up in support. House Chair Shirley Richard said it was the biggest turnout she'd ever seen for an education bill.

Needless to say, it was a total success. Now the work session comes on Wednesday, and this is when they decide what they are going to do with the bill: recommend ought to pass, ought to pass as amended, or ought not to pass. I think they will recommend OTP as amended.

It's been a long week. I've been getting calls at 9:30 and 10:00 at night—people calling to say they support my bill.

The first phase is over. The *Portland Press Herald* did an article on the hearing, as did the *Bangor Daily News*. Roberta Scruggs wrote the PPH article and emphasized the historically interesting things brought out in the testimony. The historical aspect was mostly talked about by Representative Donald Soctomah and Chief Barry Dana. The *Bangor Daily News* emphasized my testimony a bit more—the fact that I sponsored the bill, and talked about tribal-state relations. I was pleased with both articles. The *PPH* and the *BDN* both mentioned my friend Mary Griffith, who teaches at the Phillip W. Sugg Middle School in Lisbon, and the kids at her school who testified. (When the kids were about to leave after they testified, I went out into the hall and thanked them all for coming and told them they had made a difference with their testimony.)

I'm going to take it easy for the rest of the weekend and get ready to fight the good fight on Tuesday. Monday is Presidents' Day.

I FEEL LIKE I'M SWIMMING AGAINST THE CURRENT, BUT THEN AGAIN, I'VE BEEN SWIMMING AGAINST THE CURRENT ALL MY LIFE.

February 21, 2001
Wednesday

This afternoon at 2:30 P.M. is the work session for the education bill. I know the bill will lose a lot of what was in it. I'm going to try to hold on to the mandatory part and the commission part. We'll see what happens.

Yesterday Representative Paul Waterhouse gave me a book titled *Touch the Earth: A Self Portrait of Indian Existence,* compiled by T. C. McLuhan, published in October 1971. It contains a lot of the great speeches and orations by Indian chiefs. Paul had had it for thirty years. I noticed the price at the upper right-hand corner of the book: $2.95. This is a 185-page book, cover to cover.

I read a lot of the speeches during session so I could give the book back to him. When I handed him back the book he said, "Oh no, you keep it. I thought you might enjoy it."

I thanked him and asked, "You're really giving this to me?"

He smiled and said, "I was cleaning out my bookcase and haven't read it for years, I knew you would appreciate it." Again, Representative Paul Waterhouse (R) from Bridgton made my day.

This morning I was thinking about this education bill and how right it is. I know that there are people against this bill who just haven't surfaced yet. It is always a bad sign when no one speaks against your bill. If they speak against it, you at least know the objections and can counter them. I get an uneasy feeling about this one. I don't like to be blindsided. I feel like I'm swimming against the current, but then again, I've been swimming against the current all my life.

February 22, 2001
Thursday

The work session went as I had expected. They tabled the bill until the education department's bill comes up and then we will see about melding the bills into one. Representative Soctomah and I will be meeting with the education people to discuss details. Donald wants to keep my bill alive and separate just to make sure a commission is established. I will talk further with him today. I feel as long as teaching Maine Indian history is made mandatory and Maine Indians have input as to what is taught, that is all I ask. Donald is worried that my education bill may not pass and we would lose everything. I don't see that happening if we get a unanimous committee vote. I'll have to ask around to see what the feelings are. In any case I think we can get what we want.

Chief Barry Dana was at the hearing and the chair, Representative Richard, came outside the committee room and spoke to him just to make sure he was okay with what they did. I came out, too, and talked to him and everything was okay.

I escorted Chief Dana over to the Statehouse where we dropped in on my legislative aide, Ben Collings, who had worked very hard to contact people to testify. Ben is by far the best legislative aide I've had to date. *(And he remains the best aide I ever had.)* He knew Chief Dana from dog racing up north. I also took Barry to see Governor King. We all talked for a half hour or so, just about things in general, including the education bill. Governor King assured us he was behind it and would help in any way he could. He said if I needed help to just ask. I assured him I would!

February 23, 2001
Friday

I spoke with the speaker of the house, Mike Saxl, yesterday after session. I asked if the tribal chiefs could address the legislature on Wabanaki Day. He said, "My gut feeling is to say no." I was shocked by his answer. I asked him why. He said he felt he should limit who

My legislative aide, Ben Collings. Courtesy of the Clerk of the House

should address the house. I reminded him that we were a government and had a unique relationship with the State of Maine and that Montana allows its tribes to address its legislature in a "State of the Tribes Address." He asked me if I wanted him to think about it some more. I said yes, I certainly do. He mentioned he had already turned down Representative Stavros Mendros (R) from Lewiston, when Representative Mendros asked if the Greek ambassador could address the legislature. Speaker Saxl said he would ask his staff what they thought. I must say I was very disappointed with his response. I wonder if Representative Soctomah and I have taught them anything.

March 7, 2001
Wednesday
We had a bad winter storm yesterday, so bad that they canceled all public hearings and work sessions.

I did talk again with Mike Saxl and his answer was the same. I spoke with Senator John Martin about this, thinking he could enlighten me as to why Representative Saxl would not allow a tribal chief to speak. I looked upon John as a friend to the tribes. What he said surprised and puzzled me. He said, "Donna, my concern is the Micmacs and Maliseets." When he said that, I thought he would say he was worried they would not be included, but instead he went on to say, "Those Indians are not even Maine Indians; they don't have the same history as you guys." I agreed that they did not have the same history and stopped at that. He asked me to talk with him next week. Here we go again. Every time we ask for something, we end up getting other tribes or other Indian individuals thrown in our way as a roadblock, and it often causes a rift between us. Not this time! I'm not going to take the bait.

I did talk with Millie MacFarland, the house clerk, and she could not understand why the speaker was so reluctant. She said she would talk to him, since she saw nothing wrong with it and felt it was totally appropriate. She said she will get back to me sometime this week.

As for L.D. 291, I brought it before the Maine Indian Tribal–State Commission (MITSC), because I wrote them into the education bill to be the umbrella group for the Maine Indian History Commission. This Maine Indian Tribal–State Commission was added in my bill to provide staffing assistance. MITSC was concerned that it would bear all the expense and none of the reporting would come back to it. It felt that the Department of Education should bear some responsibility. MITSC members were also concerned about funding. They asked me to meet with Judy Lucarelli, the deputy commissioner of education, and Terry McTaggert, the chancellor of the University of Maine System, to try to get a money commitment. I feel my efforts to save the Maine Indian History Commission part of this bill are going to fail. The turf issues may become roadblocks that I cannot surmount.

I'm afraid that we'll end up with a bill mandating the teaching of Maine Indian history, but there will be no input from the Native communities. And you know what? It will be our own fault for not stepping up to the plate and taking some responsibility. John Banks, Penobscot Nation director of Natural Resources and Penobscot appointee to MITSC, and the other members of MITSC were in favor of including the commission. Wayne Newall, Passamaquoddy member of MITSC and former Passamaquoddy legislator, was more skeptical and felt the Department of Education and others needed to commit funds. Diana Scully and I will be meeting with Judy Lucarelli and Terry McTaggert in the next few weeks. I may talk with Speaker Saxl to see if he has any resource ideas.

The Baxter students got their public apology from the State of Maine after thirty years, but what a tremendous price they had to pay for it!

March 16, 2001
Thursday

On a tragic note, I was reading the paper today and read about a suicide in Scarborough. It was a guy named James Levier. I didn't think much about it until I saw the news on TV. They showed him testifying before the Judiciary Committee.

I remembered him instantly. He testified very passionately before our committee about how he was sexually abused at the Baxter School for the Deaf and how he suffered from suicidal tendencies as a result. We had hearings last week on whether to pass bills to give these former students compensation for their suffering.

During the testimony a representative from the state testified neither for nor against the bill but actually was testifying against it. He stated there was not enough money in the general fund to pay any compensation and said the state had problems with issuing an apology. The state felt it could be an admission of guilt. He said there were other problems with the bill, such as allowing Baxter School for the Deaf students to continue getting counseling without paying for it. Another problem was putting a time limit of January 2001. This time limit would allow anyone who had attended Baxter up until January 2001 to file for compensation if they had been sexually or physically abused.

I guess after the hearing state representative's testimony, James felt that all his efforts were totally useless and suicide was the only way he could show how traumatized and deeply affected the Baxter students were from the abuse. I remember asking the state representative at the hearing, "What is the problem with apologizing to these people since it's certainly not an extraordinary thing to do nor would it be excessively costly?" His reply was a long rambling one, finally saying something about not wanting to admit guilt. During the work session I remember suggesting that "$5 million dollars is certainly not enough—we should go for $10 million at least."

In any case, when I read the article in the *Portland Press Herald* I cried. I cried for those people who both literally and physically have no voice. The students of the Baxter School for the Deaf have been ignored as human beings, abused, and tortured by the very people who were supposed to protect and care for them. They have lived their lives with this memory. We as legislators, as well as the governor, the Department of Education, and the attorney general, have failed in our trust responsibility. We have ignored the situation and refused to listen to their voices. James Levier paid the ultimate price. He gave his life to be heard.

Did we hear him this time?

March 20, 2001
Tuesday
Yesterday the governor made a public apology to the Baxter students. I saw that on the news. The governor, from what I could observe on the television, made a telephone call to the former Baxter students and spoke to the group's representative. He apologized over the phone. I could see the interpreter and the phone on the TV monitor. I don't know if he called a special press conference to apologize, or if this was his usual press meeting. I guess at least the former Baxter students got their public apology from the State of Maine after thirty years, but what a tremendous price they had to pay to get it! This whole situation of marginalization, abuse, and the state's refusal to admit responsibility reminds me in many ways of their treatment of Maine tribes.

"Voices of change will never be silenced."
—Elizabeth (Libby) Mitchell, former speaker
of the house

March 23, 2001

Friday

Mike Saxl hasn't changed his mind about the tribal chiefs speaking
in the house. Millie, the clerk of the house, tried to say something to
him but he wouldn't let her speak. I guess that's the end of that. I
feel I should at least write him a letter with how I view this situation. He seems to equate us with foreign countries (given his comment about the Greek ambassador). In a sense, we are a foreign
country in that we are not under the U.S. Constitution and our legal
status is not that of a municipality or a state but something totally
different. (Let us not forget that Indian nations were the first nations
of this country, and from that perspective one might ask, Who are
the real foreigners?) U.S. Supreme Court Justice John Marshall, in
the 1831 case *Cherokee Nation v. Georgia,* ruled that Indian tribes
are "Domestic Dependent Nations."

But the State of Maine and the Maine tribes have had a relationship that is very different from the other tribes in this country. We
have been seated in the Maine House of Representatives since Maine
became a state in 1820. No other tribe can claim this. Maine tribal
representatives sit as representatives of their respective tribal governments. Just that fact alone should set us apart from the Greek
ambassador or anyone who *has* been allowed to address the legislature in the past!

It seems perfectly proper for tribal chiefs to address the house
given this unique status. I am not asking to address a joint session,
although that would be a tremendous sign of respect for tribal governments in this state. I am only asking that the tribal chiefs be

allowed to address the house on a day that the legislature itself has set aside as "Wabanaki Day at the State Legislature." This would be a historic moment that would certainly improve tribal-state relations. I guess I can only say I do not understand this refusal on the speaker's part. He says he wants to honor us and treat us with respect, but yet he does nothing substantive to help us or even recognize us. I am truly disappointed.

The following is a letter I wrote to Speaker Saxl:

Mr. Speaker:

This is a follow-up to our conversation approximately a month ago, when I requested that the tribal chiefs be allowed to address the house. I understand your decision not to allow that to take place has been made, and I respect your decision. I will not take this further.

I must say that I was totally shocked and disappointed by your decision. You do not take into consideration the one-hundred-and-eighty years of our presence in this house. Donald and I represent our respective tribal governments, as have tribal representatives since Maine became a state. No other state has tribal representatives in its legislative bodies. I find it amazing that in all those years, not once has a tribal chief been allowed to address the house!

In this time of devolution the states are trying to improve their relationships with the tribes. The Conference of State Legislators, in partnership with the National Congress of American Indians, has printed a sixty-eight-page document titled *Government to Government: Understanding State and Tribal Governments*. The National Conference of State Legislatures also published *Native American Issues: 2000 State Legislation*.

The National Conference of State Legislators asked Maine to be a model presenter to the State of Wisconsin. Maine is recognized as a leader in good tribal–state relations. I would like to see us keep the lead.

Mr. Speaker, allowing tribal chiefs to address the house would have recognized the importance of tribal-state relations and given visible respect to Maine's tribal governments. It would have been a very positive historic event, one that had never taken place before in the history of the legislature. I will end this with a quote from Elizabeth (Libby) Mitchell, former speaker of the house, who was in the gallery when we debated another issue, the vote in committee. She witnessed our efforts to win a vote and mentioned this experience in the *Sun-Journal,* dated January 21, 2001. She wrote: "At the end of the day, with this change in place, only the 151 duly elected representatives would be able to cast an actual vote on legislation. This time the Native Americans lost the round. They will of course, bring this back. Change comes slowly, but voices of change will never be silenced." Change truly does come slowly, and she was right, we will bring these issues forward time and time again and maybe gradually things will change.

Perhaps these changes will take place under the leadership of someone else. Voices of change will never be silenced.

March 26, 2001
Monday

Today was not a good day. I arrived at the Statehouse for public hearings at around 10:30 A.M.

The Judicary Committee (I am a member of this committee) worked the Maine Indian Tribal–State Commission (MITSC) bill this afternoon. The bill would allow MITSC to submit legislation directly and have a meeting with the governors and chiefs as well as two meetings a year with tribal councils and legislators.

Representative Roger Sherman (R) of Hodgdon made the argument that MITSC should not be allowed to submit legislation directly because it is already represented by Donald and me, and no committee should be allowed to submit legislation directly, anyway. He and Waterhouse asked if MITSC had problems submitting legislation and questioned why they'd want to submit directly, anyway. Cush Anthony, the commission chair, answered that the commission was allowed, until recently, to submit legislation and that the legislation should be attributed to the committee and not a sponsor. Waterhouse argued that a sponsor could always say that he was submitting on behalf of the commission. Our legislative analyst stated that two committees are allowed to submit legislation directly now, and they are the Child and Family Services Committee and the Criminal Justice Committee.

I explained that I am not a member of MITSC and that any one of them could attend MITSC meetings, as I have. I told them I represent the Penobscot Nation and not MITSC. I added that since two other committees are allowed to submit direct legislation, it is only fair that MITSC be able to, as well. MITSC is a creation of the Maine Indian Land Claims Settlement Act, which is a treaty between the state and tribal governments. This committee should be allowed to submit legislation directly, before any other committees, just because of its governmental status!!

The Republican committee members all voted against the bill. Sherman kept saying Donald and I represent MITSC. This infuriated me and I spoke directly to Sherman, stating very slowly that neither Donald nor I were MITSC members and he was just penalizing MITSC because he perceived it as an Indian committee. After the hearing ended, I went over to Representative Waterhouse and said, "I expect that kind of prejudice from Sherman and Ferguson but not from you."

Paul said, "I don't believe *any* committee should be able to submit legislation directly."

I said bull; that was just blatant prejudice, and I walked out of the room. My face had been just returning to its natural color and went back to a bright red. (I've *got* to start working on controlling my temper.) So prejudice still exists big time in the legislature, and this was a glaring example. It makes me very upset. *(Today, Senator Roger Sherman works very cooperatively with the Maliseet Tribe.)*

March 28, 2001
Wednesday
Today I talked with representatives Waterhouse and Madore about their votes yesterday. They both assured me they would not debate this on the floor (when have I heard that before?). They, of course, assured me that the problem with the bill was the direct legislation clause, and they felt no committee should have that right. Representative Madore said he felt that MITSC had not done a good job in the past and that he felt reluctant to give them that authority, given their record. I said, "In a way I can understand that reasoning, but we all know that legislation is fluid and if there is a problem they could always take care of that right away." That is when Representative Madore said he wasn't all that much against it and would not debate it on the floor.

I spoke to them just prior to the MITSC budget presentation before the Appropriations Committee. We, the Joint Standing Committee on Judiciary, sit as a subcommittee (when MITSC and other departments that are monitored by the Judiciary Committee are being heard) when the Appropriations Committee reviews budgets. I expected someone on either the Appropriations Committee or the Judiciary Committee to give MITSC a hard time, but Cush Anthony gave his presentation and no one asked any questions. Not sure if that's good or bad. We'll see tomorrow.

March 29, 2001
Thursday
I've spoken with both Representative Seth Berry and Senator Mary Cathcart of the Appropriations Committee, and they both seem to think the MITSC money will be okay. After the debate over the Part I budget last night (to fund ongoing costs of existing programs and services), I know that Part II (to fund new or expanded programs or services) will be a bigger debate and a harder fight. So we will see what happens.

The house had a session in the morning, then went to committees and reconvened at 5:00 P.M. and went to around 10:30 P.M., debating approximately seventeen amendments to the Part I budget that Appropriations had passed unanimously. I understand that the Democrats have the support of the governor and the support of the Republicans who are on the Appropriations Committee. That's all they really need to get anything passed. The chair of the Appropriations Committee is Senator Goldthwait of Bar Harbor, the Independent, and she will vote with their decision. So it's just a matter of time to get this budget through the senate and back and forth again today. Then it can be signed tonight. Hopefully it will be smooth sailing.

MY GOODNESS, I SOUND LIKE A POLITICIAN!

March 30, 2001
Friday
The house started its session at 11:30 A.M. to vote on the budget
when it came back from the senate. Last night the senate made
changes to the budget which I'm sure have really upset Speaker Saxl.
The fact that there are a number of seats open for election next year
was not lost on me or anyone else. Senators Bennett, Michaud, and
others are out to make a political name for themselves. I guess a few
others are, as well. It should be interesting to see how this plays out.

I had dinner at a lobbyist's house last night; there were only a
few us there and we had a good time just talking about things in
general. I heard that my friend Representative Bill Schneider did not
get the U.S. attorney position nomination from Snowe. Too bad—he
would have been great. We also discussed possible candidates for
governor such as Baldacci, Pingree, and who knows who else. I asked
what they thought of Kaileigh Tara, and they didn't think she had
the backing of the party or enough recognition. They didn't give her
much hope. They spoke highly of Pingree, but only if she ran against
Collins and not for governor. Word has it that she will announce her
run for the governorship next week. Well, I can hardly wait to see
who comes out of the woodwork on this. We will have fun times at
the legislature in any case, with legislators jockeying for a good
political position.

March 31, 2001
Saturday
Yesterday we mostly caucused and discussed the senate's decision to
make its own budget amendments. One thing I have learned is that
opinions change—one day you may feel and speak one way and the

next have a total change of heart because of what someone has told you or just because you've had time to digest something and decided your first response was not right. This happens a lot.

Yesterday and today I felt the senate totally ignored the house and an Appropriations Committee that has been struggling with budget issues and hearings for six months! I think it was totally inappropriate for the senate to do what it did. The house voted to adhere (stick with original vote) and have a committee of conference. I understand the senate is going to refuse to conference because it is afraid its amendments will fall apart. The senate amendments give everyone what they want and on the face of it, that's wonderful. The Democrats get funding for social programs and education, the Republicans get no new taxes. Oh, I almost forgot—the governor got shafted. To some that's the best part of the senate package! The governor's technology fund got put into the Rainy Day Fund to replace the $70 million or so they have raided. It would take three-quarters of the state's savings account to pay for their projects to make everyone politically happy. That would only be good until after the election; then we would be facing an almost $2 million deficit with no money in the kitty to negotiate with state employees and no cushion for a real rainy day.

My goodness, I sound like a politician! I know the thought and the study that went into this process. The decisions that the Appropriations Committee made were tough, and not everyone liked every decision, but that is what's called compromise. The house bit the bullet and voted the responsible way and for the best interest of the state. The house members were certainly not voting to be popular! The house, in my opinion, was right the first time and I think it should not go too far off track. If the budget isn't passed today then it will take a two-thirds vote in both the house and senate to get a budget passed. I don't think there will be a compromise today. The only way that could happen is if the house and the senate agree, and that is unlikely.

Democrats running for office in the senate are Senate President

Michael Michaud, Senators Longley and Nutting, Senate President Pro Tem Richard Bennett, and possibly Senator Mills. I think it's ironic the way this came about. Remember when everyone was wondering who would be senate president, and at the time, senators Daggett and Rand were running against the two men? Senator Goldthwait, the Independent, had the deciding vote. She basically designed the structure we have now because she refused to support either of the women. She chose Michaud as president with Bennett as pro tem. She then took the chairmanship of Appropriations, thought to be the most powerful committee in the legislature. Senator Cathcart had been next in line for that position. With one sweeping decsion Jill Goldthwait pushed three women aside and chose the men. The senate then proceeded to ignore the Appropriations Committee and all its hard work, and ignore the person the senate president and pro tem owe their senate positons to. In effect, they stabbed the chair of the Appropriations Committee, Senator Goldthwait, in the back!

Senator Cathcart voted in the minority to back up Appropriations because she remained a member of that committee and knew all the hard work it did. She should be applauded for that. She had a chance to stick it to Senator Goldthwait but didn't.

However, Senator Daggett went along with Senator Michaud. It is rumored and most likely true that Senator John Martin had a lot to do with this coup. Someone said his fingerprints are all over this one. Who knows, tonight or tomorrow everyone will be back in the same camps and maybe some will even have a change of heart. I guess it depends on who has the most integrity. I would hope the house sticks to its position with very few changes.

April 4, 2001
Wednesday
The past few days have been very frustrating for me, personally. The speaker made me a bit upset yesterday when we were caucusing in his office. Toward the end, he asked if anyone had anything else to

Pat Jacobs and me, having a friendly conversation in the house chamber. L-R, Representative Patricia Jacobs (D-Turner), Representative Jacqueline R. Norton (D-Bangor) in the background, and myself. Courtesy of the author

say, and I raised my hand just to comment on the importance of not forgetting the Appropriations Committee and all their hard work. He saw my hand but kept calling on other people. He dismissed the group without allowing me to say anything. I had all I could do not to just turn around and walk out. I found out later that he did the same thing to Representative Brooks. I get the feeling that he chooses to ignore anyone he thinks is going to say something he doesn't like.

On another subject, Representative Pat Jacobs (D), North Turner, submitted a bill that would ban smoking in bingo and beano halls. I asked her to submit an amendment to the bill that would exclude our high-stakes bingo. She agreed to submit one, but her bill got killed in the house. I'm hoping it does not come back to life, especially tomorrow.

I'm supposed to go to USM to meet the consul general of South

Africa. I've met her once before, when she first became consul general and had a dinner for us in her home in New York; our little group, which consisted of Rachel Talbot Ross, Tony Brinkley, and Peter Thibeault, was the first group she entertained as consul general. So tomorrow will be a busy day as I go to the legislature and then go to Portland and then back to a public hearing where Donald's bill for an extension on obtaining trust land will be before our committee. I'm sure Senator Ferguson will give him trouble, as well as a few others. It's late—almost eleven. I just got back from judging an oratory contest on Indian Island. I enjoyed it. The Indian Island students did exceptionally well. I noticed they have a showcase with quite a few trophies for winning oration contests.

April 6, 2001
Friday
Representative Soctomah's land-into-trust bill went fine—only Representatives Waterhouse and Madore had questions but they were all answered satisfactorily. Senator Ferguson was not there. The work session for this bill is on Tuesday at 1:00 P.M.

Oh yes, Representative Jacobs's bill got passed in the senate so it will be coming back to the house for debate. I'll have to be ready to give my speech on the second reading if it passes. Quite frankly, I don't know if it would make a difference or not.

I am really feeling like we don't matter much to people anymore. I guess I'm starting to feel discouraged. It seems we are losing all the really important rounds, the rounds that would give us visibility—such as the committee vote and the chance to address the legislature. I guess I'll just take a deep breath and move on.

IT'S TOUGH TO WAIT. THIS BILL IS PROBABLY THE MOST IMPORTANT INDIAN BILL THAT EVER HIT THE LEGISLATURE.

April 13, 2001
Friday

Representative Soctomah's land-into-trust bill passed the Judiciary Committee with a unanimous OTP. Representatives Waterhouse and Madore joked around a little and teased me, but that was okay; it was all in good humor and there was no problem with the bill.

Now, hopefully it will go under the hammer in both houses. Budget talks are still in progress but I think they will reach a consensus soon. We are on break until April 24.

Next week the Passamaquoddy are sponsoring a three-day seminar on environmental issues. It should be a very good seminar. Donald made sure the legislature got copies of the agenda, etc. Maybe one or two of them will show up and learn something. The court decisions have not come down yet. The chiefs are very nervous about that, and I don't blame them!! They are prepared with a plan if the decision comes down during the seminar. At least I think they are!

Today I met with Deputy Commissioner of Education Judy Lucarelli. I have been working hard to keep the fiscal note off my bill. I asked MITSC to be the umbrella agency and provide staffing and assistance and basically help facilitate the meetings of the new commission established with my bill. Diana Scully, the executive director of MITSC, has done a tremendous job with writing a proposed budget and an amendment to my original bill, as well. My meeting with Judy Lucarelli was to get the support of the Department of Education to commit funds. That was one of MITSC's requirements before they would agree to this arrangement. They also wanted the University of Maine System to commit funding as well. After a few meetings, MITSC has those commitments. Judy Lucarelli assured me that her department would come up with the cash. It was not much, $3,000 from the Department of Education and $3,000 from the university. MITSC is also counting on $15,000 in the Part II budget.

At this point it all looks good. After meeting with Judy, I went to the Education Committee's analyst, Phil McCarthy, who reviewed the amendment and thought it was very good. He also said he thought it did what it was designed to achieve, and that was to remove the fiscal note by making the commission a nonlegislative study. It takes away the money requirement because MITSC and the departments will absorb the cost out of existing budgets. Phil said he would try to get this in front of the committee our first week back, either on April 24 or 26. I truly hope we can get a unanimous OTP from the committee. That would virtually ensure the bill going under the hammer in both houses. It's tough to wait. This bill is probably the most important Indian bill that ever hit the legislature.

The MITSC bill will also hit the floor for debate. It looks like the second half of this session will be a hot one for many people because the floor debates will be in full swing. I can hardly wait.

April 21, 2001
Saturday
Phil McCarthy called me last Thursday to tell me that the education bill will be worked by the committee on April 25, Wednesday, at 10:30 A.M.

I think we're ready to go on this one but you never know what can come up to blindside you. I understand the teachers' union came out against it because they did not want another mandatory thing to have to teach. The teachers I've spoken to say that is a crock—they get mandates all the time and manage to fit things in. Indian history is especially deserving of that effort.

April 24, 2001
Tuesday

Today was a strange day—the weather was great but it seemed as if I could only get half of anything I tried for. I asked the Legal and Veterans' Affairs Committee to delete the governmental capacity part of the the bingo bill, L.D. 108, since I hadn't realized the implications of it until I really read it one day. I also asked the committee to leave the request for bingo operations on New Year's Eve and New Year's Day in. Representative John Tuttle said the bill probably wouldn't have passed with the governmental part in it.

I told him I may introduce something next session that deals with the tax part of the bill. Because high-stakes bingo is operated by the tribe in its governmental capacity, it would not be subject to state tax.

The committee didn't seem all that friendly. It's just a feeling I got while standing in front of them. They didn't intimidate me, though. My bill was scheduled to be the last one heard, but I managed to get in before Representative Michaels, because he wasn't there yet. It really bothers me to hear the same representatives who continuously vote against any Indian bingo bill talk about horse racing and off-track betting and how they are contributing one or two million to the state.

When I came up to testify, Representative Mayo asked if we could play bingo any weekend. I think he was thinking if they can play any weekend, why do they need New Year's Eve and New Year's Day? I'm sure he will be one of those who look for any excuse to vote against us. After my brief testimony, Representative Tuttle went right to the next bill and didn't ask for testimony for or against, as is the normal procedure. What was that about? I don't know whether to be glad or nervous.

Then I had to stand up and read my bingo testimony on the floor of the house. Representative Waterhouse made a motion to indefinitely postpone the amendment. I got up for the record and asked them to vote against indefinite postponement because if the anti-smoking bill passed the house this time, I needed to have the amendment attached. I really wanted the bill to be killed. The amendment got killed and so did the bill, and I got what I wanted but in a roundabout way. That's the way my day went.

Representative Waterhouse and Representative Bunker approached Donald and me about asking the body in the house to vote on tribal chiefs speaking to the house. I couldn't believe it. I told them I had promised the speaker I would not pursue the matter, but they could if they wished. They said they would, but nothing happened. Interesting day all the way around.

I go before the Education Committee tomorrow morning. I need all the luck I can get. This is a very, very important bill.

April 26, 2001
Thursday

Yesterday I went before the Education Committee. All in all, it wasn't too bad. Senator Betty Lou Mitchell didn't understand why I would want to keep the mandatory Learning Results portion in my bill when the Department of Education had the same language. I finally told them quite candidly that I understood there might be some problems with the department's bill and I wanted to be sure mine passed. Everyone laughed.

Phil McCarthy, the legislative analyst, explained that the language needed to remain in order to give legal status to the History and Cultural Commission the bill creates. Deputy Commissioner Judy Luceralli told the committee the department was in agreement and that she saw no problem with keeping the language the same. Phil told the committee that if any discrepancy came up, it could be fixed with the errors bill.

Another problem two committee members saw with the bill was the fact that it mandated another thing for teachers to do. That was Representative Weston's objection, and Representative Skoglund voted against the bill because he was against Learning Results in general. I was a bit upset because each of them had said it was a great bill in and of itself, but they just couldn't vote for it because of some other reason. I hear this a lot when introducing Indian bills. If people would just stop and think of the truly positive impact of some of the bills, this might outweigh the other considerations. Legislation like this bill could be so revolutionary in helping people know who Indian people are and that we are real people, just like they are, with a history and valuable contributions. This bill could go a long way toward healing the abuse and neglect the state has heaped upon us for so many years. How? By recognizing us as human beings who exist in the State of Maine and by acknowledging the fact that we did contribute to this state and still do, and that we are still here!

I expect there will be a debate on the house floor and maybe in the senate, but I hope we end up with enough supporters to send the message that the people of Maine want to learn about Maine Indian history and see this as important enough to make it mandatory. There was only one newspaper reporter at the public hearing, and he wrote about the tiff between the state and private schools. I'm hoping that on May 2 we'll have a great turnout and I can make a pitch for the bill then.

May 1, 2001
Tuesday

Tomorrow is the big day—Wabanaki Day. We all got notices this morning that there will be a Democratic caucus about the Part II budget at noon tomorrow. This is a direct conflict with our schedule of events, and we put out the first schedule at the end of last week. Now leadership comes out with this. I may be a bit paranoid, but I think Saxl did this on purpose! I wrote a note to the majority leader, Pat Colwell, expressed my concern, and told him I knew the budget was important but felt they could have scheduled it at some other time. I said this was a direct insult to the tribes.

He wrote back and said they would announce a second caucus on Thursday for those who chose to go to the tribal event. I had hoped they would cancel the caucus tomorrow, however I wrote back,

"Thank you for meeting us halfway." I then wrote a note to Senator Cathcart and told her the same thing I told Pat. She wrote back that the caucus was a house caucus and the senate was invited. She also said that Senator Daggett was going to talk with Saxl to see if he would cancel and change it to Thursday. Donald says that people have told him that they are just going to get up and leave at 11:30 A.M. We'll see what happens on this.

I had to go to the Legal and Veterans Committee while they decided on my bingo bill. They were late in convening but voted my bill a unanimous ought to pass. As I was walking to my car, I ran into Donald, who informed me that Pat Colwell had tabled his offensive sign bill. It was a bill that would remove the Big Squaw Mountain sign from I-95. It was in with other emergency bills. I told Donald earlier I saw no problem with it. Donald was on his way to talk to Pat to find out why he tabled the bill. I offered to go with him and he said, "Oh no, I'll talk to him." I figured Donald thought I would make Pat mad. I just said, "Okay, see you at five for session." Tomorrow will be an exhausting day.

May 2, 2001
Wednesday
Wabanaki Day was a success but not without its problems. The weather was record-breaking! It was 90 degrees! While Chief Dana was giving his speech, the fire alarm went off at the state museum and we had to vacate the building. We ended up staying outside in the hot—I mean HOT—sun. I think I may have gotten sun poisoning.

The morning portion of the program went well. I surprised my sister Beth with a sentiment. She deserved to be recognized for all her accomplishments and I was honored and proud that it was me who did it. The day was worth it just for that one sentiment. A number of legislators commented on how touched they were by it. One said she was in tears because she had lost her sister recently to breast cancer.

With my sister Elizabeth (Beth) Sockbeson (right), seated at my desk in the house chamber. Courtesy of Donald Soctomah

Some house members walked out at 11:30, but I don't think a lot did. I didn't see that many at the state museum, but then again, the crowd was a bit fluid. Representative Waterhouse stayed for the whole thing—he was still there when I left about three o'clock. I got a chance to speak briefly and talk about my education bill, and Diana Scully gave me a bunch of stickers to pass out that said "Vote YES on 291," which Sherry Mitchell had been handing out. Sherry did a great job. My niece, Rebecca Sockbeson, and her daughter, Julia, were there with my sister, Beth Sockbeson. It was a strange day in that nothing seemed to go right from the National Anthem to the fire alarm at the state museum where we all gathered. Kelly Demmones, who was to sing the Anthem, didn't make it to Augusta. The atrium of the state cultural building was crowded, noisy, and hot with stale air. Not comfortable at all. But we had a good turnout—around two hundred, I think—and the day went by fast. Not bad.

THE LAND CLAIMS SETTLEMENT ACT WAS SUPPOSED TO AFFIRM OUR SOVEREIGN RIGHTS, NOT DENY THEM!

May 2, 2001—continued

The Maine Supreme Judicial Court decision came out yesterday. It was a split decision, in that it said we had to turn over documents that were government-to-government or government-to-state. The problem is that the ruling left us with no sovereign rights in dealing with other governmental entities. Isn't that what sovereign rights are all about—being able to deal with other governments? The Land Claims Settlement Act was supposed to affirm our sovereign rights, not deny them! I find this court decision a breach of faith and I think it should make the Settlement Act null and void. Strong words on my part, I know, but the State of Maine is slowly eroding our rights through their interpretation of the act! This needs to stop.

The history the Maine Supreme Judicial Court saw and used was not the whole story. The court saw some things differently than how an Indian person would see them. They said the state had total control of the tribes for years and made thousands of laws that affected them. This is indeed true, but it does not mean the tribes were not sovereign. It simply means the State of Maine held us hostage as prisoners of war. They failed to recognize the federal law that says anything Indian people do not give up, they retain. We never gave up our sovereignty—how could we? We didn't know what the word meant. That was a white man's word and concept. We have occupied this land since time immemorial. Our governments predate the European invaders of this continent by thousands of years! We have *inherent* sovereign rights.

Anyway, enough of this. The Department of Justice filed suit against Lincoln Pulp and Paper yesterday on the Penobscot Nation's behalf, stating they polluted our river and ruined our culture. The suit could be anywhere from $400,000 in damages to $60 million in damages, depending on the cost of cleanup for the river and compensation for damage to our culture.

May 4, 20001
Friday
A couple of things happened yesterday and today. One was that Donald's offensive sign bill got tabled again—then I had to leave, so I don't know if they took it up or not. It was entered under emergency, so they would need a two-thirds vote to pass it. Pat Colwell told Donald there was some sort of problem with the bill and tabled it.

Pat Colwell also told me that there might be a procedural problem with the MITSC bill. He thought because they asked to submit legislation directly, that this was against the constitution, and he said that Speaker Mike Saxl had pointed out the problem. I told him that if other commissions were able to submit direct legislation, then this commission should be allowed to, as well. He agreed. Representative LaVerdiere was checking to see if other commissions could submit legislation and indeed they can.

I started to seriously think about this and remembered there was a ratification clause on the bill, meaning that it was an amendment to the Settlement Act and the tribes would have to agree, as well. I realized at that point that the tribes feel MITSC has too much power as it is, and they would never agree to that because they would be taking a chance that MITSC would submit something they hadn't agreed to. As it is now, MITSC has to get a sponsor for legislation and perhaps that is as it should be. I told Representative LaVerdiere that I had rethought the bill and felt the legislative part should be eliminated. He went with me to the Revisor's Office and submitted an amendment.

The Republicans who were against the bill were now willing to vote for it. I was told later in the evening that they had tabled the bill because the Democrats wanted to caucus on it tomorrow. That sounds a bit strange to me, but we'll see what's up. This is the first time this session they've asked to caucus on what may be perceived as an Indian bill. It really isn't, but because the word Indian is in it they perceive it as such. I just hope they're willing to caucus on my education bill when the time comes!

"I DON'T DRINK BEER, I DON'T PLAY GOLF, BUT I SURE WOULD LIKE TO VOTE."

May 4, 2001—continued

Tonight I had to sit through a bill that the paper companies put in that would create a new category of law called "Environmental Terrorism." It was almost laughable. The scary thing is, it passed! The only environmental terrorists around here are the paper companies themselves. The bill would make it a felony to spike a tree or violently cause damage to human life, or disrupt business. The representatives promoting the bill called the protesters bullies—can you believe it!? It took all my self-control not to get up and say something. I think if I had, it would have caused more harm than it was worth so I didn't say anything. It won by two votes. I have a feeling it will be back. (And I hope I can still keep my mouth shut.) The paper companies have polluted our river and destroyed our entire way of life, leaving us with toxic waste that I'm certain has caused the death of hundreds of Penobscot people. We had twelve people die this year alone.

May 6, 2001

Sunday

First of all, yes, the paper company terrorism bill is coming back to the floor. I've spoken to a number of representatives and they thought the same thing I did.

I worked all day Friday on a speech in reference to this bill. It will raise a lot of hairs on the paper companies' necks, but I don't give a crap! I had the speech all written Friday and planned to work on it some more this weekend if we didn't get it back on the floor on Friday. We didn't.

Friday was "Welcome Back Day," when previous legislators come to the session. We had a nice ceremony that recognized Senator John Martin and all the past speakers of the house, as well as staff, etc. There was a representative there from 1941, and I thought he might be able to answer a question Donald and I have had for a while: Why did the tribal representatives get kicked out of the house in 1941? He couldn't remember and thought they didn't have a seat anyway, so I didn't learn anything new.

I picked up my *Maine Sunday Telegram* from the mailbox this morning and on the bottom right of the front page saw a headline that read: "Tribal Rift with State Intensifies." My picture was boxed within the article on the front page! I had spoken to Bart Jansen, the reporter for the *PPH* who is based in D.C., when he had called me for comments on the court case and sovereignty. I reluctantly agreed to speak with him after he said he had tried calling Governor Dana with no success.

The line under my photo read "We have...rights," and the quote he used was, "To be quite candid, we think the state and the paper companies are too close.... Somebody said they were in bed with each other, and I tend to agree." I'm sure Governor King will not appreciate that comment! But it's okay; I truly believe that, so I guess it's about time the general public knew. I can defend that position.

The newspaper also came out with an editorial stating that the tribes had a victory in the court case because our leaders' contempt charges were vacated and they wouldn't have to go to jail. It went on to say that our tribal governments should conduct their business in a more transparent manner and be less secretive, and that open government is simply good practice. I find this editorial outrageous—it simply shows the ignorance of the dominant society. I will explain this further in detail when I write an op ed to the paper.

May 7, 2001
Monday
Well today they did not get to the environmental terrorism bill again. They will most likely do it tomorrow. It was a long session,

from nine in the morning to six in the evening, with a couple of hours off for lunch. The longest debate was one that we thought would be shorter, and that was a bill to allow the sale of alcohol on golf courses. It lasted about two hours!

Finally a representative stood up and said, "I don't drink beer, I don't play golf, but I sure would like to vote!" Everyone laughed and he got applause. The bill passed the house—I guess because people realized it was reality, and that people were drinking on the courses anyway.

May 10, 2001
Thursday
They didn't get to the terrorism bill yet. They will debate it on Monday the 14th.

Next week they will have sessions up until 9:00 P.M. People's tempers will be short when they get tired. (Should be an interesting week.)

Today they passed the MITSC bill in the house for the last time. They also passed under emergency L.D. 618, An Act to Remove State Road Signs with Offensive Names from Interstate Route 95 and the Maine Turnpike. The vote was something like 109 to 11. I'd be interested in who those eleven were. Tomorrow the tribal chiefs will be honored at a People's Alliance dinner in Portland and I plan to attend. That should be interesting as well.

THE NOTES FROM MY COMRADES MADE ME FEEL VERY GOOD, AND FOR ONCE, EVEN IF THIS IS SHORT-LIVED, I MADE A DIFFERENCE.

May 15, 2001
Tuesday

We finally got to the environmental terrorism bill. I was a bit confused at first because Representative Clark put his amendment on the bill and then Representative Povich moved to indefinitely postpone the amendment. I wasn't certain what I should do—speak on the amendment or wait until the bill came up for vote after the vote on the amendment. I understood they were going to move indefinite postponement of the bill itself, as well.

I decided to speak while I had the chance. I listened to other speakers and they were not just speaking on the amendment, so I figured I could speak on the bill as everyone else had. Luckily, Representative Etnier was the speaker pro tem and didn't know that much about protocol or didn't care, so we got away with arguing the bill as well as the amendment at the same time. No one called "point of order." A lot of people debated the bill and after the debates and after I made my speech (which I changed a few times), Representative Soctomah said, "You could hear a pin drop after your speech." I fully expected at least three paper company loyalists to stand up and say something, but they didn't.

Here is my floor speech:

I would be remiss in my duties as the Penobscot Nation Representative if I did not speak on this bill and this amendment.

The words "Environmental Terrorism" within the title of this bill are inappropriate and misleading. When I heard this term in the bill title I thought, "We are finally going to enact a policy making those big corporations and paper companies felons for their devastation of the environment and rape of our forests and natural resources."

Needless to say I was wrong.

I heard the words damaging to property, human health, life threatening and violence. Those words do indeed define environmental terrorism. They are words that are descriptive of the devastation, disease, and human suffering caused by the paper companies and the big corporations who directly release toxic materials into our water and air. This bill gives them an extra recourse, a "special legal remedy" to use against those who destroy property or interrupt business while protesting. We already have criminal laws in place to cover property damage or criminal activity. I submit to you that if you pass this "special remedy," then you are providing a special right, a special remedy to the paper companies and big corporations that the general public does not have, and if you pass this special remedy then to be fair you must also enact a "special remedy" for the rest of the people of Maine, including tribes and communities throughout the state who are being affected daily by the release of toxins into their environment.

Years of toxic release by these companies have led to death and devastation in our communities, particularly within the Native communities. Our very culture is on the verge of extinction because of these poisons that are released into our waters and have built up over the years infecting the fish, plants, and animals that are so important to our way of life.

Where are the "special legal remedies" for our people? Where are the special remedies for Maine people who have been victimized by real environmental terror?

The companies who have released and continue to release toxins into our water and air are the real environmental terrorists!

They should not be given an extra recourse or a "special legal remedy." To give them a special legal remedy would truly be dangerous public policy! I ask you to indefinitely postpone this amendment and go on to the indefinite postponement of the bill itself.

Thank you.

The vote was taken and the amendment was indefinitely postponed and so was the bill. The final vote on the bill was 80 to 60. It now goes to the senate. I hope this bill doesn't raise its ugly head again. I did say some harsh things about the paper companies in my speech, but they were all true. I felt that I was right on and that I hit the bullseye. I got a lot of notes from other reps telling me what a great job I had done.

Representative Susan Hawes wrote, "Hear! Hear! Thank you for exposing the bill on 'ET' for what it is! Thank you!" Representative Skoglund from St. George wrote, "Rep Loring, Very interesting and colorful talk!" Representative Ross Paradis wrote, "Donna, Excellent speech! You *absolutely* convinced me to vote to kill that environmental bill. Bravo!" Representative McLauglin wrote, "Donna, Well done." Representative Jacobs wrote, "Donna, Excellent!" Representative Lillian LaFontaine O'Brien wrote, "Dear Donna, Great info, well delivered, very succinct. *Excellent* Floor Speech. Have a good day, Your friends at seats 55/54/53."

The notes from my comrades made me feel very good, and for once, even if this is short-lived, I made a difference.

The bill's sponsor, Representative Joseph Clark (D), Millinocket, was not exactly happy—in fact, I think he was upset. I don't feel sorry because I truly do feel that this bill was to give the paper companies special rights in the court system which the ordinary Maine citizen does not have.

EDUCATION WILL HELP PREVENT HATRED AND
PREJUDICE. IT WILL SHINE A LIGHT ON THAT DARK
PLACE WHERE INDIAN PEOPLE HAVE BEEN HIDDEN
FOR ALMOST TWO HUNDRED YEARS.

May 18, 2001
Friday
I have to deal with the education bill, which I found out today had a
fiscal note put back on it. I spoke to the Education Committee's legal
analyst and the fiscal office. They are reviewing the bill. I also ran
into Judy Lucarelli, the deputy commissioner of education, and she
said she would do what she could to get the note removed. She did
say that there was a section of her Learning Results bill that specifies
Native subjects to be taught, and she asked if she could take them
out of the bill. She said she needed to get a majority and was working the committee. Representative Weston insisted that she could
not vote for the bill if that specificity was there referencing Native
history, since it's not there for any other subject. I told Judy I would
rather she try to get a majority and only eliminate it if she absolutely had to. She promised she would try. Things that seem easy at
first never are.

May 19, 2001
Saturday
I found out yesterday that the education bill will have to have a fiscal
note on it. This means that it needs a preamble stating that the state
will pay 90 percent of the costs of the new subject matter. It also
means that two-thirds of both houses will have to vote in favor.

That's going to be tough to get, but this bill is *so* important to
Indian people in Maine. I'll have to get out the troops and do my
best to persuade people. The senate is the body that worries me the

most, however the house can sometimes surprise me as well.

As soon as I know when the bill hits the floor I will let people know that they should be calling or writing or e-mailing their senators and representatives, and we need a big group in the halls when this hits the house and the senate. This will happen on two consecutive days. I guess the fight is on!

The other thing I've been involved with since last January is creating an entity for the Penobscot Nation that will help members finance small business loans and small individual loans. It will also help the tribe to start up some business ventures. These types of organizations are called Community Financial Development Institutes, CDFIs. We created an interim advisory board to lay the groundwork for establishing a CDFI of our own. We had an advisory board meeting with the interim board on this past Thursday. It was a very, very good meeting. We had representatives from FannyMae, Bangor Savings, the U.S. Treasury, Coastal Enterprises, Inc, and a national group with monies for advocacy that can also help us with technical assistance.

This was the first time I had sat at a meeting with money people who were willing and able to help us—and not try to cheat us out of anything. During our discussions with the advisory group I brought the idea forward about an employee credit union for the tribe, possibly to include all the Maine tribes. This would keep our monies in our communities. Everyone thought it sounded good and was something to be considered and studied. I feel good about this, as well. The group is forming a non-profit 501 C-3 and has called itself the Four Directions Development Corporation (FDDC).

I missed legislative session for that evening because of this CDFI meeting, and the next day I found out that the house had considered my bingo bill. I spent a few hours trying to find out what happened to it and discovered it passed in the house and senate for enactment and is on the governor's desk awaiting his signature. I hope he signs it. I'm sure if he has problems with it he will let me know.

Next week we will be back in session again from early morning to late at night. Speaker Saxl let us out early yesterday, around 2:30 P.M., so everyone could rest up over the weekend and be ready to work hard on Monday.

May 30, 2001
Wednesday

Time is flying by. Last week, around the 22nd, I went to speak with Phil McCarthy again about the Maine Indian education bill and we actually came up with some language that could help. I then went to the fiscal office and spoke with Jim Dixon, and we left it that the bill is a mandate and the committee will decide what to do. Their options are: (1) put a mandate preamble on the bill, which would require a two-thirds vote; (2) put a money amount on the bill, which would make it go to Appropriations for a decision on whether or not to fund it; and (3) let it go as is with some language on it to help the schools out with costs.

The committee met on the 23rd and chose the new language we worked out, and also allowed the bill to go forward on its own, so only a majority vote is now needed. The new language was satisfactory to representatives Skoglund and Weston, so they voted for the bill!! Only Representative Stedman was not there, and he will vote tomorrow. I spoke with Representative Schneider today, and he called Representative Stedman and asked him to vote in favor. I hope we get a unanimous on this. I'll know tomorrow.

The lobbyist for the People's Alliance came up to me and said the alliance was backing the bill and was happy to lobby for it! Now we just need to know when it will hit the floor. I'm getting letters and e-mails about the bill every day now, people wondering what's happening with it. I think we'll have a lot of support.

Another bill was debated on the floor on the 21st, L.D. 14, An Act to Prohibit the Use of Juveniles in the Enforcement of Laws Governing Tobacco Sales. It was Representative Waterhouse's bill. I felt strongly that juveniles should not be used in police sting operations, so I stood up and said the following:

Representative Waterhouse and I do not agree on many things, but on this issue I agree with him.

In the Penobscot culture we respect our elders and plan seven generations ahead to protect our children. There is something inherently wrong with using your children in such a way. I cannot fathom a tribal council even deliberating such a program for their children. If I could vote, I would vote with Representative Waterhouse.

The vote was taken after I spoke, and Representative Waterhouse's bill passed, 98 to 41. Representative Waterhouse sent me a note right after the vote saying, "Donna, thanks! I really appreciate it! Paul (P.S. You carry great weight here!!)"

I told him later I'm sure the bill would have passed anyway, but he insisted that what I said made a difference. It made me feel good, anyway.

I got a second note on that bill from Representative Schneider, the minority leader, which read: "Donna, That was really great! Thanks! Bill."

The senate, however, voted against the bill.

I met with Congressman Baldacci at the Liberal Cup in Hallowell for lunch. He arrived around 1:30 P.M., but better late than never. We had a very productive meeting. We talked about education, which was mostly about my bill, and we talked about environment, namely inviting the chiefs to be on one of the panels he's having in different parts of the state. I complimented him on supporting Chellie Pingree and told him that was what gave him my vote. I told him I would help him in any way I could, and then I mentioned I thought a Native person should be on his cabinet when he becomes governor. He said he thought that was a good idea and asked if I thought perhaps a bureau of Indian affairs would be a good idea. He said he was just throwing that out as food for thought. I said maybe an office to deal with Indian matters. I told him I'd think about it.

June 3, 2001

Sunday

On the 29th the Education Committee had voted to allow the bill to go without a identifying it as a mandate, which would require a majority vote. I was very relieved and now just needed to get Representative Stedman's vote.

I found a note on my desk from Phil McCarthy, who wanted to talk with me about my bill. I went immediately to his office and we decided that we would keep the last paragraph in. That paragraph required schools to report to the Department of Education if they cannot afford the course, and also requires some proof.

I saw Representative Stedman and he read the amendment and signed the bill OTP as amended—that made it unanimous! Now all that was left was to get a copy of the amendment, which I found out would not be available until later that day or on Friday. We were not going to be in session on Friday, but I planned on stopping by and checking on the amendment.

When I did, it was in and I needed to find out when it would hit the floor. I asked the speaker and he said there should be no problem with the bill since it was unanimous and should go under the hammer. He said it would be on the consent calendar for Monday morning. I said I would have liked to have it on Thursday, to give people enough notice so they could be there to lobby for it. He said it will go on Monday but suggested we could have people there on Thursday to witness the house enacting the bill. I thought that was a great idea and thanked him.

I hope he's right and we get no opposition. My aide, Ben Collings, has let people know and hopefully we'll have a great turnout on Thursday. It has not been easy to get this bill passed—we haven't yet, but if things go well maybe the governor will sign it on Thursday and we can have a press conference with a signed bill. *(That was very naïve of me.)*

June 5, 2001

Tuesday

I spent about two hours in the Appropriations Committee hearing room defending my education bill. I spent one hour waiting and the other one explaining the bill in detail. The bill had to go before this committee because it had a fiscal note on it, and the committee would decide whether or not to put it on the table. When a bill goes on the table, it gets considered for funding—and if it's not funded it gets killed. I had to make sure it did not go on the table. The Part II budget is really contentious this session and nothing new would pass. I requested my bill be taken off the table because it required no General Fund expenditures.

Representative Belanger (R) from Caribou was one of the most hostile questioners. He and Representative Windsor (R) from Norway suggested the bill be amended so that the first part of the bill that actually requires Native history to be taught is deleted from the bill, leaving only the commission!

I shook my head, looking at Senator Cathcart (D) from Orono for some help. She came to my assistance and stated that the Education Committee voted for this unanimously and we shouldn't mess around with the bill this late in the process.

Representative Nass (R) from Acton chimed in something about team mascots and if the schools didn't implement the program then the Indians might try to make them feel guilty. I sat there in disbelief; this man's ignorance was exactly why we needed Indian history in our schools! I did not say anything, because that would have only made him madder and his intent to hurt the bill even more focused.

Senator Goldthwait, the senate chair of the committee, got to the heart of the matter when she said the bill was in front of the committee for the committee to decide whether or not it would go on the table.

Representative Etnier said he agreed and the bill had already gone too far in the process to be pulled back now. Representative Belanger kept insisting it was a bad idea. Representative Windsor said he thought it was a good idea and particularly liked the commission. In the end, Representatives Nass (R), Belanger (R), and Mailhot (D) from Lewiston voted against the bill. It was a majority vote to take the bill off the table.

I spoke to Representative Mailhot later in the evening and asked why he voted against the bill. He said, "Nothing against you, Donna, or the Native people. It's just that you didn't follow procedure. [I had heard this argument about not following procedure before and it cost us a vote in committee.] Some of the members wondered why there was no mandate preamble on the bill."

I told him that the Education Committee had voted to let it go without one, since it had no money amount and only required a majority vote. (The Department of Education, the University of Maine System, the Maine Indian Tribal–State Commission, and the tribes would pick up the cost of the commission members, as well as provide technical assistance with website development and grant-writing. The commission members would also search for grant monies to develop and distribute educational materials. The Appropriations Committee felt there should have been a preamble on the bill and that the Education Committee was just trying to get around the mandate.)

I suggested to Representative Mailhot that the procedure argument was bull, and he, of all people, being on the Appropriations Committee, should realize this after what the senate did to Appropriations by ignoring them in the Part I budget process! I was a bit upset with his argument and said, "I bet you voted for Learning Results the last time, didn't you?"

He said, "Yes, but I didn't know they had the same language as your bill."

I said, "Why is it that a bill like Learning Results, which costs the state millions of dollars, does not get scrutinized as closely as an Indian bill that costs nothing? It's a real double standard to let huge bills like that go by without the close scrutiny that they give to Indian bills, and because of this microscopic approach to all our bills,

Indian bills get killed. You should consider this and give us a break!"

Representative Mailhot said, "I voted the way I felt was right, but just tell me how I can get your bill passed."

I said, "Thank you, but it's already passed the house twice and hopefully will be enacted in the senate on Thursday morning." I added that I appreciated his willingness to help.

It's now 7:00 P.M. and I'm in the house. I'll stay tonight just in case the senate takes up my bill. I'm hoping no one in the senate will argue against it because of the mandate. If they do, it will call into question the Learning Results bill. The Maine Learning Results are already being implemented across the state and are law. There are also millions of dollars being invested in the program. I don't think the senators will want to open that can of worms.

I have a news conference scheduled for Thursday at 1:00 P.M, and I hope the news I have to give will be good. I knew this was going too smoothly!

June 7, 2001
Thursday
This morning at approximately 11:30 A.M. the senate enacted L.D. 291, "An Act to Require Teaching of Maine Native American History in Maine's Schools." The press conference was about forty-five minutes late, since we tried to get the house out but that didn't happen as they were all tangled up in the milfoil issue, which they ended up sending back to committee. Pleasant Point Governor Richard Doyle, and Houlton Band of Maliseet Chief Brenda Commander were in attendance, and this surprised me! It shouldn't have, because those two are always there for any big event Donald and I have conducted. Mary Griffith and her kids from Phillip W. Sugg Middle School in Lisbon were there; although they didn't get to be interviewed, at least they got to be on TV.

Some representatives came, even though the house was still in session: representatives Joanne Twomey, Marie Laverriere Boucher, Lisa Marrache, Deborah Hutton, Susan Dorr, Glenn Cummings,

Shirley Richard, Mabel Desmond, Lillian O'Brien, Deborah Simpson, Monica McGlocklin, and Senator Mary Cathcart. Speaker Mike Saxl said a few words, as did the chiefs and Senator Cathcart and Representative Richard.

Representative Donald Soctomah spoke after me. We decided this time that I would do the boring part of explaining the bill in detail, and he could do the more interesting part and talk about the bill's implications. It was a small group but it filled the camera view.

June 7, 2001, is truly a historic day. I don't think any of us realize the full impact of this education bill. Governor Doyle said we probably won't see the results for years, but once we do they will be impressive. Sherry Mitchell and Gail Dana Sockabasin also came. Sherry said something very nice to me and Donald—she said we were the most effective tribal legislators ever. I thought that was quite a compliment.

June 11, 2001
Monday
I received notice from the governor's office last Friday that the signing ceremony for the bill will take place on Thursday, June 14, at 1:00 P.M. All the tribal leaders should be in attendance for this, and perhaps the governor will draw more media coverage. Media coverage for this is important in the light of the bigger picture. I hope that other states will see what Maine has done and look to this bill as a model.

June 14, 2001
Thursday
Representative James Tobin, Jr. (R) of Dexter stood and thanked fellow legislators for their support last week after the passing of his mother. He said his mother had been in a nursing home for the last eight months, that he was a mumma's boy, and he and his mother were very close. He would stop by the nursing home every morning and give his mother ten kisses good-morning and every evening he

would stop by and give her ten kisses goodnight. He said, "For those of you who are lucky enough to still have your mothers, reach out and give them a hug and a kiss." There wasn't a dry eye in the house.

Then Representative LaVerdiere stood up and announced a Judiciary Committee meeting on the errors bill, and legislative announcements went on. During Representative Tobin's talk I couldn't help but think of my own mother and how she died at a very young age, just thirty-five. People who are lucky enough to have mothers who are still alive and have actually known their mothers for years are very, very fortunate. I can only imagine what it would have been like to have my mother, Julia Elizabeth Neptune, for so many years. I was ten years old when she died.

Today at 1:00 P.M. Governor King will sign the Act to Require Teaching of Maine Native American History in Maine's Schools, a bill that I sponsored and worked through the system, and that bill will become law today! I know this bill will change history in the future because children will grow up being taught that Maine Indian people exist and that we have made valuable contributions.

Education will help prevent hatred and prejudice. It will shine the light of knowledge on that dark place where Indian people have been hidden for almost two hundred years. I know my mother and our ancestors are watching today and they are proud of the work we have all done to get this bill passed and signed into law. It will make a difference

This one's for you, Ma.

Governor King signed the bill! The media was there and so were all the chiefs except Billy Phillips and Richard Stevens. Chiefs Barry Dana and Brenda Commander, and Governor Richard Doyle were there and said a few words. There were quite a few people attending, and we had the ceremony in the governor's cabinet room. Governor King gave me the pen after he signed the bill.

After leaders spoke we went outside on the steps of the capitol and had a press conference. We again spoke and repeated much of what we had said inside. Everyone was just so happy that we were finally going to get some recognition in the school system. The signing of this bill into law marks the end of this session for me. It is the most significant Indian bill since the land claims. I truly believe this.

Addressing a gathering outside the Statehouse after Governor King signed the bill into law.
Courtesy Donald Soctomah

Left: My mother Julia Elizabeth Neptune, holding my brother Adrian Malcolm Loring. Right: my mother with the kid next door, Bruce Door, and her faithful dog Tippi, at the home my father built at 110 North Brunswick Street in Old Town. Courtesy of the author

WHO ARE THE REAL HUMAN RIGHTS ABUSERS?
ALL THIS TIME WE THOUGHT IT WAS CHINA!

June 19, 2001
Tuesday

Yesterday I attended another Tri-council meeting. The attorneys called the meeting to figure out what to do if the federal court, the 1st Circuit, finds against us on the Freedom of Access case relating to tribal documents. The two Passamaquoddy tribal councils have already voted not to turn over any documents, no matter what the courts decide. I'm starting to agree with them at this point. We are tribal governments, and to date we have not been acting like governments. There is a treaty that exists between the state, the tribes, and the United States of America, but we have sat back and let the state define it in its courts and in its system.

I think it's time to say this treaty is not working for us and they have not abided by their end of the treaty, and therefore we are voiding it. We no longer recognize this treaty. We have to make a stand here, because if we don't, we will end up being just another municipality and a sub-political entity of the State of Maine. I don't know how this will play out, but I do know it's time to do something serious. If we make this stand and void the treaty, I believe we will be the first Indian government in history to void a treaty.

In the past we have allowed the U.S. to renege on treaty obligations, while all along we have followed these agreements to the letter. It's time for the Penobscot to take a strong position on this as well. I also feel that for the state to be hearing these cases is like the fox guarding the henhouse. The World Court should be hearing these cases. The Penobscot council has yet to meet on this, and I hope they don't wait until the last minute. Chief Dana thinks they should wait. I think they should not wait. The decision is expected within the next two weeks. This Friday I will be going to my last Flemming Fellows retreat. It will be in West Virginia until the following Monday. I sure hope the decision doesn't come down while I'm away.

The session should end this week. I see no reason for me to return to session, since they just have the budget to vote on and that should be done by the end of the day tomorrow.

June 21, 2001
Thursday

Well, guess what? The decision came down today. I heard it through the grapevine last night. The U.S. District Court found in favor of the state by choosing not to hear the case, since the Maine Supreme Judicial Court had decided already. How convenient for them not to make an adverse decision that would reverse a Maine Supreme Judicial Court ruling. Yes, it's the fox guarding the chickens.

This legal system used to mean something to me. Now it means nothing and I have no respect for it anymore. When the U.S. Supreme Court gave Bush the presidency by disenfranchising all those black voters in Florida, I knew something was wrong with the system and we could never expect to get justice. Now, more than ever, I feel an outside entity should be hearing our case—the World Court, perhaps, or even just a panel from the UN. Someone should have jurisdiction other than the states and the U.S. federal government. How ridiculous is this? We as tribal governments have for almost two hundred years have been dictated to and controlled by the U.S. Congress and its laws as well as state laws. Tribal governments have not had one iota of say in any of these laws or decisions. What kind of democracy is that? Who are the real human rights abusers? All this time we thought it was China!

I have to go to West Virginia in the morning for that retreat. I'll be back on Monday. I don't think the court will do anything this weekend.

ANITA'S POEM

July 6, 2001

Friday

I haven't written anything since I returned from the Flemming Fellows retreat. It was a very powerful experience for me. I have debated with myself whether or not to include this experience in my journal, because it was so personal, but sometimes personal events are important to express, so here goes.

The retreat was a sad experience in that Wes Watkins, one of the founders of Flemming Leadership Institute, passed away a few weeks before our retreat. The cofounder of the Flemming Leadership Institute was Wes's partner in life for seventeen years, Anita. She insisted on coming to the retreat and doing her part in the program. It was a very emotionally draining event for her, but something she needed and wanted to do.

It was particularly difficult for many of us when one of the exercises we had to do was write our own obituary. I know it was tough for Anita, as well, but it was indeed a regular part of the program before Wes's death. Anita spent a lot of time crying. I felt she needed some energy, so I was one of many who went up to her and gave her a hug. (This took place on the second night.) One of my weak areas, as I soon learned from Myers-Briggs, is feelings. I do not let my emotions rule my decision-making nor do I get touchy-feely, but this was an exception. To this day I don't understand why.

We were assigned places to stay when we first arrived at Coolfont, a resort in the Blue Ridge Mountains. The housing was mostly cottages of different varieties; some were actually houses that the owners lease to Coolfont for the summer. I was assigned to one house with two roommates. On the first night I slept upstairs in the cottage, but the next day I discovered that there was a full bath and empty suite in the basement, so I moved all my stuff. It was very private; it was also very dark, although there was a small entranceway with French doors leading outside, which brought some light into the basement.

On my first night sleeping in the basement, I was sound asleep when I felt something touch my arms. I was sleeping on my back with my arms crossed and my legs crossed. I reached for whatever was touching me—and felt a hairy arm, then a hand. At first I was shocked, but then I felt the hand melt into my body and the sensation was like two 220-volt live wires touching each other. A super wave of electricity surged through me. I felt very peaceful. I was certain it was Wes's spirit that had touched my arms.

This experience left me with a desire to do something for Anita. I thought about what to do for her all day. We broke at four-thirty in the afternoon that day and did not have to be back until around seven in the evening. I spent that time meditating, and out of the meditation came the words of a poem. I have some of the poem but not all of it, since I found out later I had inadvertently torn some of it up. Here is what I saved:

Anita's Poem

Our spirits soar together over clouds, and wind, and storms.
We glide on the wings of the eagle as we fly to meet the dawn.
We are on an infinite journey and our spirits are as one.
We dance and laugh and sing and talk and go on and on and on.
Our spirits soar together upon the eagle's wings and our souls
    enjoy a solitude that
Only love can bring. So we will stay together on our never-
    ending flight
And we will fly with souls entwined beyond the deep dark night.

So close your eyes my darling and fly with me tonight
Upon the eagle's wings we'll glide on our never-ending flight.
We are on an infinite journey and our spirits are as one.

We dance and laugh and sing and talk and go on and on and
    on—
We glide on the wings of the eagle as we fly to meet the dawn—

The above is not exactly what I gave to Anita. I have added some lines, but it is close to the poem that Wes inspired me to write for Anita. I gave Anita the poem that night and she told me the next day that she read it and cried.

I know that some people may not understand what happened to me during this retreat, and all I can say is this was my true experience and yes, I did spend the next two nights in the basement suite with no further incidents.

It seems whenever I am under duress the eagles speak to me. They were to come again to me on September 11th. And they are the reason for the title of this book.

JUDGE CROWLEY'S DECISION AND THE MAINE SUPREME JUDICIAL COURT'S DECISION WERE DEAD WRONG.

July 19, 2001
Thursday

On Monday the 16th I drove up to Indian Island and had a brief meeting with Chief Barry Dana. We began to talk about the paper companies and the possibility that they could push this case and have Judge Crowley rule against us. If that happens, there is a huge possibility that the chiefs will go to jail. Barry didn't want that to happen, and we talked about how we could defuse the issue. I told Barry it might be too late, but at least we could talk to the governor and the attorney general.

Barry felt that we should offer to drop our demand that the EPA not allow the state direct permitting status, on the condition that we be allowed to monitor the river and have input into the process. At first I thought this was a sign that we were giving up our sovereign status, but Barry seemed to think it would be quite thee opposite— that we would be holding on to it. We would at least be having a say in how our water was being taken care of. It sounded like a valid point to me in that right now, since the courts have ruled against us on everything, this might be a way of salvaging something. We decided to give this tactic a try. Barry said he would call EPA with the suggestion and see what they say.

August 6, 2001
Monday

A lot has happened since July 19. We had a meeting with the original negotiating team for the Land Claims. We met on Indian Island with Tom Tureen, Jim Sappier, Andrew Akins, Butch Phillips, and John

Stevens. The purpose of the meeting was to review the history and intent of the act from the negotiators' perspectives. We were particularly interested in the "municipality" designation. Every single member said when he negotiated this issue it was accepted with the intent that the tribes were not to become a sub-political entity of the State of Maine. This designation was to make sure the tribes were eligible for funding for schools and road maintenance and other funding that might come up.

They reviewed in detail their feelings on the issue, and they all agreed that we are not municipalities in any sense of the word. Their consensus was that Judge Crowley's decision and the Maine Supreme Judicial Court's decision were dead wrong. The Maine courts had failed to consider federal Indian law.

On August 7th the Penobscot Tribal Council met with the Department of Justice to talk about the case they were litigating on our behalf against Lincoln Pulp and Paper. They told us that they felt it would not be in our best interest for them to pursue the case, and suggested they go forward to try to recover what they could by filing on behalf of the federal EPA. They explained that the paper company attorneys told them they would bring up the question of whether or not we were municipalities. The Department of Justice attorneys' concern was that this would be heard in a federal bankruptcy court, not the proper venue for any decision on our sovereign status. The decisions the federal courts were coming down with dealing with tribes have not been good.

We felt we hadn't been given enough time for consultation with them on this case and we were very disappointed. They said they understood and would make a record of that. They said they were behind us 100 percent still, but that this was not the time to bring up the question of sovereignty. I asked them if they would help us litigate the question of municipality status, since it appears in the Settlement Act, and they said they would do whatever they could to help us. They said they believed the United States government has a trust responsibility to us and that they would strongly say this to the media or in a letter to us. The council said that because of the short consultation period we could not make a proper decision on what they had put in front of us and would follow up with a detailed response.

We also had a Tri-council meeting earlier in the day to discuss the upcoming meeting that the attorneys were going to have with Judge Crowley. The council told the attorneys to ask for a stay until the U.S. Supreme Court rules on our case. The attorneys had no idea of what Judge Crowley would do, but that was all the council authorized. Luckily, the state had agreed to come in on our side to ask for the stay, and Judge Crowley has allowed them to submit briefs. I think by the end of August everything will have been submitted from both sides. The tribes are using every tool and avenue they have. I truly believe the state courts are wrong in this case and wonder how we will ever get a fair hearing.

September 6, 2001
Thursday
A great deal has happened since my last entry. First, Judge Crowley ruled that the stay would happen partially. We were to start gathering our documentation and Assistant AG Bill Stokes would draft the order. In the meantime, no documents would be turned over. Judge Crowley ruled that he would set the timeline for documents to be turned over after he had heard from Bill Stokes and reviewed the order. Judge Crowley was in a much better mood than the last time I saw him, but he continually referred to the tribes as Indians instead of using their names. He has shown no respect or recognition for our tribal governments.

The World Trade Center and the Pentagon were attacked by terrorists.

September 14, 2001
Friday
On September 11, 2001, the World Trade Center in New York City and the Pentagon were attacked by terrorists. The twin towers at the World Trade Center were leveled and the Pentagon has a gaping hole in it!

First reports say over five thousand dead. A horrible, horrible tragedy! I have shed tears many times this week but always alone in my car or at home alone when I hear the stories of individuals who lost their loved ones or talked to them for the last time knowing they would never see the, again. There is nothing in my lifetime, not even Vietnam, to compare to this—we were attacked on our home soil and thousands of innocent civilians have been killed.

The United States and the world will rally and hunt down terrorists worldwide. It will be a long, drawn-out affair, but in the end we will win. We will never be the same again. Nor will they. I felt I needed to write so I wrote this poem a few days after the tragic events. It helped me. and I hope it will help whoever reads it.

Ten Thousand Eagles
Ten thousand eagles flew that day across the bright blue sky
to meet the spirits on their way from fiery smoke-filled tombs.
They soared above the dark, black, clouds
billowing from the earth and hovered for a moment there
and saw the face of doom.
Ten thousand eagles gathered and swooped down beneath the
clouds.
They found the spirits one by one and plucked them from their
plight.

They carried each new spirit through the black and hate-filled
    clouds.
They gave them each a shelter wrapped in warm wings oh so
    tight.
They gave them strength and comfort too on their unexpected
    flight.
On swift wings they flew towards their final destination
where each spirit knew without any hesitation
There would be peace and love and harmony—
they would forever be
wrapped within the eagles' wings through all eternity.
Ten thousand eagles flew that day as all the world stood still
and watched in shock and horror as the tragedy unfurled.

Now we are left here on this earth to face the billowing clouds
and our eyes search for the eagles as we say our prayers out
    loud.

May our spirits soar on eagle's wings above the dark black clouds
of hatred, murder, and revenge that keep us hatred bound.

Ten thousand eagles flew that day as all the world stood still.
The eagles flew above those clouds.
Perhaps someday—we will.

October 3, 2001
Wednesday
Last week, September 27–30, I attended the Vietnam Women
Veterans second reunion in San Antonio, Texas. Yes, I did fly, and
yes, I was a bit apprehensive, but there was no way I was going to
cancel. I felt this was something I could do, a small act of defiance
that stated I was not going to let terrorists rule my life or prevent
me from attending an event that was so important to me and to
other women veterans. I attended the event with a friend from

Maine, Roseanne Tousignant, who presented retired general Wilma Vaught, the director of Women in Military Service, with a ceremonial State of Maine flag. General Daniel James III was the keynote speaker. His great-grandfather was the commander of the famous Tuskeekee Air Squadron during WWII. He is presently the adjutant general of the State of Texas. It was quite an honor for all of us to have him present. He also recognized former captain Joanne Murphy; she was the second commanding officer of the Long Binh WAC Detachment in Vietnam. (She was my commanding officer while I was stationed there and is now a close personal friend.) He

Below left: Captain Joanne Murphy, CO WAC Det Long Binh, Vietnam, 1968. Right: Joanne with her 92-year-old mother, Johanna Elizabeth Latham, who made the teddy bear I'm holding in the photo below. They both live in San Antonio, Texas.
Courtesy of Joanne Murphy and the author

Above: My WAC Basic Training graduation photo. Below: In front of the WAC Det Company Office, Long Binh, Vietnam, 1968. This photo was taken by another tribal member, Terry Lolar, who had just returned from three weeks in the field.. Courtesy of the author

Roseanne Tousignant, chair of the Maine Commission on Women Veterans. Roseanne presented a State of Maine flag to the Women Vietnam Veterans at their conference in San Antonio, Texas.
Courtesy of the author

presented her with a medal of appreciation and read a legislative sentiment by Representative Glenn O. Lewis of the Texas House of Representatives. It was by my invitation and a personal request of Representative Glenn Lewis (who is a close personal friend and supporter of General James) that the general accepted my offer to speak at the reunion. I had met Representative Lewis at the Flemming Institute retreats. Glenn was very gracious and cooperative and I owe him one.

October 26, 2001
Friday
The past weeks have been a time of paranoia in this country. Anthrax has been detected as the cause of death of a news media person in Florida, and other cases in the post office in D.C. and the capital have turned up. I think it's the work of locals, not the Taliban. Hard to tell

though; this will take a long time. I hope we don't self-destruct. The media and our country's leaders need to project a strong America, not a wimpy one that is afraid of its own shadow. The Taliban already thinks we are cowards. We need to quit whining and start making statements of strength and fearlessness. "When the going gets tough, the tough get going!" We also need to start saying that we will find Osama bin Laden sooner or later, rather than, "The Taliban should have surrendered by now. It's a lot tougher than we thought." Hogwash!

The state is taking Maliseet children from their homes in record numbers—five times the national average.

November 6, 2001
Tuesday
Yesterday I testified before the Subcommittee on Judiciary for Child Protective Services. I testified about how the state is taking Maliseet children from their homes in record numbers—five times the national average. The testimony from Chief Brenda Commander and me made the front pages of the PPH and the BDN. My testimony was as follows:

> I am here today to bring to the committee's attention the situation that exists in Houlton between the Houlton Band of Maliseet Indians and the State of Maine.
> First I would like you to hear a little bit about the Indian Child Welfare Act, 25 USCA Sec. 1901, which states: "Recognizing the special relationship between the United States and the Indian tribes and their members and the Federal responsibility to Indian people, Congress finds—(1) that clause 3, section 8, article I of the United States Constitution provides that 'The Congress shall have power to regulate commerce with Indian tribes' and, through this and other constitutional authority, Congress has plenary power over Indian affairs; [Plenary is a legal term meaning complete and total. Of course many tribes do not agree with that interpretation of the law.] (2) that Congress, through statutes, treaties, and general course of dealing with Indian tribes, has assumed the responsibility for the protection and preservation of Indian tribes and their resources; (3) that there is no resource that is more vital to the continued existence

and integrity of Indian tribes than their children and that the United States has a direct interest, as trustee, in protecting Indian children who are members of or are eligible for membership in an Indian tribe; (4) that an alarmingly high percentage of Indian families are broken up by the removal, often unwarranted, of their children from them by nontribal public and private agencies and that an alarmingly high percentage of such children are placed in non-Indian foster and adoptive homes and institutions; and (5) that the states, exercising their recognized jurisdiction over Indian child custody proceedings through administrative and judicial bodies, have often failed to recognize the essential tribal relations of Indian people and the cultural and social standards prevailing in Indian communities and families."

The whole purpose of the act is to protect Indian children from being taken away in great numbers from their culture and their heritage. The Indian Child Welfare Act was crafted and passed by the U.S. Congress and supersedes any conflicting laws.

Today in Houlton the Houlton Band of Maliseets faces an unprecedented taking of their children by the state, twenty-nine children in the past five years. I see this not only as a failure on the part of DHS to place Indian children in extended families, but also a failure on the part of the judicial system to implement the Indian Child Welfare Act. The loss of that many children to a tribe numbering approximately six hundred members is nothing less than genocide. When an Indian tribe loses its children, it loses its future.

These numbers are more than five times the national average. The vast majority of children taken are being placed in non-Native foster care homes. Parental rights are being terminated at an alarming rate. I ask this committee to focus its attention on this issue and ask you, Why is this happening? Are DHS workers following Indian Child Welfare Act procedures? More importantly, are the proper procedures being followed by the court system? Are judges informed and are they implementing the Indian

Child Welfare Act procedures in their Indian Child Welfare hearings?

As some of you know I am a member of the Joint Standing Committee on Judiciary. Last month we held judicial confirmation hearings. During those hearings I asked at least two judicial candidates if they were familiar with the Indian Child Welfare Act. One of the candidates was honest enough to say no, he was not. I received a letter from that individual a few days later wanting me to know that he had become familiar with the act. He said, and I quote: "In particular, I am now mindful of the underlying purposes of the act to protect the interests not only of individual Indian children and families, but also the interests of the tribes themselves in achieving long-term tribal survival. Among other things I am also now mindful of the heightened evidentiary standard of proof beyond a reasonable doubt as a precondition to the termination of the parental rights of an Indian parent. I hope that I am never called upon to apply this law in the performance of my judicial responsibilities, but should that occur, I have you to thank for calling the Act to my attention and I do thank you for this contribution to my continuing legal education."

I would think that if this judge did not know about the Indian Child Welfare Act then there must be others.

I do not like to criticize without offering some recommendations. One of my recommendations to you would be to provide training to the judiciary on the Indian Child Welfare Act. The training could be accomplished by using experts in the field on a national level. There is a disconnect between the state court system and the tribes on many levels. There should be an Indian advocate placed within the state court system to be a liaison between the courts and the tribes. An Indian advocate could help fill this void.

Finally, the Houlton Band of Maliseets does not have its own court system to hear their child welfare cases. I have submitted a bill this session that will allow the Houlton Band of Maliseets to bring their child welfare cases to the Penobscot Nation's tribal court until they can create their own court system. I strongly urge this committee's full support of that bill and the above recommendations.

Thank you.

Today I attended a breakfast in Portland for a delegation from Palestine. They were sponsored by the U.S. Department of State. Portland hosted them and they were presented with a key to the city. This truly upset the Jewish faction in Portland. One lady stood up and started saying a lot of negative things about the Palestinians and how they did not keep their promises and how they were a bunch of terrorists, basically. It changed the whole tone of the nice, peaceful breakfast atmosphere. There was a lot of healthy discussion.

I had to stand up and say that this situation reminded me of how the U.S. treats Native Americans. The U.S. has broken every treaty it has ever made with a tribe. They've stolen our land and our resources and built this country on the bodies of our ancestors. We as Native people have something in common with the Jewish people and that is, we suffered the first holocaust. We lost five times as many people as the Jews did during the holocaust in Germany. Yet the U.S. does not acknowledge this nor will they talk about it.

How can this country even think they can solve the Middle East problem until they acknowledge and own their own genocide and human rights abuse of the First Nations on this continent? I had lunch with the Palestinian delegation, and we had some interesting conversations. One delegate said, "There is a joke in the Middle East that the Palestinians are the Indians of the twenty-first century." I think this is very true.

That same day I noticed two front-page stories in the *Portland Press Herald*. The stories were set side by side at the bottom of the page. The headlines were: "Tribe Faults DHS Placement of Kids in Non-Indian Homes" and, to the immediate right of that, was

"Palestinian Delegation Visits Maine to Explain Goal of Peace, Homeland."

November 8, 2001
Thursday
Today I had lunch with Bill Stokes, assistant attorney general. I first met Bill when I was police chief at the Penobscot Nation. I had arranged a workshop for the tribal police, game wardens, and the AG's office. Bill was one of the presenters. We have spoken on a number of occasions since. The first question Bill asked me was, "Why isn't the Land Claims really settled? Isn't it written in black and white?" We talked about this for a good two hours. My response to Bill was:

> The Land Claims Settlement Act now defines the relationship the tribes have with the state. When it was written it created a commission called the Maine Indian Tribal–State Commission. The reason the commission was created was because the negotiators of the act knew there were areas that were unclear and that there needed to be more discussion on those gray areas. The commission also had jurisdiction over a few other areas as well, such as hunting and fishing in certain areas and approving new Indian territories. In the past this commission has been unable to function very well because they dig in and cannot move on issues. Why can't they move on issues? Because they represent their respective governments and the views of those governors and chiefs. The commission has started to move, but it has been very slow. The fact is there is a lack of trust on the tribes' part, and they view everything the state wants suspiciously. The tribes have every reason to be suspicious, given the past history of how the state treated the tribes prior to during and after the Land Claims.
>
> When Maine became a state it agreed to take over the responsibility that Massachusetts had to the treaties and obliga-

tions with the tribes due to the tribes' participation on the American side during the Revolutionary War. Maine agreed to take over these obligations and Massachusetts gave Maine $30,000 dollars toward those obligations. One of the first things Maine did was to take tribal lands without consent, and lease tribal stumpage and shore lands without tribal permission. The state established a trust fund for the tribes from these monies. The state told the tribes they would each have to settle in one main village, and then they assigned an Indian agent to each village. The agent was there to monitor the tribes and to hand out vouchers for food, clothing, fuel, etc., all from monies earned from the theft of Indian land. After a few decades the state had the attitude that it was giving the Indians all this free service, and the Indians had the attitude that they were paupers, and many lost all self-respect.

The filing of the Land Claims brought new hope to the tribes, hope of self-sufficiency and economic development. Until the Land Claims were filed the state had control over the tribes and the living conditions on the reservations were inhumane.

A few months prior to the filing of the Land Claims the Maine tribes became federally recognized; with this recognition came federal monies and great improvement to their living conditions.

The posture taken by the State of Maine once this suit was filed was that it would not pay one penny, it would not give up jurisdiction, and it would not be held accountable for any past abuses. The Land Claims met all three requirements. It was the best deal the State of Maine could have made. The federal government paid all the money, and the state lost very little jurisdiction and is held harmless for any past actions or abuses.

Bill said he had a better understanding where the tribes were coming from but felt we could still work cooperatively on issues. I agreed, but said trust was still missing and the state has to earn that. It would be unfair of me to say that there is lack of trust only on the tribes' part. The state also lacks trust in us. The state needs to change its paradigm of the tribes. Times have changed and it is now time for the state to regard us as productive and potential partners in an ever-increasing global competitive market. The state and the tribes need to communicate often and recognize the value of partnership. They have to establish a trusting relationship. Bill and I felt we had both reached a better understanding of the situation, but we both needed time to digest it and figure out what to do to improve tribal-state relations. We agreed to set a up meeting with Steve Rowe, the attorney general, and talk further.

November 14, 2001
Wednesday
On Monday the 12th another plane went down. This one crashed on takeoff to the Dominican Republic. Officials say there is no indication of terrorist activity, but they can't rule it out. People are becoming more and more leery of flying. I'm scheduled to fly to D.C. on December 7. I am a bit apprehensive but will go anyway.

Yesterday I had to appeal a bill that I had submitted to clarify the fact that the tribes are exempt from the Maine Freedom of Access Act. If this bill passes, it will at least guarantee to the tribes that we will not be in court again on this issue and it will secure our internal tribal matters. The Legislative Council only allows bills of an emergency nature to be submitted during the second session. They voted 6 to 4 against allowing this bill in to be debated.

I spoke with Representative Bill Norbert (D), the house whip from Portland, who was the only Democrat to vote against allowing the bill in. He said he would vote to allow it in. I then spoke to the Republican representatives Bill Schnieder and Joseph Bruno, and Senator Mary Small from Bath. None of them would give me the answer I wanted to hear. They would only say they would think about it. That usually means no. When I testified before the Legislative Council yesterday, I used the following argument:

A potentially explosive situation exists between the state and the tribes as a result of a pending court case. This bill would not affect the pending court case, however the tribes fear that the state and the paper companies are trying to extinguish their existence as tribal governments and make them political subdivisions of the state. This bill would calm those fears and would recognize their right to exist as tribal governments and their right to protect internal tribal documents and council minutes. I urge you to recognize the importance of this bill as a tool to address the real fears of the tribal governments.

The Legislative Council voted 5 to 5, which meant the bill was voted out of the legislative process for this session. The vote was along party lines—the Republicans voted against the bill. I immediately left and went home. When I arrived home I had a message on my answering machine to call Chief Dana. I called and he told me that the U.S. Supreme Court had issued a short refusal to hear the case. The impact of the Supreme Court's refusal to hear a case is that it leaves the case decision made by the lower court standing and in effect. I called our attorney and spoke to him about next steps, and then called Ben Collings, my legislative aide, to ask him to get a note to Representative Saxl telling him of the Supreme Court decision. I felt that this certainly put the bill in an emergency category. *(But I guess the tribes' emergency was not the state's.)*

I then returned to the legislature and spoke briefly with Representative Saxl, who told me the Republicans would not reconsider. I went to the Republican office and found Representative Schnieder, Representative Bruno, and Senator Bennett in Representative Bruno's office. I told them of the Supreme Court decision. They acted as if they had never been told about it. They were surprised and wanted to caucus. I left and waited for them in the Legislative Council chambers. They came out a few minutes later and told me they decided not to reconsider, since they felt the bill might escalate the situation. I had no time to protest that line of thought, since bill hearings were in progress. I practically begged them to let the bill in, and they refused. I did everything I could.

I have decided to work with a lobbyist to try to get the bill in later in December, when the makeup of the Legislative Council changes to favor the Democrats under the power-sharing agreement in the senate due to the tie in membership this session. I don't know what will happen next. I do know that we will try to appeal to Judge Crowley. How many appeals he will accept is anyone's guess. I would think he will run out of patience very shortly. I fear we will have a national situation on our hands. The tribes will not turn over these papers to the paper companies. We *cannot*. Our existence as tribal governments depends on the fact that we have internal tribal matters and certainly our private files and documents are not open for the general public to walk in and look at.

November 19, 2001
Monday
Yesterday morning I got a call from our tribal attorney, Kaighn Smith. I thought it was unusual since it was Sunday and he never calls me on Sunday unless I've called him. I said, "Are you going to make my day?" He laughed and said, "I don't think so." We talked about the case for about thirty minutes or so. Kaighn explained that he wanted to talk with the AG before the next filing. He felt the AG would be upset that we are appealing yet again. I don't know if he reached anyone in time. I saw an article on the appeal in the next day's paper. The appeal is based on reservation entry. I haven't read it yet—I promised Kaighn I would. Kaighn feels that the Maine Freedom of Access Act is written with the normal Maine citizen in mind, and that the citizen—by Maine law—is allowed to enter a public office and go through and tag whatever files they want copied and have them copied. The title of the newspaper article was "Catch-22." The Catch-22 is that even though the Maine Supreme Judicial Court has ruled that the Maine Freedom of Access Act applies, the documents are not accessible because the public is not allowed to

enter tribal government offices and go through their private files. That's what the appeal is based on. The next move is Judge Crowley's. I wonder if he will entertain this appeal.

We'll have to wait and see.

December 6, 2001
Thursday
On the third of December John Baldacci had a policy advisory meeting in Portland. I attended. along with ten or fifteen others. The advisory committee is made up of what John refers to as the best minds in the state; it has over eighty members. This may be the first time in the history of the state that an Indian representing the tribes has been in on the policy-setting for a future governor of the state. I am excited about the possibilities. I wrote an initial policy paper for John, which I will include in this diary. I will be sending additions to it from time to time.

On December 4 I had a follow-up meeting with Steve Rowe and Bill Stokes in the AG's office. We talked for over an hour and agreed upon a course of action. We felt that we should start to look at areas where we can have cooperative agreements rather than litigation. Bill and I will work toward bringing some key people together to discuss possible areas of cooperation. Steve wanted me to be aware of the fact that we will still have our differences and may even have to go to litigation, but he really wants to improve the relationship between the attorney general and the tribes. I felt this was a very productive meeting.

I did mention toward the end of the meeting that I had changed my mind about casinos. I told Steve the state was very hypocritical, earning well over $40 million—maybe even close to $100 million—a year on gambling and refusing to allow the tribes to have the same opportunity. I know both Steve and Bill disagree with allowing casinos in Maine for all the reasons that are cited over and over again. Crime, prostitution, organized crime. I use to think the same way. Yes, there is that danger, but I believe with participation in the planning process by the AG's office and the state police, we can have an honest casino business that will benefit everyone. I believe the benefits outweigh the risks, especially in light of the downturn in the Maine economy. This year Maine is looking at close to a $250 million budget deficit.

Maine does not have a huge population. In order to support our school system, our infrastructure, and our health care requirements, Maine needs another source of money besides taxes. A casino would help provide some of that. It has to be done right and only be placed in a town or city that wants it.

I think we should ask the cities and towns to compete for the casino business and see what benefits they would be willing to give to entice a casino into their town or city.

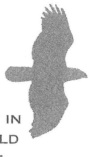

...JUST THINK, FOR THE VERY FIRST TIME IN MAINE HISTORY THE TRIBAL CHIEFS WOULD BE ADDRESSING A JOINT SESSION OF THE LEGISLATURE!

December 21, 2001
Thursday

Last Friday I received a letter from Chief Brenda Commander of the Houlton Band of Maliseets. The Maliseet Tribal Council had voted not to support my bill, the bill that would allow the Penobscot Nation to hear their child welfare cases. The reason given was they feel they have a right to decide what court to have their hearings in without permission from the state. They feel that this could be accomplished with just an agreement between the tribes. They do not want to compromise their sovereignty by allowing the state to tell them what court the child welfare hearings are to be held in.

When I first submitted the bill I was up against a deadline of a few days. I had talked with Chief Commander about the bill, and she thought it was a great idea. Since then, the Houlton Band tribal attorneys have expressed concern. I totally understand their concerns and will withdraw my bill. My thought in submitting the bill in the first place was that the state courts have been hearing the cases all along for the Maliseets and therefore we needed a law on the books that would mandate to the state courts (not to the tribal courts) that the Houlton Band child welfare cases must be heard in the Penobscot Tribal Court, and in the future, the Houlton Band Tribal Court. I guess the Houlton Band tribal attorney didn't feel comfortable with the bill.

The Penobscot Council had voted unanimously to support the bill, even though its members felt the two tribes could make the agreement on a government-to-government basis. The question was not so much jurisdiction or sovereignty, but the immediate welfare and retention of Indian children within the Houlton Band.

I may be wrong on this, but at this moment I feel the legislation I submitted was correct and would have been a great step in state-tribal relations. I will withdraw the bill and make a statement to the effect that after further study of the issue we feel that a change in the Settlement Act is not necessary and we can deal with this immediately with cooperative agreements between the tribes.

If the state expresses concern over jurisdiction, we will work out an agreement with them as well. I believe the AG's office and DHS will cooperate. This was an issue everyone was concerned about, and it made the front page of Maine's two major newspapers. It even was a topic in their editorial sections. The Legislative Council, fellow legislators, as well as the AG's office, were all lined up to help.

January 8, 2002
Tuesday

I stopped by the speaker's office to drop off my timesheet and was informed that the speaker had been looking for me.

The secretary went in to see if he wanted to talk to me immediately or if he wanted to set up an appointment. He came out from a meeting he was having and asked me to sit down. I sat down and he looked at me and smiled and said, "I have been trying to figure out all summer how to accommodate your request about the tribal chiefs speaking." He suggested that next Wabanaki Day they could address the whole legislature for about twenty minutes. He said if that sounds good, would I look at the invitation and see if it's okay.

I said that sounds very good—except that Wabanaki Day wasn't scheduled again until next year. The speaker replied that it didn't matter, we can schedule a special day this session. I quickly agreed and said we could do something simple like having a few booths with tribal brochures and information.

He said, "It doesn't have to be something simple and it *shouldn't* be something simple. It should be important and we'll work on it together."

I shook his hand and said, "Friends?"

He said, "We were always friends."

I'm very excited about the possibility of the chiefs making history by speaking to the legislature. I hope he means what he says. I remember at the beginning of the 120th Legislature, how he had recognized the tribal reps, and how I thought this legislative session was going to be different. I was bitterly disappointed when the speaker had refused the chiefs time to speak to the house on Wabanaki Day. I began to think he didn't care about the tribes. Now I guess I have to rethink that. Aren't politics strange?

January 16, 2002
Wednesday

I spoke to Millie MacFarland, clerk of the house, yesterday, and we firmed up March 11 as the date the chiefs will speak! I also spoke with Senate President Richard Bennett. Senator Bennett said he would check with leadership in the senate to see if they would okay a joint session. He also said he wasn't sure if the speaker of the house would agree to one or not. I told Rick I was certain Mike would agree. I left with a positive feeling that this might happen—just think, for the very first time in Maine history the tribal chiefs would be addressing a joint session of the legislature!

I asked Rick what he thought of the day being called "State of the Tribes" day. He seemed to be okay with it but said he'll talk with Mike. I'm sort of holding my breath, not quite believing this will happen. I told Rick I felt the State of Maine and the tribes were entering a new era—one of partnership and progress. I mentioned areas where we could work together, such as child welfare, the court system, tourism—and the fact that the attorney general was willing to explore other areas of cooperation. I also mentioned a meeting I had with the new chief justice on Monday and how she felt the same as the AG, that we could explore areas of cooperation such as the child welfare and drug courts. I will be seeing Chief Dana this morning in Harpswell. I can't wait to tell him the good news.

January 25, 2002
Friday

On January 23 we had a Tri-council meeting. We discussed the upcoming Freedom of Access hearing before Judge Crowley. The hearing is set for next Wednesday, January 30, in Portland.

I fear that this time the judge will not entertain any further appeals and that he will indeed censure our attorneys. If the judge decides to demand that documents be turned over and sets a date for that to happen, then there will be resistance from the tribes. This has the potential to explode. There are Indian people across the country who are waiting to come to the aid of the Maine tribes, if need be. My fear is that someone or a number of people will be seriously injured or even killed. One of the Tri-council members asked how it is that one man has power to destroy everything we (tribes and state) have worked for in one single decision. Clearly, if force is used to gather those documents, the tribes will never forget it and much damage will be done to tribal-state relations, not only in Maine but across the country.

The State of the Tribes Address is scheduled to happen on March 11 (coincidently, six months to the day after the World Trade Center attack). I hope to see the tribal chiefs there to address the body. They may not come if the FOA situation turns ugly. They may be in jail. Donald and I have talked about this possibility and will ask that we be able to address the session if our leaders are jailed. Again, this is another wait-and-see scenario.

The chiefs have sent the AG a letter requesting a meeting to discuss the NPDES situation, the issue that is really behind this whole thing. The AG has agreed to at least come to the table. I had hoped it could be done before Wednesday, but I understand from our attorney that this discussion will take some time to organize. So before Wednesday is out of the question.

I just got back from the session. I found a note on my desk in the house from Senator Bennett asking to see me. I went looking for him and found him walking up the stairway. He looked at me and said,

"Donna, I've talked with senate leadership and we're having a joint session."

I said, "That's great!"

He responded, "I thought you'd be happy with that."

I certainly was happy with that and went to make sure Mike Saxl knew. I saw the clerk of the house, Millie MacFarland, and told her what Rick had said. She said that she and Mike had sent the letters of invitation to the senate, to be signed as a joint session invitation.

I told her they will be signed. I then went to talk to Mike and asked him if we could invite Governor King and the chief justice. He said certainly. He also said he would help with the publicity leading up to the event. He wants me to make a list of invitees, which I will be very happy to do. This is just too good to be true! I really hope nothing spoils this, like the chiefs ending up in jail. I must get to work writing my list. I think I'll invite the congressional delegation, former Senator George Mitchell, former Governor Ken Curtis, and I think I'll send a special invitation to Senator James Jeffords of Vermont. I had met Senator Jeffords at his niece's wedding here in Maine. We had a long conversation about Native issues. I liked his thoughts and I liked his conviction. It took real guts to change parties. Maybe he would come if I tell him what a historic event this really is in Maine history. It's worth a try.

JUDGE CROWLEY JUST BASICALLY SIGNED THE PAPER COMPANIES' ORDER AND CHANGED THE DATES.

January 31, 2002
Thursday
Yesterday the hearing in front of Judge Crowley took place in superior court in Portland. The weather was bad, and it was very slippery driving—and much worse on the Portland sidewalks! I ended up walking on the road. The attorneys were there but no one else except a single reporter and me. Our attorney presented a convincing argument, I thought, and the paper company's attorney was very curt and to the point. They simply want the documents and enough is enough.

The judge heard the arguments and did not render a decision on the spot but said, "I will write my decision and you will hear shortly." I take that to mean in a few days. I wonder if he had most of the decision written before the arguments were heard. (He did— the decision was what the paper companies had submitted, only with his signature added.) I am still worried but hope the judge has enough fortitude to be fair. I think he has to be careful, because the Law Court has written an opinion and on appeal this will go back to them. This time there is a different chief justice—Leigh Saufley— although she did write the court opinion in this case. (The cards were stacked against us throughout the judiciary.)

February 1, 2002
Friday
This morning public hearings and work sessions were canceled due to weather conditions. The legislative session was going to be a quick open and close. I decided to stay home and work here.

Our attorney just called me and informed me that Judge Crowley basically signed the paper companies' order as is and just changed the dates. I find it very suspicious that Judge Crowley used the March 11 date in his order—the day the chiefs will address the joint session. He stated that "Defendants shall make the records identified in section I above available for inspection and copying by plaintiffs no later than *March 11, 2002" (the emphasis is mine)*. The rest of his order reads "...during regular business days and hours, and continuing until plaintiffs have completed their review. No later than February 25, 2002, defendants shall send plaintiffs a written notice as to where all records requested to be inspected will be located and made available for inspection and copying, beginning no later than March 11, 2002." He said that if problems arose between the February 25 and March 11 dates, he could be reached immediately by telephone, a telephone conference could take place, and he could issue an order upon request without a hearing.

Judge Crowley has written his order in such a way that events will unfold before the March 11 date if we do not comply. He does not say anything about jail or contempt, but we understand that is what will come next. He did leave the option of costs open, meaning we would end up paying court fees and attorney fees if we did not comply with his order or if we gave the plaintiffs a difficult time. He stated he could revisit it in the future.

I can't help but believe he is aware of the historic event to occur in front of a joint legislative session and is using that event as another gun to our heads to do what he wants. This judge has a knack for doing things like that. Remember how he forced the chiefs into using the state court system after placing them under arrest? He gave them the choice of turning over the documents, jail, or appeal in the state court system, which the tribes did not want to recognize. I'm hoping our attorneys can figure out something that will carry us beyond the March 11th deadline. Failing that, I guess we will have no alternative but to refuse to turn over documents that we believe represent internal tribal matters. In the meantime I will introduce legislation to address this issue so it does not ever happen again.

This is a recipe for disaster, depending on how we handle it. I would think a Tri-council meeting would be called as soon as we can all get together. Chief Dana and the other chiefs are still in D.C. I'm not sure when they will get back, since the weather has been bad and flights have been delayed and canceled. We clearly have a lot to think about.

February 8, 2002
Friday

The Tri-council met yesterday and we discussed different approaches to the judge's order and what we want our attorneys to do. We asked our attorneys to file stays and appeals in Crowley's court and in the Maine Supreme Judicial Court. We can only hope the Maine Supreme Court will hear us. Tribal Council members are referring t o the order deadline as 3/11 and are starting to dread the day.

We see it as the possible end of tribal governments in Maine, because if we are made to turn over these documents, we are nothing more or less than a municipality. Many tribal members are prepared to resist what they consider to be total disregard and elimination of their sovereign rights, but we do not intend to commit any violent or criminal acts. We know that presently the majority of the people in the state are on our side.

It is my hope the chiefs will be able to address the joint session and make us visible as sovereign tribal entities recognized by the Maine State Legislature and the government of Maine. This will be the first step in a long healing process. It will signify a new era and a new beginning in tribal-state relations. I find it ironic that at the time of this event full of hope for our future, a parallel event is threatening our very tribal existence. We are indeed in a perilous situation, one we need to measure and address carefully and methodically. We are like a tightrope walker who is doing a balancing act between two worlds with a fiery pit below. If we make it across we will have a bright and productive future as tribes; if we fall we will burst into flames and cease to exist. Indeed 3/11 is very significant.

February 21, 2002
Thursday
We met today with Attorney General Rowe, Assistant AG Elizabeth Stout, Assistant AG Chuck Dow, a representative from DHS, as well as Houlton Band Chief Brenda Commander, their attorney Doug Luckerman, Judge Gary Grow from our Penobscot Court, and George Tomer, also from the Penobscot Court. Erlene Paul, Penobscot Human Services director and a Penobscot child caseworker, was also present. We discussed the possibility of Indian child welfare cases being transferred immediately to the Penobscot Court. The meeting went well and AG Rowe stayed for the entire three hours. We set a next meeting date for March 21. This will be an all-day meeting. The morning will be to talk about funding for Indian child welfare cases and the afternoon will be to talk about process. I have asked Elizabeth Stout to consider acting as a facilitator for the second meeting. I am hopeful that we can work out cooperative agreements and start hearing Houlton Band child welfare cases in the Penobscot Nation Tribal Court.

February 22, 2002
Friday
The Tri-council met on Valentine's Day and discussed the FOA court case but made no final decision. The Passamaquoddy were going to go back and discuss things further with their entire council, and we agreed to meet on the following Tuesday with our council. We also talked about a meeting that was scheduled to take place with the AG and the governor on that same Tuesday afternoon to discuss the NPDES issue and to see if the tribes and the state could agree to work together within the permit process. We felt this meeting was key, because it was a chance to work with the state and come to terms on some sort of process that would recognize and allow our input. We discussed withdrawing our objections to the state getting a

direct NPDES permit delegation for the entire state. This NPDES issue was the sole reason behind the paper companies' suit against the tribes. Perhaps we can work with the state and have the state broker an agreement with the paper companies, which would result in the withdrawal of their suit.

Tribal chiefs and their staff met with Governor King, Attorney General Rowe, and their staff on Tuesday, February 19, at 2:00 P.M. in the Bangor city council chambers. The meeting lasted for three hours. It opened with Governor Doyle of the Passamaquoddy Tribe giving a traditional opening prayer. We made introductions and the chiefs took turns talking about what they wanted to see happen at the meeting.

The chiefs basically wanted the state to recognize the tribes' cultural and traditional relationship with the rivers surrounding their reservations. They wanted the state to allow input from the tribes in the NPDES process, and they wanted special consultations. The governor said he saw no problem with recognizing our special relationship with the river, and that our cultural and traditional uses of the water could be taken into consideration. When the governor said that, he looked directly at Commissioner Kirkpatrick, who nodded her head in the affirmative. After he said this, the chiefs and tribal governors, as well as staff in attendance, felt we could really develop a meaningful agreement. If the tribes could get the state to honor their cultural uses of the rivers, then there was something worth talking about. Without this, we all felt it would be an empty process.

The meeting went very well and we discussed a process that mirrored our relationship with the federal EPA. It was agreed that there was a good chance we could work together, and a small technical working group was designated to work out a proposal. The governor said he felt he could speak with the paper companies and perhaps persuade them to either settle or withdraw. Attorney General Rowe also felt good about the meeting and said he would speak to the paper companies, also. We all left the meeting feeling good about our ability to work cooperatively with the state. We all thought this was the first time in the history of the state that the governor, the attorney general, and commissioners left Augusta and traveled to Bangor to meet with our chiefs and governors. It was truly a good faith gesture. We felt heartened.

Later, around 6:00 P.M., we had our council meeting to discuss the results of the earlier meeting and to decide what our response to Judge Crowley would be. Our attorneys were also at this meeting. Every one of us felt it would be a breech of our sovereignty to turn over the required documents to the paper companies. The council had previously passed a resolution that would hand over specific documents directly to the state only, and not to the paper companies. We would do this only if the paper companies would drop their suit and if we could agree on a NPDES process with the state.

After four and a half hours of debate, we decided to incorporate the wording of this resolution in the response letter to Judge Crowley. The Penobscot Nation's letter would basically say we were a sovereign nation and internal documents would remain on our reservation. It would state that we would keep the traditions and customs of our tribe. The letter would be signed by the entire tribal council and chief. The deadline for this letter to be given to the court is February 25—this coming Monday. We knew this letter would not conform with Judge Crowley's order, and we would be found in contempt.

I had spoken to our tribal attorney to see if he had any more news about the FOA case. He told me that there was going to be a conference call on Monday at 11:00 A.M. between his office and the paper company attorneys. He said they would let him know what they were willing to do. If we cannot agree on whatever their offer is, then the letter from the tribe will be mailed. We are all hoping we can come to some sort of compromise and that this situation won't escalate to another level. Otherwise the situation could explode.

February 23, 2002
Saturday
This weekend's *Bangor Daily News* had a front-page article on the

Houlton Band of Maliseets and their child welfare issues. The head-line of the article read: "Fostering Heritage Connections," and it was a huge article with a picture of Larry Robichaud, a member of the tribe who had been placed in a non-Indian foster home at a young age. The picture took up almost half of the front page! I think it was a good story and hopefully it will open some people's eyes to the sit-uation that exists in Houlton. (The story covered two whole pages on the inside of the paper, as well.)

February 25, 2002
Monday
This morning I wait and wonder what the results will be of the phone conference our attorney will have with the paper company's attorney.

I am also thinking about what I will say tomorrow at noon, when I'm scheduled to speak to eleven or so Democratic legislators who are in leadership or are influential to other legislators. Donald and I are sponsoring a luncheon on economic opportunity for the tribes. Yes, we will be discussing the dreaded Indian casino! This is a venture the Penobscot and Passamaquoddy tribes have been talking about and researching now for almost two years. Tom Tureen will be giving the actual presentation. The possibility of a casino will add another element to things that are already brewing. The tribes have not decided what they are going to do this session. They may put in a bill or wait until next session to do so. We will know more by the end of the week.

February 26, 2002
Tuesday
I spoke with our attorney yesterday afternoon about the court case and he says he understands the paper companies will be joining the state and the tribes in requesting a thirty-day extension to negotiate an end to the case. The attorney for the paper company was not very cooperative, and the comment from our attorney was, "Don't be too

optimistic about a quick settlement." But if they are joining us in asking for a thirty-day delay, then hopefully the judge will grant it and we won't have to give him our letter and be found in contempt. This delay will at least allow the State of the Tribes Address to take place without fear of the chiefs being arrested on the same day.

Got to run—I have a busy day ahead with the economic luncheon for legislators and attending the Coastal Enterprises annual dinner tonight in Portland.

March 8, 2002
Friday
A great deal has happened since I've last written. Judge Crowley granted our request and we are given until March 27 to file our response on complying. We had a council meeting with our attorneys present and decided that since we had the extension granted, we would withdraw the appeal to the Maine Supreme Judicial Court, since we do not want the state court ruling on sovereignty issues. Their decisions have been mostly against us.

We are also hoping we can reach a settlement with the state on NPDES delegation, and if we can, the paper companies have publicly stated that they will withdraw the court case. This is the best possible solution we could get at this point.

The tribes did appeal, and while the Maine Supreme Judicial Court ruled that yes, we had to turn over documents, it found that "internal tribal matters" pertained to some things and recognized our sovereign status in those areas. The Maine Supreme Judicial Court also reached out and took the arrest threat off the table. They remanded the case back to Judge Crowley who proceeded to insist that the documents be turned over and gave the paper company attorneys the right to go into our offices on our reservations and go though our administrative files. The tribes stated that these attorneys would not be allowed on tribal property, and by granting that kind of access the judge was again ignoring our sovereign status.

Our attorneys filed a motion to appeal his ruling and the paper companies came back with a countermotion asking the judge to sanction our attorneys for frivolous motions and wasting the court's time. This had a chilling effect on our representation. The tribes decided to remove the files from the reservation and turn them over in Augusta. The frivolous motion by the paper companies was never ruled on. The conduct of this judge in this case certainly does not reflect a judge who respects and treats people with civility and respect in his courtroom.

"KITTERY SITE WOULD EMPLOY 4,000 AND FETCH $100 MILLION A YEAR FOR STATE." —BDN

March 8, 2002—continued

On another front, on February 27 the *Bangor Daily News* came out with front-page headlines: "Tribes Discuss $300 Million Casino Plan—Kittery site would employ 4,000, fetch $100 million a year for state."

These headlines were a result of what *we* had planned to be a very low-key meeting with a few Democrats to see what they thought of the idea. We wanted to get a sense of how they would react and if there was any possibility of bringing a bill forward this session.

I knew that the press would get it. You can't meet with a bunch of legislators in the Statehouse over an issue as huge as this and expect that they will keep things quiet. The press of course was waiting outside in the hall and interviewed legislators as they left the meeting. In any case, it has been a big draw for the press, and, as one press person put it, "Thanks for making this session so interesting to the media." There have been articles in the *Portland Press Herald* and the *Bangor Daily News* every day so far about the casino issue.

Tom Tureen, the former Land Claims attorney for the Penobscot and Passamaquoddy, is spearheading this project. The tribes got together with each other last year sometime to research the question of marketability and financing, but we got nowhere until a tribal member approached Tom with the idea. Tom met with the Passamaquoddy council, researched the project himself, and liked it so much he has spoken to the movers and shakers in the financial world of Maine. Tom has set up an advisory board and talked with lobbyists such as Severin Beliveau and Jon Doyle. The casino's advisory board is made up of well-known, respected people: former

Governor Ken Curtis; Madeleine Corson, former chairwoman of Guy Gannett Communications and former owner of the *Portland Press Herald*; and Neil Rolde, a former Curtis aide and legislator who is now chairman of the board at Maine Public Broadcasting.

This project has really taken off. Everyone Tom talked with liked the idea. The tribes are concerned that it is going too fast and they don't have a good handle on what's happening. We met on March 5 and expressed our concerns to Tom, who explained that he just got caught up in the excitement and the positive way in which people were reacting, and just decided to take action while the iron was hot.

A bill to submit to the legislature is being drawn up and revised. It is on a fast track because we were not sure if we were going to submit a bill this session It is my gut instinct—and Jon Doyle's and Tom Tureen's—that we should wait until January. The good side of waiting is that we can make the bill better and include more details. It will not be a rush job. We will also have time to plan an effective strategy and put our casino plans out to the public. The negative side of waiting is the unknown factors that can come up and bite you. The Christian Civic League and Angus King are formidable opponents. If we wait, this gives them time to form a better offensive. Governor King has been adamantly against gambling from day one.

Donald Soctomah had a bill in that would give the Passamaquoddy Tribe a twenty-year extension to buy trust land in Calais. The bill went before the Judiciary Committee, and the Calais town manager and a few town council members testified in favor of it. The language of the bill was written in 1994, and it mentioned economic development and a casino in Calais.

The Judiciary Committee left the casino language intact, and the only change was a request to extend the deadline from 2001 to 2020. When the committee talked about the bill, the casino was mentioned and we said we had no plans to build a casino in Calais but wanted the option left open if we should want to in the future. The committee voted unanimously to pass the bill. The bill went under the hammer in both houses and landed on the governor's desk for signing.

Governor King's chief of staff, Kay Rand, called me at home and told me the governor was going to veto the bill because of the casino language. Sure enough, he vetoed it on March 4, and on March 7 the trust extension bill came before the body for a legislative override. It would have taken two-thirds of both the house and senate to override the governor's veto.

Representative Charles LaVerdiere came to see Donald and me and told us that we should not recall the bill to the house; that we should table it until next year or recall it back to committee. Some Judiciary Committee members felt they were not told the whole truth about the extension bill and some others felt that, because of the upcoming casino bill, Donald and I had bamboozled them. I told Charlie that we were perfectly upfront with them and that I would be happy to talk with the committee about it. I was rather offended by their reaction.

Our lobbyist advised us not to fight the veto on the Passamaquoddy extension bill, since it would look like we were asking for a preliminary vote on the Kittery casino proposal. We worried that some Judicary Committee members would stand up on the floor of the house and say they were lied to, and that would just muddy the waters for the casino bill.

We talked about this in our caucus before the vote, and caucus members were upset that Judiciary Committee members would treat another committee member like that, and after the caucus meeting five or six of the legislators came up and shook our hands and apologized for the committee. When the vote to override the governor's veto came up on the floor, Donald and I both stood and stated we would not oppose the veto. Some house Democrats were confused because they had not attended the caucus; they came up to us later and said they had been ready to vote to override and were confident we could have overridden the veto. I just said we needed to focus on the casino bill and not let the trust extension bill muddy the waters. We can always reintroduce that bill next session.

When the Kittery casino possibility came up in the papers in the days following the first story, the papers were very much ready to give the casino idea a fair hearing, thanks to Tom Tureen and Chief Dana attending editorial board meetings. Those meetings went far in helping the papers to understand the position of the tribes.

Tom Tureen, Chief Dana, Donald Soctomah, and I had a meeting with Governor King at 2:30 P.M. on March 5. He listened to us and said we had given a very good presentation and he was impressed. He said the best argument we made for him was that, if a casino were going to happen, he should be involved just to make sure there was no proliferation of casinos throughout Maine. He said he would seriously think about what we had said.

Two days later, on March 7, Governor King called a press conference and said there was no way he could support a casino, that he was very much opposed to the idea, and that he didn't want to leave a legacy to the Indians of a casino. He basically threw down the gauntlet and declared war. The surprising thing about his press conference was that he did not say he would veto a casino bill if one should pass—but maybe this was a strategy move in case he found himself in a situation where he could not stop a casino. Anyway, I think it will all be a moot point by Monday, since everyone, including Tom, is now leaning toward waiting until next January. I just spoke with Donald, and he wants to go with it this session, as does Ken Curtis. I know Donald wants to be part of things in the legislature, and that's why he wants it to go now, but I'm not sure why Ken feels it should go.

When I spoke with Representative Bruno, the minority leader in the house, he said we have twenty-five votes in the Republican caucus but they don't want to deal with the bill this session, probably because it's an election year and they don't want gambling to be an issue. They can't afford to lose seats because of it. I think that we would lose a lot of the twenty-five Republication votes this session and not have enough to override a veto. We are better off not alienating the Republicans and keeping some friends for next session. That's my thought on this. We'll see if others agree.

ON MARCH 11, 2002, THE LEGISLATURE OBSERVED THE "STATE OF THE TRIBES" FOR THE FIRST TIME IN MAINE HISTORY.

March 15, 2002
Friday

On March 10 I met Chief Barry Dana, Governor Richard Stevens, Governor Rick Doyle, Donald Soctomah, Tom Tureen, Rex Hackler, Trevor White, and former governor George Stevens of the Passamaquoddy Tribe at the Senator Inn in Augusta. The plan was to have dinner and then go to Severin Beliveau's office to work on the speeches for the State of the Tribes Address the following day. Before going to dinner I had spoken with Barry and we had decided that the word casino should not appear in his speech—and hopefully not in the speeches of the others, either. We would have a press conference afterward to talk about the importance of the State of the Tribes Addresses and then say something about the casino decision. This was the game plan before I arrived at the Senator to meet them at 6:00 P.M.

Barry, Tom Tureen, Rex (our PR advisor), and Rick Doyle were upstairs in their rooms talking. I waited in the lobby with Trevor White, George Stevens, and Richard Stevens. We decided to go ahead and get a table around 6:30 P.M., and around 7:00 Barry came down with his wife and children. Barry's wife sat next to me and Barry came up to me and said, "Rex wants us to talk about the casino in our speeches and he does not want us to have a press conference afterward."

I was a bit upset but didn't show it. I waited until Tom came to the table and we started talking about what the content of the speeches should include. I said I strongly felt that the casino should not be mentioned in the speeches, since we need to focus on a government-to-government relationship; these speeches needed to be dignified and diplomatic.

Tom said, "I don't understand why we shouldn't say anything."

I said, "I know this legislature, and I'm telling you to keep the casino out of the speeches. If you want to go against my recommendations, go ahead, but I'm telling you it would be a mistake. We need to be viewed as diplomats and we need to be respected."

Tom finally agreed and saw the wisdom of it, since we needed to win and maintain the respect of the legislature. I said, "We can mention the casino at the press conference afterward." We all agreed the best course was to not mention the casino and to go ahead with the press conference.

Barry left the table to inform Rex of our decision. Dinner ended around 8:30 P.M. or so, and with the exception of Barry's family and George Stevens, we all met at Severin's office to go over the speeches. We looked at each speech and made comments and changes. We finished around 10:30 P.M. I was so excited I couldn't sleep. I was exhausted the next day.

The historic day came and I arrived at the Statehouse around 8:30 A.M. The house was due to start at 9:00 A.M. with the National Anthem being sung by Loran Stevens of the Passamaquoddy Tribe, followed by the Pledge of Allegiance, and finally the blessing by Butch Phillips, a Penobscot elder and former representative to the house. As 9:00 A.M. drew near, Donald Soctomah informed me that Butch was nowhere to be found. We had to start on time. Did I know anyone who could do the blessing? After a few panicked moments, Mike Saxl suggested I read my "Ten Thousand Eagles" poem in place of the prayer. I agreed.

We were still missing Loran Stevens, the soloist, but then realized she was up in the balcony. She was prepared to sing from the balcony as she was used to doing in church. When she was told she would be singing from the podium—in front of all those people—she got very nervous, but she came down and joined the procession that was getting ready to march into the well of the house. I actually

I read "Ten Thousand Eagles" as the opening blessing in the house on State of the Tribes Day. Courtesy of the Clerk's Office

thought she might faint at one point. She was dressed in a dark brown buckskin dress, moccasins, and a beaded headband.

I stood with the speaker and the clerk and we followed the sergeant-at-arms into the well of the house. We all stepped up onto the podium together, Loran was escorted to a seat on the left of the podium, and I sat in a chair to the right of the podium with my eagle feather in hand. I looked into the house chamber and to the balcony above and remember seeing my sister, Beth Sockbeson, and her husband, Jack Loftus. I momentarily wondered what they were thinking. The speaker called the house to order and said, "The prayer will be delivered by the representative of the Penobscot Nation, Representative Donna M. Loring."

I didn't have much time to get nervous or even think about what I was going to say. I had planned on having some time at my desk and writing a quick introduction and a few words. Now I was standing before the legislature and all the people in the balcony. I'm not sure exactly what words came out of my mouth, but it was something to the effect that today was the six-month anniversary of September 11, that I had written a poem three days after the event, and that I would like to read in place of a prayer and hoped it would be of some small comfort to all of us. I felt unusually calm and collected and the reading went very well. After I had finished reading, I stood to the side as the speaker introduced Loran. She sang *The Star-Spangled Banner* and did a wonderful job.

Governor Richard Stevens from Indian Township in Princeton was introduced first by Speaker of the House Michael Saxl. When he was introduced he received a standing ovation, as did Governor Doyle and Chief Dana.

Governor Stevens started his speech by holding his wampum belt and explaining that it was a sign of truth and any one who holds the belt and speaks must speak the truth. His speech was very short but full of information about the hopes and expectations of the Passamaquoddy at Indian Township. He spoke of the struggle to maintain their culture and to access good-paying jobs, adequate housing, and good education. He gave a life-expectancy figure for tribe members of forty-eight years, unemployment at 50 percent, and a median income that was far below that of the rest of Washington County, which is $25,000. He talked about the health care situation and the fact that many tribal members were dying from diabetes and cancer. He recalled the events of September 11th when he said:

> The world today is a place of uncertainty and upheaval. We as Americans remember the awful events six months ago today in New York, Washington, and Pennsylvania. As our people struggle with fears, doubt, and worry about the future, it is our responsibility as the elected officials of the people of Maine and the Passamaquoddy Tribe to foster stability and accomplish a new era of mutual respect and cooperation between ourselves. It is my tribe's responsibility to work with the State of Maine, to find common ground, and to broaden our horizons while practic-

ing our individual culture. It is my belief that the Passamaquoddy people and the people of Maine expect no less.

I wondered is it during wartime only that the state would be
willing to work with us and treat us as an economic partner. The
theme of working together to find common ground and as partners
would prevail throughout the speeches of each governor and chief.

Governor Richard Doyle, Passamaquoddy Tribe at Pleasant Point
was the next to speak. He recognized the historic occasion and said:

> This is a historic occasion and a historic opportunity for the
> Passamaquoddy people and the people of Maine. My hope is that
> this is the beginning of a new era of cooperation, trust, and part-
> nership as we move forward and look to the future. While our
> past has been colored by distrust, we are willing to walk forward,
> together in friendship to help raise the quality of life of my peo-
> ple and the people of the State of Maine.

He then talked about the Maine Indian Land Claims Settlement Act:

> Unfortunately, the Settlement Act has not achieved its goal. It is
> a failed experiment in my mind. We seek only to maintain and
> exercise our sovereignty to protect our way of life.... I would
> urge the Maine Tribal–State Commission to review the Settle-
> ment Act and to suggest changes to help bring into a new era
> and clarify the questions of jurisdiction that were left open.
> These questions have led us to our current situation. We want to
> ensure that we have clean water. Plain and simple. The current
> court cases and the arguments made by the paper companies are
> not about documents to us. It is about our right to clean water. It
> is about the health and safety of our people.... If I must be
> imprisoned to protect the river and the water, then so be it. This
> is worth fighting for. Money and power are fleeting. Nature is
> forever. My people are forever. We will not back down. We will

Above, L-R: Chief Richard Stevens, Chief Barry Dana, and Chief Richard Doyle, holding a wampum belt. All photos in this section courtesy of Donald Soctonah.

Below, L-R: Governor Angus King and Chief Barry Dana.

Above, L-R: Butch Phillips, Robert Dana, Chief Doyle, and Chief Stevens lining up in front of the speaker's office to march into the house chamber.

Below, L-R: Speaker of the House Michael Saxl, Chief Stevens, and Chief Doyle.

Above, L-R: Robert Dana, Penobscot Council member and brother of Chief Dana, Senate President Pro-Tempore Richard A. Bennett (R-Norway), and Butch Phillips, tribal elder and former Penobscot nation representative. Butch opened the historic joint session with the opening prayer.

Below: Chief Barry Dana gives his State of the Tribes Address.

continue to fight for our right to clean water, no matter how long, and no matter what the cost....Whenever we were asked we came willingly to the aid of the State. We ask for your assistance now. Help us protect our waters. Help us to grow economically. Help us to protect our traditions and culture. And most importantly, let's help each other to become better neighbors and partners.

As I listened to Governor Doyle's speech, the words of Chief Orono came to mind. On June 2, 1775, after George Washington requested our warriors to assist him during the Revolution, he held council and Chief Orono addressed the Penobscot warriors just before they were to participate in the American Revolution with these words:

The Great Spirit gives us freely all things.

Our white brothers tell us they came to Indian country to enjoy liberty and life but a Great Sagamore is coming to bind them in chains, to kill them. We must fight him for should he bind them in bonds, next he will treat us like bears. He will tear away from us Indian liberties and land.

We must help his ill treated sons for they will return good for good and the law of love runs through their children....

Look down the stream of time. Look up to the Great Spirit. Be kind, be valiant, be free, then are the Indians sons of Glory!

What has the stream of time revealed to us today? Certainly not what Chief Orono and our ancestors fought for. We are still asking for help and holding our hands out in friendship. We are still filled with hope 227 years later. Amazing.

Last to speak was Chief Barry Dana of the Penobscot Nation. He spoke along the same lines as the previous speakers but talked about his mother and grandfather and told the story of Gluskabe and the frog monster. He also talked about the importance of the river in our culture:

Today's address symbolizes what I truly believe to be a new era in tribal–state relations. Relationships are based on communication. Today's forum allows for direct communication. Perhaps our greatest days lie before us.... Only through education can we ever hope to eliminate stereotypes and put an end to all forms of racism. The Penobscot Nation is a tribe. Tribes here in this country pre-date the creation of the states and the federal government. In the creation of the U.S. Federal Government, the founding fathers recognized the tribes as distinct forms of government, with inherent sovereign powers to ensure the birth-given rights to be self-determined. The 1980 Settlement Act recognizes these protections of inherent sovereign powers. The United States Senate Committee on Indian Affairs, in their view of the 1980 Settlement Act, recognized and ratified our retained sovereign powers and cited the 1st Circuit Court's decision, 'That the Maine tribes still possess inherent sovereignty to the same extent as other tribes in the United States.' Thus, rather than destroying the sovereignty of the tribes, by recognizing the power to control their internal affairs and by withdrawing the power which Maine previously claimed to interfere in such matters, the settlement strengthens the sovereignty of the Maine tribes. The very essence of tribal sovereignty is the ability to be self-governing and to protect the health, safety, and welfare of our people, within our own territory. We are a distinct people with a unique history.... From thousands of years ago, the bones of our ancestors still lie on the shores of Maine's rivers and ocean frontage. We still carry on their dreams, their pride, and the traditions of self-determination—and these we hold sacred. We will continue to fight to safeguard these rights, in honor of our ancestors and in order to preserve a future for our children. Failure to do so would mean surrendering the very essences of who we are as Indian people. We are proud of our place in history and many contributions we have made to the larger society by assisting in common goals. We are still here.

As Chief Dana explained our concept of sovereignty and how vital it is to us for our survival, I wondered if any of these legislators, government officials or members of the general public really understood what he was saying. Did anyone get it? Did anyone care? Would this historic day make a real difference in future tribal–state relations?

I AM PROUD OF ALL THE WABANAKI WARRIORS WHO HAVE SERVED AND WHO REMAIN ROLE MODELS FOR FUTURE GENERATIONS.

March 21, 2002
Wednesday

I was asked to give a speech on Memorial Day by the American Legion Post commander, and today I delivered the speech at the gazebo located on the Richmond waterfront.

I began by honoring those who have died in our nation's service in wars such as the Revolutionary War, the Civil War, the Spanish American War, WWI, WWII, the Korean War, Vietnam, the Gulf War, Somalia, Kosovo, and Afghanistan, as well all other military personnel and civilian personnel who lost their lives in service to this country. I paid tribute to those who lost their lives at D-Day, Pearl Harbor, and September 11th and honored the Gold Star mothers and family members who have lost loved ones. I also honored women and Native Americans who have served out country, and below are some excerpts from my speech.

> I stand before you as a Native American and a woman veteran. Very little is mentioned about Native or women veterans, and I would like to give you a glimpse of their contributions, which helped make this country what it is today—a country founded on the principles of freedom and democracy and the most power-ful nation in the world.
>
> I will first speak about women veterans. Women have served in combat and as combat support since the Revolutionary War, when women like Margret Corbin and Mary Hays McCauley, aka Molly Pitcher, who, without official status accompanied their

husbands into battle and stepped behind cannons and continued the fight when their husbands fell.

There were also women during the Civil War who organized to form military-like units and trained with weapons in order to protect their homes.

Prior to WWI the U.S. Navy, anticipating that women would be needed to fill their manpower needs, figured a way around a law that prohibited women from serving in the military. Over 11,000 women enlisted as yeomen.

During WWII over 250,000 women volunteered to join the enlisted ranks of the military. The idea was to free up men for combat. Women's duties consisted of secretarial duties, parachute packing, repairing guns, driving trucks, making maps, and even flying supply planes. Some worked in top-secret intelligence jobs and built and used early computers. By the end of WWII women had served in every theater of the war from North Africa and Europe to China, Burma, and India.

It is estimated that approximately 1,234 enlisted military women served in Vietnam and throughout the war.

Today women serve in every branch of the armed forces and continue to give their lives in the service of their country.

I am also a Native American.

Native Americans have served with honor in all of America's wars. Members of the Penobscot, Passamaquoddy, Micmac, and Maliseet tribes fought to help this country gain its independence from England.

Since the early 1800s the United States government had sent missionaries to the tribes in order to help them assimilate into the larger society. Indian tribes resisted this and maintained their languages and cultures. This very resistance was to play a major role in winning a world war.

Eight thousand American Indians took part in WWI. Their patriotism caused Congress to pass the Indian Citizenship Act of 1924. Since Native people were fighting and dying for this country, Congress felt it only right to grant them citizenship.

In WWII more than 44,000 Native Americans served with distinction in both the European and Pacific theaters. More than 40,000 others left their reservations to work in ordinance depots, factories, and other war industries. At that time there were only 350,000 Native Americans in the entire United States, including children. Approximately 12 percent of the Native American population, or one third of all able-bodied Indian men, served in WWII. This is the highest percentage of any racial group. Several hundred Native American women also served with the Women's Army Corp, Army Nurse Corp, and the U.S. Navy.

Native people contributed to winning WWII in a unique way. The Japanese were adept at breaking our military codes and because of this ability they were winning the battles. It was imperative to winning the war that we have the ability to communicate with our forces without our messages being decoded by the Japanese.

Navajo code talkers used codes derived from Navajo and other Native speech which were unintelligible to the enemy. While most codes were considered unusable after one day, Navajo codes were never broken.

I can't help but wonder what would have happened if assimilation of all the tribes were complete and all tribes spoke English only. Would we be speaking Japanese or even German today?

More than 42,000 Native Americans, more than 90 percent of them volunteers, fought in Vietnam. Native Americans see duty today wherever our armed forces are stationed.

I don't think many people know about the military contributions of Native Americans. My own family was a military family. My uncles served in the Marine Corps, the air force, and the army. My father George M. Loring, Jr., served in the 10th Mountain Division and was in the Po Valley on D Day when they took Mt. Belvadere. My uncle Frank Loring served in the Marine Corps in the Pacific during the

Harald Prins (center) and Bunny McBride with Charles Shay. Harald and Bunny nominated Charles for the Légion d'Honneur, the French Medal of Honor. Courtesy of Donald Soctomah

Korean War. I served in Vietnam. I am proud of all the Wabanaki warriors who have served and who remain role models for future generations.

On June 6, 2007, Charles Norman Shay, a Penobscot elder and WWII veteran was awarded France's highest honor, the Légion d'Honneur medal. He was presented with the medal by President Nicolas Sarkozy of France at the French ambassador's residence in Washington, D.C. He received the medal for extraordinary bravery shown during the war, especially at Normandy's Omaha Beach on D-day, June 6, 1941. This honor came on top of the Silver Star the U.S. military awarded him during the war for his heroism on that fateful day. His official citation states: "Private Shay subordinated

I present a legislative sentiment to Charles Shay at my home in Bradley, Maine. Courtesy if the author

personal safety for the welfare of his comrades...plunging repeatedly into the treacherous sea and carrying critically wounded men to safety."

Charles Norman Shay is indeed a hero and role model, for all.

THIS CARTOON WAS DEHUMANIZING. IRONICALLY, IT WAS IN THE PAPER THE DAY AFTER THE FIRST-EVER STATE OF THE TRIBES ADDRESS.

March 28, 2002
Thursday
A bill to study the feasibility of a casino was introduced by the opposition through Representative Rod Carr (R) of Lincoln. The legislative leaders and the chiefs felt it was a good idea to have a study.

I am now waiting to see when the casino study bill will hit the floor for debate. I asked the speaker about it, and all he would say was, "It's funded." I still need to get something more from him because I have to be prepared when and if this hits the floor.

The *Portland Press Herald* has come out against the casino and has had an article in the paper every day to keep the issue alive. I sent in an op ed about one of their dehumanizing cartoons, and so far they have not printed it. I feel they are deliberately silencing us. They would never do this to any other group or race of people. I will include the op ed in my journal so that at least it will get read by someone:

I am writing in response to your editorial cartoon on March 12, 2002. The cartoon was titled "Steve Meyers' View."

I am writing because there was something terribly wrong with the image and the very subtle message it sent.

No, I am not going to ask the paper to print an apology, nor am I going to call for Mr. Meyers' resignation. (I know people who would.) The reason I am not asking for his resignation or an apology is that Native people since Columbus have simply learned how to forgive.

There is a saying, "a picture is worth a thousand words." In this case it's a cartoon. I would like to use some of those words to describe the picture I saw.

The picture was of Governor Angus King holding a can of poison marked VETO in big letters. (I wonder what that container with the skull and crossbones held? It was obviously something toxic like dioxin, mercury, or cadmium.) There were small insect carcasses all around him. I think these were supposed to be roaches, and they presumably depicted attempts at other gambling proposals. There were some images I did not see depicted that should have been, such as live roaches with the letters LOTTERY, HORSE RACING, OFF-TRACK BETTING. I have never seen a cartoon with the governor exterminating those depicted as insects!

I then saw a jumbo-size insect—perhaps eight to ten times the size of the others. The words CASINO PROPOSAL were written on its shell, along with the word YEWWHOOooo! There were music symbols depicted as coming from the insect. I cannot figure out what the meaning of this is, except that when Native people are being made fun of they are mocked with similar words.

The good governor looks as though he was taken by surprise and is getting ready to exterminate the jumbo insect with the poison canister marked VETO.

What could possibly be wrong with this picture? I will explain from my perspective as an Indian. Indian people are real people, we are human beings with the same dreams and desires as anyone else, and we should never be dehumanized. This cartoon was dehumanizing. Ironically, it was in the paper the day after the first-ever "State of the Tribes Address." The chiefs spoke to the entire legislative body and to the entire state through the media. Maine Public Radio carried their speeches live and in their entirety.

The chiefs spoke to Maine people from their hearts and spoke the plain truth. They were genuine and honest, they offered their hands in friendship, and they spoke of partnerships and working together for the common good. They invited the people of Maine to a place they had never been before, into their hearts, their spirituality, and their humanness.

There are people who will take advantage of our tribes' casino proposal to make us look less than human. Some will even see a political advantage in using the Indian people of this state like a political football. But I would like to think Maine people have progressed. I would like to think Maine people are smarter than that. I would like to think Maine people are fair.

The word casino has been synonymous with Indians ever since the success of the Pequot's casino in Connecticut. I know this is true in Maine, because every time my colleague Donald Soctomah and I introduce a bill, it is heavily scrutinized to make sure there is no casino involved. It has been this way ever since we were elected to represent our people in the state legislature.

The word Indian and casino are synonymous to some. I wonder, has anyone thought of equating words such as: Indian and children, Indian and mother, Indian and father, Indian and family, Indian and home, Indian and partner, Indian and future, Indian and equality, Indian and dreams, Indian and human being? *(They printed the op ed on April 2.)*

April 8, 2002
Monday
We are coming up on the end of session. The casino study bill has passed in the house and senate and has been sent to the Appropriations Table. Determination was made to fund the study and the bill is back in the senate for final enactment.

The bill has been changed somewhat, and the Christian Civic League is still very strongly opposing it. I think there will be another senate fight on this bill today.

May 20, 2002
Monday

The casino study bill passed and the governor signed it.

A group called Casinos No has been formed to fight the introduction of a casino to Maine. People are not even waiting to study the issue. The people in Kittery and York and other southern towns are whipping themselves into a frenzy. Some of the towns have even held a nonbinding referendum to stop the casino. Sometimes I think the issue is not a casino but an "Indian Casino." There are those who would say I'm just playing the race card, but let's look at the big picture here in Maine, the whitest state in the country.

Maine has a lottery that brings in $40 million a year and other forms of gambling such as horse racing, scratch cards, and off-track betting that add up to over $100 million a year. I have heard it said that horse racing isn't even gambling! It's more of a tradition. If it's a tradition, it's a gambling tradition. Horse racing is a sport. Right? It's entertainment. Right? I could say the same for a casino. It is similar to a sporting event in that when you go, you know you will be spending your money to be entertained. When you look at Maine as a whole and see that the state is already into gambling in a big way, you wonder why all of a sudden is a casino so terrible?

I've had fellow legislators tell me, "Donna, I just can't go along with this casino thing; it's gambling. I just can't support gambling." These same legislators have never once submitted a bill to eliminate the lottery or any other form of gambling. I could say the same about Governor King, who on many occasions has told me how much he despises gambling. I asked him once why he didn't submit legislation to get rid of it. He told me, "We are addicted to it. We can't afford to get rid of it."

Maine Indian people are hoping a casino will improve their economic situation. Why is it that Indian people can't use this tool? The State of Maine can no longer use the excuse that it's anti-gambling. The State of Maine is being hypocritical and using a double standard. The State of Maine can gamble but not the Indians.

I find that most people who are against a casino are well-to-do or are against it for moral reasons. In Kittery, for instance, they are often people from out of state who have moved to Maine to retire or who are wealthy and have moved to Maine to be left alone. I can see where a casino in their town would not be welcome.

Maine people who are poor or who have lost their jobs are more willing to consider the casino alternative. The casino would bring in thousands of jobs. The jobs would first be in the construction industry, and construction jobs pay well. The money put into building a casino and employing thousands of people would stay in the state. This project would be one heck of a shot in the arm to the community that hosts it and to surrounding communities. I believe this could be a bonanza if it is done right—with input from the surrounding communities as well as state planning and economic experts. In the end we could create a casino that would benefit the whole state. I firmly believe that once some people get over their prejudices, this will be a wealthier state in so many ways.

"I AM PLEASED TO APPOINT YOU AS HOUSE CHAIR OF THE CASINO STUDY COMMITTEE."

August 3, 2002

On July 25 I picked up my mail with the thought that I would read it while getting the headlight replaced on my VW Beetle. While in the waiting area at the car dealership, I started to review the mail and noticed a letter from the majority office. I figured it was a letter from the speaker appointing me to the Casino Study Committee, since I had asked to be on it. I opened it and started to read.

It said, "I am pleased to appoint you as house chair of the Casino Study Committee." I had to read it two or three times to really believe it was saying what I thought it was saying. My first thought was, "This is a mistake." I decided to call the house majority office to make certain they were serious.

I called and they were serious. I spoke with Billy Brown, one of the speaker's aides, and he confirmed the appointment stating, "You were chosen because of all the legislators that signed up to be on the committee, you were the most qualified for the chairs seat."

At that moment I was ecstatic! I thought, "A tribal representative has actually been appointed to co-chair a very highly visible and important committee!" I thanked Billy and told him to thank the speaker for his confidence in me and that I would not let them down.

I was thrilled. I considered the fact that this was an election year and the chair of this committee would be in the hot seat, since every gubernatorial candidate had come out against the casino idea and the candidates running for office were waiting to see what the overall public sentiment would be before they declared a position. It was actually brilliant strategy on the speaker's part. I had nothing to lose and even if I did, I would not hurt the party or the candidates in any way. It didn't matter to me what the reason was, I certainly was not going to turn this down. I viewed this as a chance for a tribal representative to finally have not only input but visibility in a very important decision that the state—through its legislature and citizens—would have to make.

The ironic thing here is that when the study commission was proposed it was proposed by the opposition. Representative Roderick Carr (R) from Lincoln sponsored the resolution and Senator Mary Small (R) from Bath made a number of amendments to it. The study, at that point in time, was looked at as a way to get rid of the idea of a casino. The economic impact was not on the public radar screen at the time.

But since the committee has been formed, the economic condition of the state has rapidly declined and now the casino study has become a huge media topic. The media has zeroed in on the fact that I am a tribal representative and co-chair of this study. There have been editorial comments that the study commission results are therefore tainted and cannot be relied upon. They feel the study commission should be abolished.

To date the committee has heard testimony from state economic experts who are considered tops in their field. These experts stated that the tribes' economic information was good and based on acceptable economic models. Yes, the tribes paid for the study and the expert opinions. To suggest that this economic study and these experts are not telling the truth because they were hired by the tribes, and then to question my honesty and integrity as co-chair because I am a tribal representative, is both ludicrous and racist. Why would the tribes want to have a resort casino if it was not going to be profitable? I would think that the legislature and the people of Maine would want the best and most accurate information possible. The tribes were very generous in paying for the study and then allowing this information to be shared with the legislature.

Any business worth its salt is going to do an economic study. No other economic impact study on a resort casino located in Maine exists. The tribes are only doing what any other business entrepreneur would do. The makeup of the committee is such that there are pros and cons; therefore the chairs would have been either pro or con. As co-chair it is my obligation to ensure that the best and most accurate information is presented to the legislature and to the citizens of Maine. This issue is too important to be smothered by innuendo and hearsay.

To be perfectly candid about it, the opposition, in the guise of "Casinos No," has failed to present factual information to the state and to the commission. They have no expert testimony from state economists or any other Maine state entity that is fact-based. They are using fear and innuendo as fact. I guess what bothers me the most is that they are using these tactics to say that because the tribes paid for the study, it is tainted and cannot be believed, and because I am a tribal representative, I am biased and cannot be fair in conducting a hearing. The message is that a tribe cannot conduct a fair and accurate economic study and a tribal representative cannot be fair and ethical. These accusations smack of racism.

I see this resort casino as a way in which to sustain our sovereignty, and I use the term "sustainable sovereignty." I also see it as a means to address the huge economic problem the state is facing.

Two years ago the word casino could not have been used in the halls of the legislature without incurring wrath. It was never used in the wording of a bill; it would mean sure death for the bill. The Penobscot and Passamaquoddy tribes brought this idea forward when no one else dared or even thought about it. There are rumblings now among some legislators that perhaps Indians should not be allowed to benefit from their own proposed project, but rather the state should take over these potentially lucrative resources. Wow! What a novel idea! Sounds like history repeating itself.

I hope the citizens of Maine remain open and fair about this idea and unbiased by the rhetoric that desperate, venomous, mean-spirited people are espousing. I find it ironic that these people find a resort casino so horrible but not one of them fought the idea of state-owned lottery, horse racing, or liquor stores. The same people screaming about the murder, fraud, and prostitution that a resort casino might bring are not at all concerned about the problems in Maine that alcohol causes. That carries with it a much bigger social cost in terms of crimes and addiction, yet I've heard them say alcohol is okay because people enjoy it and it is entertaining.

It is easy to criticize, point fingers, and take shots at a person's integrity and character. It is far harder to find solutions. The tribes have proposed a partial solution to the ever-worsening economic problem this state is facing. It would be much better to work together in partnership, with the tribes using knowledge from other states and other casinos. The knowledge and the tools are out there; we need only have a willing spirit and a positive attitude. Together we could create a resort casino unique to Maine and one that would help rekindle Maine's economic fire. The Penobscot Nation and Passamaquoddy Tribe have proposed this project in good faith.

EPILOGUE

The biggest and most expensive campaign in Maine history followed
in November 2003 as the question of a casino was put to referendum. The casino referendum is a story within itself although it was
defeated two to one. The naysayers and those who used every trick
they could—even lies—won the battle. It was an easy battle to win
when racist scare tactics were used. Ironically, on the same ballot was
a "racino" proposal for Bangor, Maine, which was approved. Maine
people chose horses over Indian people.

Maine is still struggling economically with no real answers. Oh
yes, there is a racino in Bangor and it is doing very well. It is
expanding its operations and will be making a large contribution to
the state coffers. But this contribution is nowhere near what the
state could have had if they had passed the Indian casino referendum. The resort had planned to spend $100 million a year buying
goods from Maine companies. It estimated it would pay Maine taxes
of $130 million a year as well as employ 2,000 during construction
and have 5,000 permanent full-time jobs within the resort itself. The
best part of the Maine Indian proposal was that the money would
have stayed in Maine.

We now see other New England states approving their own
Indian casinos—in Rhode Island and Massachusetts. I do not know if
Maine Indians will ever get a casino or racino, or even be allowed to
have slot machines in their bingo halls, but I do know that as long as
Maine Indians are being kept out of the economic plans and
progress, Maine will not prosper as a state and only the wealthy will
thrive. The average Maine citizen will have to work for low wages or
move to another state, maybe somewhere where Indian people are
economic partners not forgotten relics of the past.

THE STRUGGLE CONTINUES

Today, almost a decade later, Maine tribal governments are facing the same issues. We struggle to gain economic sustainability and social equality. Today I am faced with the same opposition I was faced with almost a decade ago. I could literally take the same speeches I wrote back then and not change a word. They would still be pertinent and on target today.

The gaming issue is still being debated, although some progress has been made with the majority of the legislature and the majority of Maine citizens. In spite of the negative outcome of the 2007 referendum vote on a racino in Washington County, I truly believe that Maine people finally understand that the state is heavily dependent on its gaming profits. I also believe they have come to terms with the fact that the tribes are being treated unfairly on this issue. But it's called a "matter of fairness" rather than what it really is: "economic discrimination."

I was interviewed by MPBN on November 8, 2007, and they asked me for my thoughts on the racino vote. I told them it was a bit of a surprise to me that the racino referendum lost, and by a narrow margin of around 8,000 votes. The turnout was low, the weather was bad, and it was an off year. All of that considered, the vote was lost because people were not motivated by jobs or economic development, or by concern for Washington County or Indian people.

But clearly something more compelling than the common good of Washington County residents motivated those who *did* come out. Many of those who voted against the racino did so because they felt that money was going to go out of state or felt that not enough money was going to various causes in the rest of the state. Others voted against the bill simply because Indians were involved. Yes, I believe that there is still racism in this state. I also believe that most Maine people are not racist and they simply want what's best for Maine. Those people did not vote.

The racino bill lost for all the above reasons—but there were other factors as well. Money, for instance. It seems that out-of-staters funded Casinos No very well. They were able to put out a highly effective negative ad in the last week or so of the campaign. Why did a former member of the gaming commission show up in TV ads at the last minute? He said that just a small amount of money was staying in the state and that Bangor was only getting a little over $300,000 dollars a year. He also claimed that the gaming commission was not doing its job monitoring the racino in Bangor. He made many such misleading accusations at the last minute.

The Passamaquoddy Tribe and Washington County people did not have the funds to counter that kind of nasty rhetoric. People of Maine ate it up, at least those who were motivated by negativity and those who didn't pay close enough attention to who he was and what he was saying. If, indeed, what this fellow said about the gaming commission was true, then we have a problem that needs to be addressed immediately and the gaming commission needs to answer those accusations. The sad thing is that this person planned this for months. He resigned from the commission to take this position on the racino bill. If the commission was managing things so badly, why didn't he call for an investigation right off the bat? His real purpose was to sabotage the Washington County racino vote. In the end, good people in Washington County were left without hope and with even deeper wounds.

The Penobscot Nation is also facing some critical economic realities in that we are losing federal dollars that once funded our infrastructure. We need a source of revenue we can use to ignite our economic engines and enhance our social welfare. Gaming is that initial boost we need.

In 2007, in the first session of the 123rd, I put in a bill that would allow the Penobscot Nation to have 400 slot machines. I testified many times in front of the Joint Standing Committee on Legal and Veterans' Affairs and on the floor of the house. I explained the need for the revenue of these machines and the fact that the tribe was losing money to Bangor's Hollywood Slots. We simply needed the machines to help us survive economically and allow us a competing chance. The slot bill passed in both houses but again would have fallen short by one or two votes in the senate when a two-thirds vote was needed to override the governor's promised veto.

Governor Baldacci has constantly vetoed or threatened to veto any tribal effort to use gaming as an economic tool. I find this reprehensible and very hypocritical, since he was the one who added "Powerball" to the lottery to help balance the state budget. He and the legislature are now using Hollywood Slots as an economic tool to create jobs in the Bangor area and to balance the state budget. This was very evident when the Appropriations Committee tried to make Hollywood Slots pay an extra percentage toward state taxes. Hollywood Slots was in the process of building a brand-new hotel and gaming facility in downtown Bangor. Penn National, the parent company of Hollywood Slots, shut the whole construction site down, stating it could not afford to subsidize our state government and stay in business. Governor Baldacci stepped in, the Appropriations Committee withdrew its demands, and the governor agreed to discuss options with Penn National that would guarantee that the state wouldn't tax them out of business. The new construction project started up again, and many people went back to work.

Now if gaming in this instance is not an economic tool, I don't know what is. The Penobscot Nation and the Passamaquoddy Tribe are still trying to gain the same economic tool that the people of Maine have given to Bangor and the governor has given to the state.

The Penobscot Nation's slot machine bill was saved to come back in the next session (spring of 2008) by a vote in both the house and the senate to allow the bill to go back to committee. In committee it can be amended to be more palatable to legislators who voted against it in the previous session.

Maine tribes are still struggling to be treated equally and fairly on this very important economic issue.

* * *

The environment is still a huge issue for us, and the battle with the paper companies continues. In July 2007 the Penobscot Nation discovered a giant blue-green algae bloom in the Penobscot River. It stretched for over seventy miles, from Millinocket to the coast. These blooms can cause eye, ear, and skin irritation, as well as gastrointestinal problems if ingested. They can also cause serious harm to pets and livestock. The Penobscot Nation issued a hazard warning to its tribal members advising them not to eat the fish or swim in the river, and sent samples of the bloom to be analyzed. The Maine Department of Environmental Protection (DEP) stated that it is safe to fish in the water and it does not believe the algae blooms to be toxic, but we're not so sure. It is, however, certain that the paper company was discharging a very high level of phosphorous and not being properly monitored by the state. I find this incredible!

This is doubly ironic since in August 2007 the 1st Circuit Federal Court came down with a decision in favor of the State of Maine against the tribes. The court found that the tribes have no say over the rivers and the water quality of the rivers flowing through their reservations. It let stand the paper companies' "one-stop-shopping" request to get its discharge certification from the state directly, without going through the national Environmental Protection Agency as a parallel process. The EPA process had allowed the tribes to comment and force the paper companies to comply with environmental law before they could be issued a discharge permit. The one-stop-shopping scenario is a total injustice, not only to the tribes but also to other Maine citizens who live near the Penobscot River and use it for recreation.

It has been proven that Maine has not monitored these paper companies well—or even at all, in some instances. The DEP has pretty much left monitoring up to the paper companies themselves! The state DEP needs to stop being so trusting and start enforcing the water quality laws that this state brags are more stringent than the federal law. It is clear that the struggle for a clean and healthy environment goes on as the DEP turns a blind eye toward paper company toxic discharges.

* * *

These issues all revolve around the question of sovereignty. The Maine Indian Land Claims Settlement Act is the document that defines the relationship between the state and the tribes. The name itself is a misnomer. It was an act to solve the dispute between the tribes and the state over land ownership of two-thirds of the state. What the act did do was solve the dispute of land ownership, but it was also used as a tool to keep the tribes in handcuffs, so to speak, and under state control. It was, in fact, a document that ended up being used as a tool via court decisions to maintain the state's jurisdiction over the tribes in every area of law, even internal tribal matters. This total control was never the intent of the tribes or the intent of Congress. The intent of Congress was to recognize and enhance the tribes' culture and sovereign status.

The Senate Select Committee on Indian Affairs put into the Congressional Record answers to some concerns. One concern was that the settlement amounts to a "destruction" of sovereign rights and jurisdiction of the Passamaquoddy Tribe and the Penobscot Nation. The committee's answer in part was, "While the settlement represents a compromise in which state authority is extended over Indian territory to the extent provided in the Maine Implementing Act, in keeping with these decisions the settlement provides that *henceforth the tribes will be free from state interference in the exercise of their internal tribal affairs.* (The emphasis is mine.) Thus, rather than destroying the sovereignty of the tribes, by recognizing their power to control their internal affairs and by withdrawing the power which Maine previously claimed to interfere in such matters, the settlement strengthens the sovereignty of the Maine Tribes." (Federal Record, August 14, 1980, on S.2829)

The Land Claims Settlement Act is a document that left more questions than it answered. The ironic part is that its ambiguous phrases and legal questions are being adjudicated in state courts, which are totally ignoring federal Indian law and applying state law insead. The case of *Bottomly v. Passamaquoddy Tribe* (1st U.S. Court of Appeals, cir. 1979) speaks to this issue (599 F.2d 1061 [1979] II Tribal Sovereign Immunity [1]): "...we find the conclusion which the state draws there from—that only the fierce independent tribes of the western frontier who have been 'federally recognized' enjoy sovereign immunity—to be unpersuasive...the powers of Indian tribes are, in general 'inherent powers of a limited sovereignty' which has never extinguished." (F. Cohen, *Handbook of Federal Indian Law*, 122, 1945.)

As the state courts take over more and more cases involving Settlement Act issues, federal Indian law is being ignored and federal judges are actually recognizing and concurring with the state judges' decisions! The Land Claims Act is being used to leverage these arguments. Any case that results from the Land Claims Act should be settled in federal court without the influence of state court judges. The act is an agreement between three sovereign entities and it is clearly questionable that a state court should be ruling on any issues of the act.

There is a phrase that was added to the Settlement Act without tribal approval—by then Senator William Cohen. It was added to federal Indian law, as well, and is as follows:

USC 25 1735 (b) General legislation
The provisions of any Federal law enacted after October 10, 1980, for the benefit of Indians, Indian nations, or tribes or bands of Indians, which would affect or preempt the application of the laws of the State of Maine, including application of the laws of

the state to lands owned by or held in trust for Indians, or Indian nations, tribes, or bands of Indians, as provided in this subchapter and the Maine Implementing Act *shall not apply within the state of Maine unless such provision of such subsequently enacted Federal law is specifically made applicable within the State of Maine.*

This addition to the federal Indian law by Senator Bill Cohen has isolated the Maine tribes from the rest of Indian Country. The Maine tribes were not included in the Federal Clean Water Act or in the Indian Gaming Act. The effect of this law is to continue to keep Maine Indians totally under state control. This addition to federal Indian law and its negative effect on the Maine tribes is an act of bad faith that undermines the intentions of the Settlement Act and interferes with congressional intent.

The Land Claims Settlement Act has been an instrument of abuse and continued subjugation for the tribes. The long record of discrimination against the tribes both economically and socially is there for anyone to see in the report on "Federal and State Services and the Maine Indian—A Report of the Maine Advisory Committee to the United States Commission on Civil Rights, December 1974." This report makes it clear how the tribes were controlled and marginalized. The Settlement Act was the result of the tribes' efforts to break free of that total control. The tribes did have one brief moment of freedom, as it were, when they became federally recognized and before the Settlement Act was signed into law—a brief historic moment when Maine Indians had the same rights as any other Indian tribe nationwide.

The Settlement Act was written with gray areas—that were yet to be defined—on purpose by the negotiating team. The thought was that the two sides would discuss and negotiate issues, not that the state would totally take over and make rulings in its own favor. The act did not and does not fulfill its intended purpose according to the Congressional Record and intent of Congress, and therefore the wounded party, the tribes, should take lawful steps to make the Settlement Act null and void.

* * *

Education is another issue that Maine tribes are still struggling with. The three Ivy League Maine colleges—Bates, Bowdoin, and Colby—are not recruiting Maine Indian students. Graduates of these institutions can be found in top levels of our state government and in places of power throughout the country. Very few Maine Indian students have ever attended these colleges. The University of Maine System, by contrast, offers a scholarship to Native students who qualify for admission.

Yes, we've made some progress in Maine. The Maine State Legislature passed into law a bill that would require all public schools to study Maine Indian history. That bill is a great beginning for students to learn about Maine Indian people. I would like to express my deepest appreciation to Diana Scully, former executive director of the Maine Indian Tribal–State Commission, and Cushman Anthony, former chair of MITSC, for the wonderful job they did in helping the Maine Indian History Commission in those first few months. Their support gave the commission time to get organized and to accomplish a tremendous amount of work. Even more work has been done since those first few months to develop curriculums and resources for teachers. James Eric Francis, tribal member and historian for the Penobscot Nation and former staff person for the Maine Indian History Commission, has taken the lead in creating and developing teaching materials for the Penobscot Nation. James, with the help of Maria Girouard, Cultural Center director, Connie Manter, former curriculum developer for the State of Maine, and others have developed twelve units for teachers K–12 and they are working on twenty-four more. The educational kit they have created is extensive and most impressive.

The Passamaquoddy Tribe has also done a great deal of work in curriculum development and their kit has won a national award. The Penobscot Nation Cultural Center as well as the Passamaquoddy Cultural Center have held workshops throughout the state in the past few years to teach the teachers. There is still much work to do in outreach to the schools and the teachers, but with the help and aid of organizations like the Maine Humanities Council, the Maine Department of Education, the University of Maine's Wabanaki Center, the Abbe Museum, Acadia National Park, and the tribes, the work is being done and the message is getting out. Maine's children will know the history of Wabanaki people in Maine. They will come to know who we are and know our struggles and our accomplishments. We will become real human beings to these children and they will honor Maine's first people when they become adults.

The next step is to have the colleges and universities make Maine Indian studies a part of their required curriculum just as they have made African American studies a requirement. The University of Maine System is starting to make improvements on at least two of its seven campuses. The flagship campus in Orono has created the Wabanaki Center for Native students to study and to find a cultural connection with Maine Indian communities and with each other. The University of Maine has also created a Native Studies Department where those wishing to study Native issues can find a course of interest. The University of Southern Maine has created a Native Student and Multicultural Affairs program where Native students can go to study and socialize. But the most important piece that is missing from the entire Maine college and university system is the academic piece, where Maine Indian history is a required course.

***

It is a struggle that takes place worldwide, not just in Maine. On September 13, 2007, after twenty-five years of negotiations, the United Nations adopted the Declaration of the Rights of Indigenous Peoples, which states, in part, that Indigenous peoples are equal to all other peoples and affirms further that all doctrines, policies, and practices based on or advocating superiority of peoples or individuals on the basis of national origin or racial, religious, ethnic, or cultural differences are racist, scientifically false, legally invalid, morally condemnable, and socially unjust. There were forty-six articles in the declaration protecting Indigenous lands, resources, and rights.

The vote at the UN was 143 in favor, 4 opposed, and 11 abstaining. The United States, Canada, Australia, and New Zealand all voted against the declaration.

In spite of this, Native American organizations in this country were excited and hopeful. The majority of the world now recognizes Indigenous peoples' rights, although the struggle continues in the United States, Canada, Australia and New Zealand. Joe A. Garcia, president of the National Congress of American Indians, said, "The passage of the declaration today acknowledges the individual and collective human rights of the world's Indigenous peoples. It gives hope that the dark days of colonization and forced assimilation are behind us."

We need to study and understand the First People and First Nations who lived here long before colonization, know their history, and recognize the importance of their culture in their lives. We need to face the fact that this country was built on the bodies of Indian people—indeed, there was a holocaust on these shores. Once we know our country's history, we can work to improve policy and practice. Then and only then will we be capable of empathy with other countries and cultures. Then and only then will we be prepared to look outside our protected shell and actually help other countries. Then and only then can we start building a new legacy of respect within the global community.

The struggle to educate and be educated continues.

Acknowledgments

I would not have had the opportunity to keep a recorded journal of my legislative experiences if it were not for the Penobscot people who elected me to this office. I thank you all for allowing me this experience and opportunity. The following Penobscot Tribal members were of much appreciated assistance: James Francis and Carol Binette, for their help in providing accurate information about past Penobscot representatives to the State Legislature; Martin Neptune for his beautiful photograph of Katahdin; and Sebastian Clayton Francis, Jr. (SC), for allowing his sculpture, "Soaring Free," to be used on the cover.

Donald Soctomah, the Passamaquoddy representative, was also a great help to me. We have worked well together and totally support each other's efforts. He has contributed photos to this book and he is the person who first called my attention to the wealth of information that is located in the Maine State Archives and the Maine Law Library in Augusta. He is a constant researcher of Passamaquoddy and Wabanaki history. Thank you, Donald, for all your help, support and advice over the years.

I thank my publisher, Tilbury House, and my friend Neil Rolde for seeing the potential of this book, and Neil for graciously agreeing to write the foreword. I especially thank Jennifer Bunting, who patiently and expertly guided me through this sometimes frustrating yet rewarding process and supported my efforts in so many ways.

It is impossible to live and write about such an experience without the support of family and friends. I thank my partner of twenty-nine years, Deborah A. Bouchard, who is my rock and my heart and was and is always there for me. Thank you to my sister Elizabeth Sockbeson and her husband Jack Loftus, my nieces Rebecca Sockbeson and Julia Sockbeson, and Julia's daughter, my grandniece

Maulian Dana. They actually made the trip to Augusta on several occasions to testify and to be a part of the events that unfolded. I would especially like to thank and recognize my partner's family: her mother Jeanne Cloutier, her mother's partner Forrest Reddy, Deborah's brother Philip Cloutier and his wife Nicole, who supported me in so many ways including sharing their home, and their daughter Bailey Cloutier, who provided me with many hours of entertainment and amusement. Also, Deborah's brother Michael Bouchard, an assistant professor and cancer researcher at Drexal School of Medicine ,for his support and for just being Michael. Finally, the other two members of my family for the past twelve years, my two dogs: Chance, a golden retriever, and Nedabe, a chocolate lab. They were always there for me and always happy to see me when I came home.

I would like to acknowledge Ron Phillips, president of Coastal Enterprises, Incorporated, who has been a true friend to the tribes and a welcome ally in our economic battle to become self sufficient. I would also like to thank my friend Susan Hammond, who I could always talk to, who always had some good advice, and who I could always count on. Susan was the sole mover and shaker that made the vision Ron Phillips, and I first conceived of, come true. It is a non-profit corporate financial institution (CDFI) known as Four Directions Development Corporation. This company has become a very successful economic tool for Maine Indian people. Thank you, Susan, for all your hard work and for all the Maine Indian people you and Four Directions have helped.

A special thank you to my friends Nola Weston, who believed in me enough to chair my senate campaign in 2004, and to Roseanne Tousignant, who contributed greatly to the Maine Women Veterans first conference ever.

Every once in a while I get a call from a wonderful elderly lady. She is an ardent supporter of Maine Native people and their issues. She has a very fine sense of humor and can make me laugh. She loves to talk about the Beetles, her home in the UK, and those handsome Penobscot men. Thank you, Sylvia Butler from Belfast, for your calls and your kind thoughts. They have made the rough road just a little bit easier.

Bunny McBride and Harald Prins were invaluable in their support and advice over many years. They were always there when I needed some information or even just to air my frustrations. They have contributed greatly to the understanding of Wabanaki people through their writings and research. They have become trusted friends and confidants. Thank you both.

Finally, there were many times when I had to just get away to the woods and water to renew my spirit. My favorite retreat is located on Hopkins Pond in Clifton, Maine. My friend has a camp there and we have shared many wonderful times talking and solving the world's problems. Those respites renewed my strength and allowed me to keep fighting the good fight. Thank you, Jane I. Peasley, for your friendship and for just being there.

INDEX

Page number references to illustrations are in italics.